IMAGES
of America

Historic Vermillion and Clay County

IMAGES
of America

HISTORIC VERMILLION AND CLAY COUNTY

Elizabeth Theiss Smith

ARCADIA
PUBLISHING

ISBN 978-0-7385-2027-8

Published by Arcadia Publishing
Charleston, South Carolina

Printed in the United States of America

Library of Congress Catalog Card Number: 2002109583

For all general information contact Arcadia Publishing at:
Telephone 843-853-2070
Fax 843-853-0044
E-mail sales@arcadiapublishing.com
For customer service and orders:
Toll-Free 1-888-313-2665

Visit us on the Internet at www.arcadiapublishing.com

Contents

Acknowledgments

Publishing this book became possible because of the generosity and time commitment of three outstanding women of Vermillion who superintend local photographic archives. Dorothy Neuhaus, Director of the W.H. Over Museum, kindly provided invaluable assistance in finding and identifying photographs with in the museum's extensive collection. This book would not have been possible without her help. Her patience with our occupation of her workspace over a period of weeks is most appreciated. Cleo Erickson, who serves as President of the Clay County Historical Society and staffs the Austin-Whittemore House, gave of her time and expertise unstintingly to unearth some of the wonderful photographs printed here and also provided workspace while we pored over boxes of photographs in the dining room. She is a most generous local historian, sharing her knowledge with many of us who impose on her time. Finally, thanks to Special Collections Librarian and Assistant Professor Dr. Gayla Koerting of the I.D. Weeks Library who guided us through the photographic archives at the University of South Dakota. Without her assistance and enthusiasm, this would have been a much less interesting book.

I am in debt to local historians who have painstakingly documented Clay County's history. Herbert S. Schell, Everett Sterling, A.H. Lathrop, and members of the Clay County Historical Society wrote the histories that made this book possible and I acknowledge here their important contribution to our heritage and this book. Anna Kerner's excellent history of downtown Vermillion formed the basis for that chapter.

Thanks are also due to the Political Science Department at the University of South Dakota and its Chair, Bill Richardson, who provided both practical and moral support as I attempted to juggle teaching, a research project, and this book at the same time.

Very special thanks are due to my spouse, Laurence Smith, who bravely followed me to South Dakota several years ago and continues to be central to my life. He kept the home fires burning and put dinner on the table while I inhabited local archives and spent long hours in my office.

Last but not least, my thanks to Shane Penfield, who scanned and organized all of these photographs while simultaneously finishing his second year at the University of South Dakota's Law School. I am most appreciative of his hard work.

Elizabeth T. Smith
Vermillion, South Dakota

Introduction

The area known as Clay County was once part of a vast inland sea. After the waters receded, glaciers covered the land. Today, the county is blessed by its geological past with fertile soil of rich black loam on the prairie and alluvium in the bottomlands of the Vermillion River valley.

More than a thousand years ago, a semi-sedentary people settled in the area. The Omaha and Ponca tribes inhabited the area. The Dakota later displaced earlier residents. Dakota means allies. However, the Ojibwa referred to them as *nadouessioux*, or enemies, the name for the tribe adopted by later settlers. The Dakota lived along waterways and relied on the buffalo for food, shelter, and clothing. Clay County was home to the Yawkton Sioux.

At the time of the Louisiana Purchase, President Thomas Jefferson commissioned Meriwether Lewis and William Clark to lead a Corps of Discovery into the new region for the purpose of finding a northwest passage to link the Mississippi River to the Pacific. They also provided a detailed record of the geography of the region and the flora and fauna encountered along the way. In the course of the expedition, Lewis and Clark passed through the area and provided the first written record of Clay County.

The earliest inhabitants of Clay County were fur traders of the Columbia Fur Company who had a trading post at the mouth of the Vermillion River. Additional fur trading posts followed. The first permanent settlers arrived as soon as the ink was dry on the Indian Treaty of 1859. Thirty-one families gathered at the Nebraska border awaiting the opening of the area for settlement.

In 1861, Dakota Territory was created by an act of Congress. Shortly afterwards, the first Territorial Legislature created Clay County. The new County's population boomed with the coming of the railroad and the Homestead Act of 1862, which granted 160 acres of land for farming to those who would live on the land and farm a quarter section for five years. The discovery of gold in the Black Hills in 1874 created wealth in Clay County as well. Residents formed wagon trains to move necessary commodities such as food, clothing, and equipment to growing mining camps out west.

In 1880, the County voted to adopt township government and created twelve townships: Bethel, Fairview, Garfield, Glenwood, Meckling, Norway, Pleasant Valley, Prairie Center, Riverside, Spirit Mound, Star, and Vermillion.

The history of Vermillion and Clay County that follows is a selective one that is based on available photographic records from 1868 to about 1940. Thus, Native American history is not recorded, nor are the lives of the earliest homesteaders. Nonetheless, the record is a fascinating one as it evokes the vanished era that is the shared heritage of Clay County.

One

Lewis and Clark in Vermillion

The Lewis and Clark expedition arrived in Vermillion on August 24, 1804, the first whites to appear in the area. The following morning, expedition members walked ten miles north to Spirit Mound, a site sacred to local Native Americans who believed that small mischievous *chanotila*, or little people of the woods, inhabited the mound. In the words of the Lewis and Clark Journals, dated 24th August Friday 1804:

> *In a northerly derection from the Mouth of this Creek in an emence Plain a high Hill is Situated, an appears of a Conic form, and by the different nations of Indians in this quarter is Suppose to be the residence of Deavels. That they are in human form with remarkable large heads, and about 18 inches high, that they are very watchfull and are arm'd with Sharp arrows with which they Can Kill at a great distance; they are Said to kill all person who are So hardy as to attempt to approach the hill; they State that tradition informs them that many Indians have Suffered by those little people, and among other three Mahar men fell a sacrifice to their murceless fury not many Years Sence. So Much do the Maha, Soues, Ottoes and other neighbouring nations believe this fable, that no consideration is Sufficient to induce them to approach the hill.*

Although no devils were sighted, the journals of the Lewis and Clark expedition remarked on the fine view and the sea of buffalo to be observed as far as the eye could see:

> *The Surrounding Plains is open Void of Timber and leavel to a great extent, hence the wind from whatever quarter it may blow, drives with unusial force over the naked Plains and against this hill; the insects of various kinds are thus involuntarily driven to the Mound by the force of the wind, or fly to its Leeward Side for Shelter; the Small Birds whose food they are, Consequently resort in great numbers to this place in Surch of them; Perticularly the Small brown Martin of which we saw a vast number hovering on the Leward Side of the hill, when we approached it in the act of catching those insects; they were so gentl that they did not quit the place until we had ariv within a fiew feet of them....from the top of the Mound we beheld a most butifulll landscape; Numerous herds of buffalow were Seen feeding in various directions; the Plain to North N.W. & N.E. extends without interruption as far as Can be seen.*

(Excerpted from the Journal of Capt. Clark, dated 25th August Saturday 1804)

Today, visitors are welcome to explore Spirit Mound, which has been acquired with National Park Service funds and returned to tall grass prairie. It is located on Highway 19 about eight miles north of Vermillion. A footpath allows walkers to ascend to the top of the mound and stand where Lewis and Clark once stood to survey the territory.

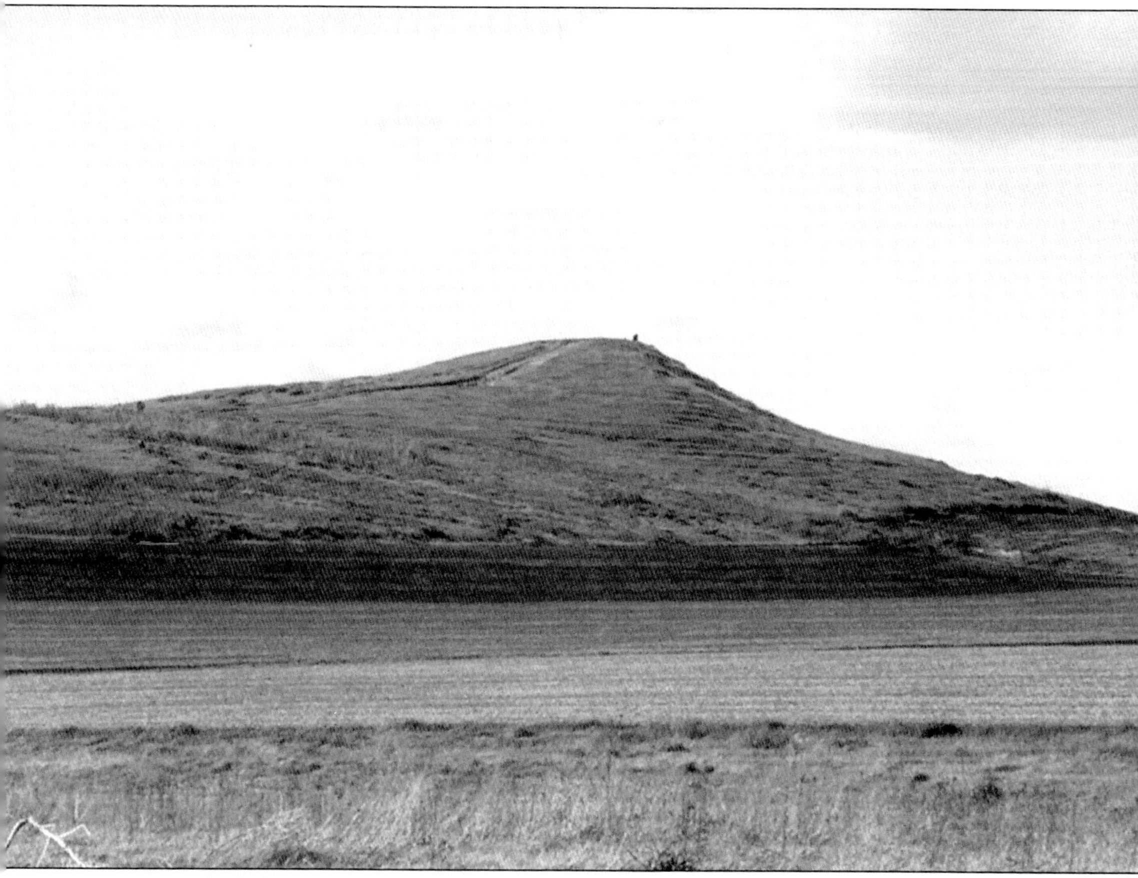

Lewis and Clark stood at the top of Spirit Mound (above) and surveyed the "butifull landscape" with its "herds of buffalow" as far as the eye could see. Today Spirit Mound has been returned to tall grass prairie and is open to the public. It is one of the few places where one can stand in the footsteps of Lewis and Clark.

Two

EARLY SETTLEMENT

Various peoples have inhabited the Clay County area for some 12,000 to 15,000 years, beginning at the end of the last ice age. The earliest settlers were probably a nomadic people—Paleo-Indians—who hunted big game with Clovis points attached to wooden shafts. Later migrants into the area include an Archaic people who used many different food sources, a Woodland people who used pottery, bows and arrows, and learned to grow maize, beans, and squash, and Plains Village people who built substantial villages in the area. The Arikara and similar groups were descended from people who migrated from the south. Finally, the Dakota, Nakota, and Lakota migrated to the area during the 1600s and 1700s.

Earliest records of settlement in Vermillion suggest that the area just below its steep bluffs was a camping ground for bands of Yankton Sioux where they cultivated corn and stored supplies for the long cold winters. The Lewis and Clark expedition arrived in Vermillion on August 24, 1804; they were the first whites to appear in the area. Later, a fur trading post was built at the junction of the Vermillion and Missouri Rivers.

After the Indian Treaty of 1858 cleared the way for settlement, a small river town began to grow along the Missouri at the foot of the bluff near what is now Dakota Street. That same year, Captain Joe Blair Todd and Daniel Marsh Frost established a trading post at the mouth of the Vermillion. At least one other trading post also existed in the Clay County area.

Early settlement was dominated by farmers of Scandinavian heritage In 1859, a group of 31 Norwegian families settled on land in the extreme southwest corner of what is now Clay County. Swedes, Danes, and Finns would follow. The Irish settled in Lodi. The first Territorial Legislature met in 1861 and formed Clay County, designating Vermillion as its county seat.

Early businesses catered to the steamships that docked at Vermillion's pier and included the St. Nicholas Hotel, as well as provisioners of the meat, grains, eggs, produce, and dairy products needed by those undertaking the journey west. The area's first subscription school was in a small log building in 1860. The Territorial Legislature designated Vermillion as the site of the University of Dakota in 1862, though no funds were designated for the enterprise. Several decades would pass before citizens of Vermillion would take matters into their own hands and construct the first building with locally-raised funds.

Early settlers in Clay County's tall-grass prairie faced unfamiliar challenges of harsh weather and meager rainfall. However, meat and wild honey were easily procured and the rich bottom land provided fertile soil for crops. By the 1880s, corn had emerged as the most important cash crop in the area. In addition, the land's natural affinity for producing hay in abundance led many farmers to add livestock to their operations. Meckling Township, in particular, was heavily engaged in stock-raising.

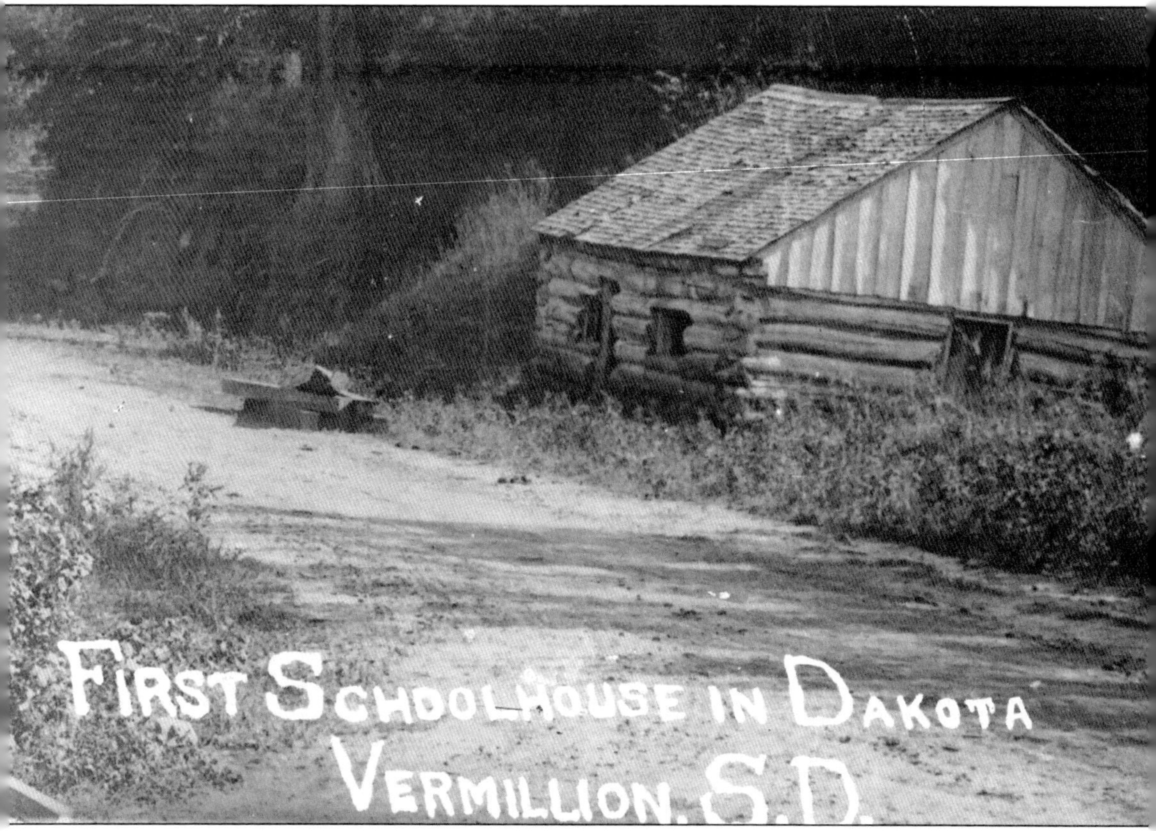

The first schoolhouse in Dakota Territory was built of logs below the bluff on the east side of what is now Dakota Street. (Courtesy of W.H. Over Museum.)

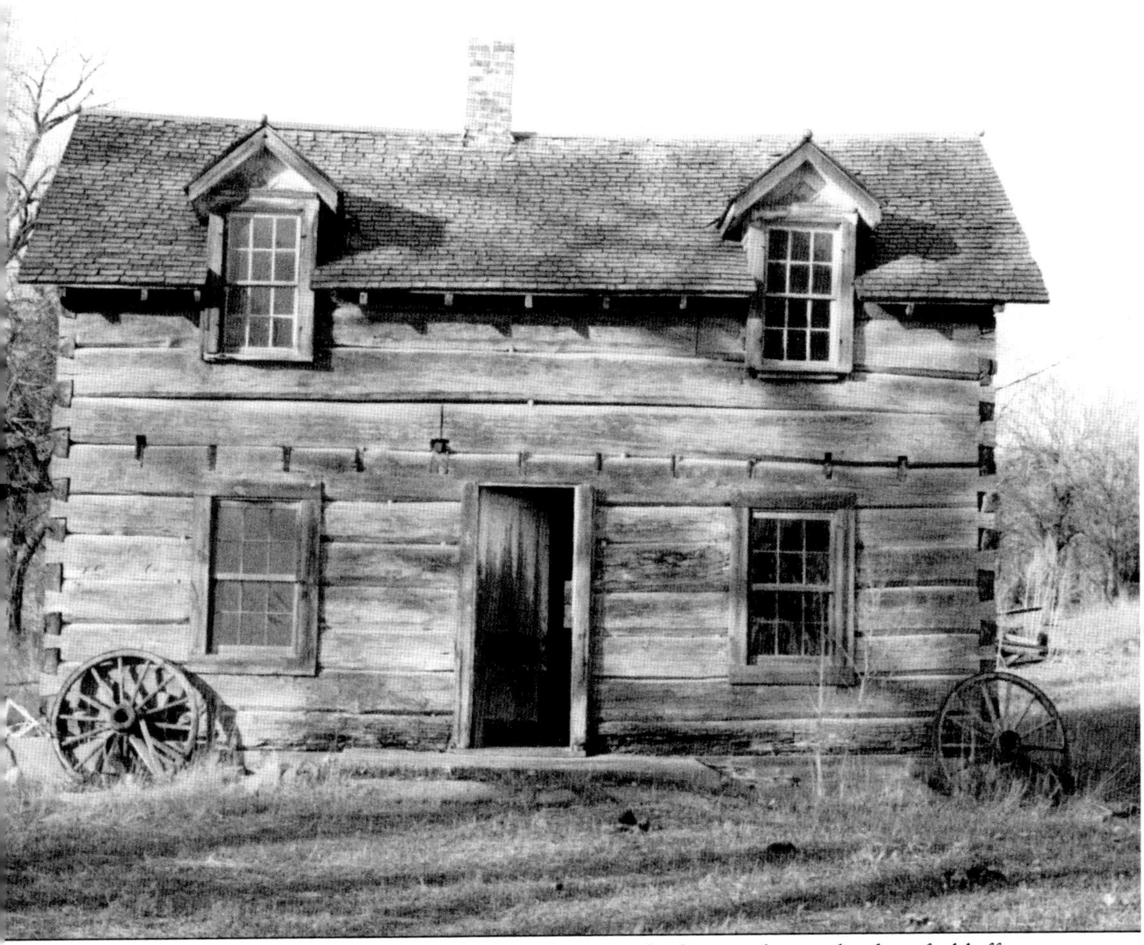

This one-and-a-half-story log house was built to the east of a draw at the south edge of a bluff on a homestead purchased by Inglebrit Severson in 1869. The unchinked squared logs were joined at the corners by dovetail notching, a feature suggestive of Scandinavian influence. The dormers were probably added at a later date. Severson sold the farm to his two daughters, one of whom was Gurina Rice. It is known locally as Rice Farm. (Courtesy of the W.H. Over Museum.)

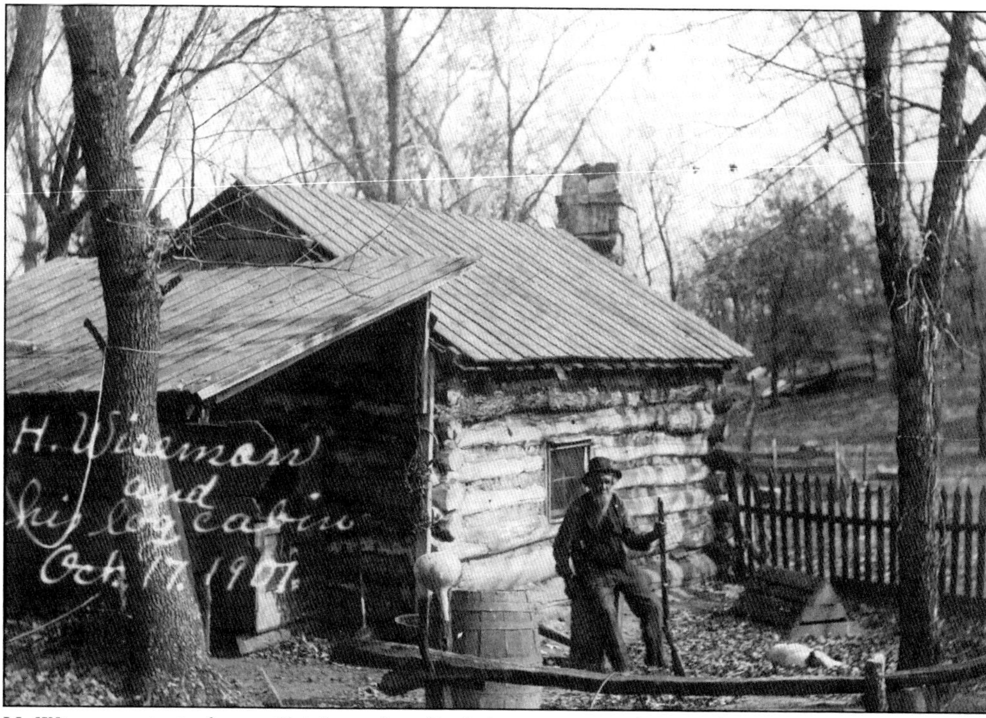

H. Wiseman sits in front of his log cabin. Early homes were often made of rough-hewn logs from cottonwoods and other old growth trees along riverbanks. In many cases, the logs had to be transported great distances. (Courtesy of Clay County Historical Society.)

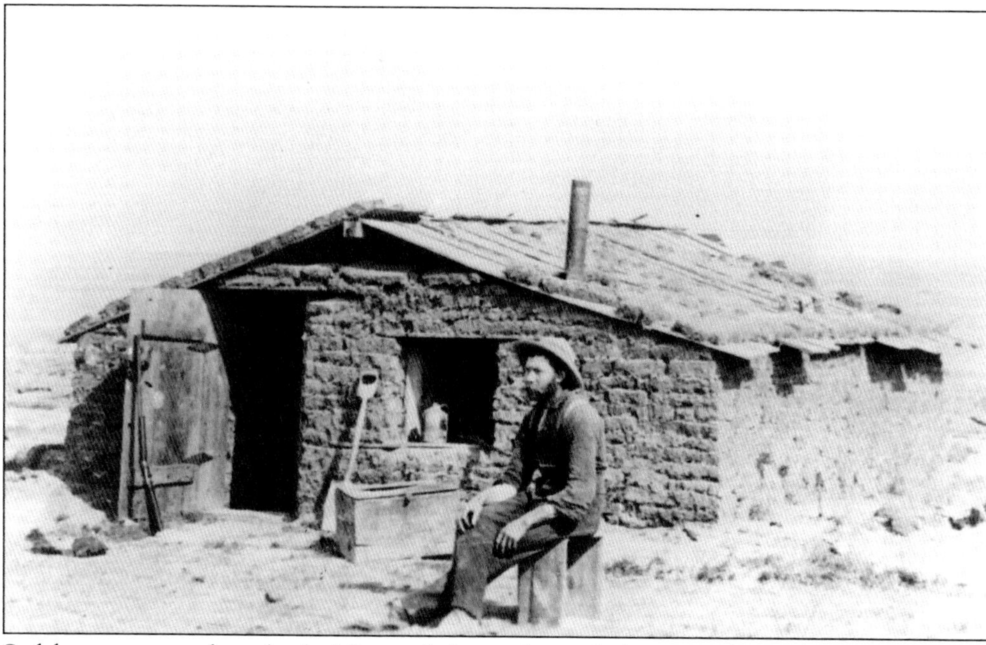

Sod houses were often the buildings of choice for early homesteaders. The materials were on-hand and free. This man rests for a few minutes on a bench in front of an early sod house. (Courtesy of W.H. Over Museum.)

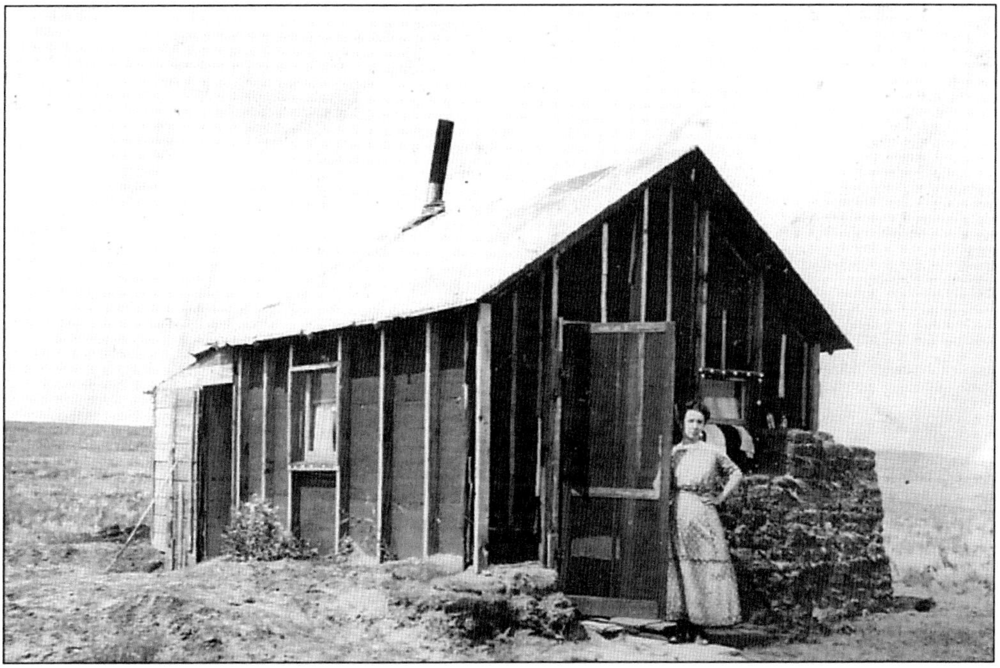

A young woman stands at the door of a shack that is still under construction. Notice the sod stacked out in front.

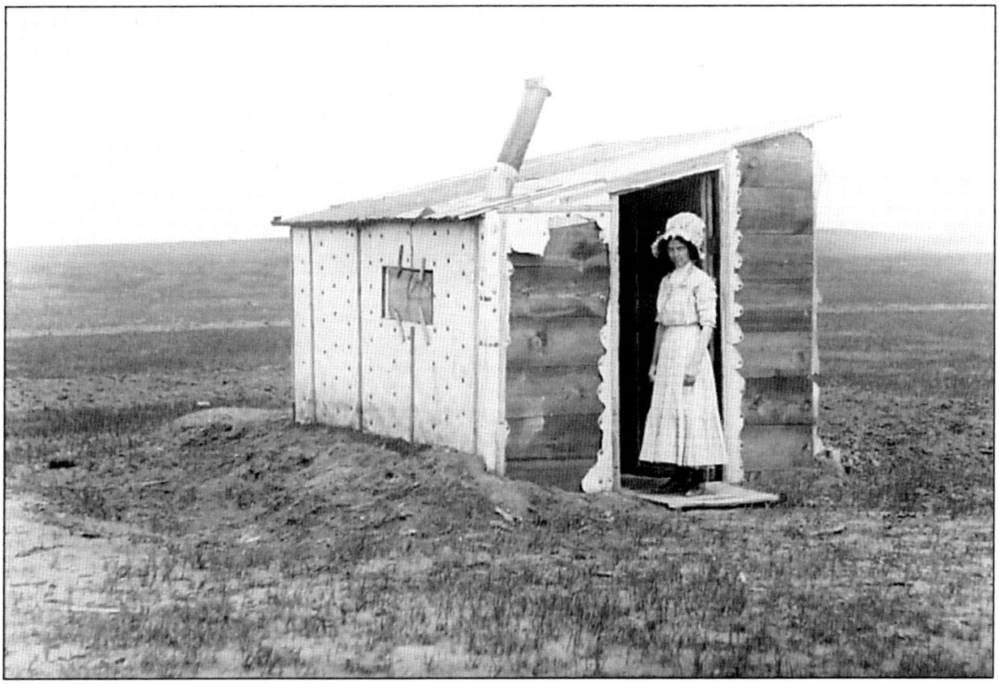

Pictured here is a young woman with prairie bonnet in a little shack on the prairie.

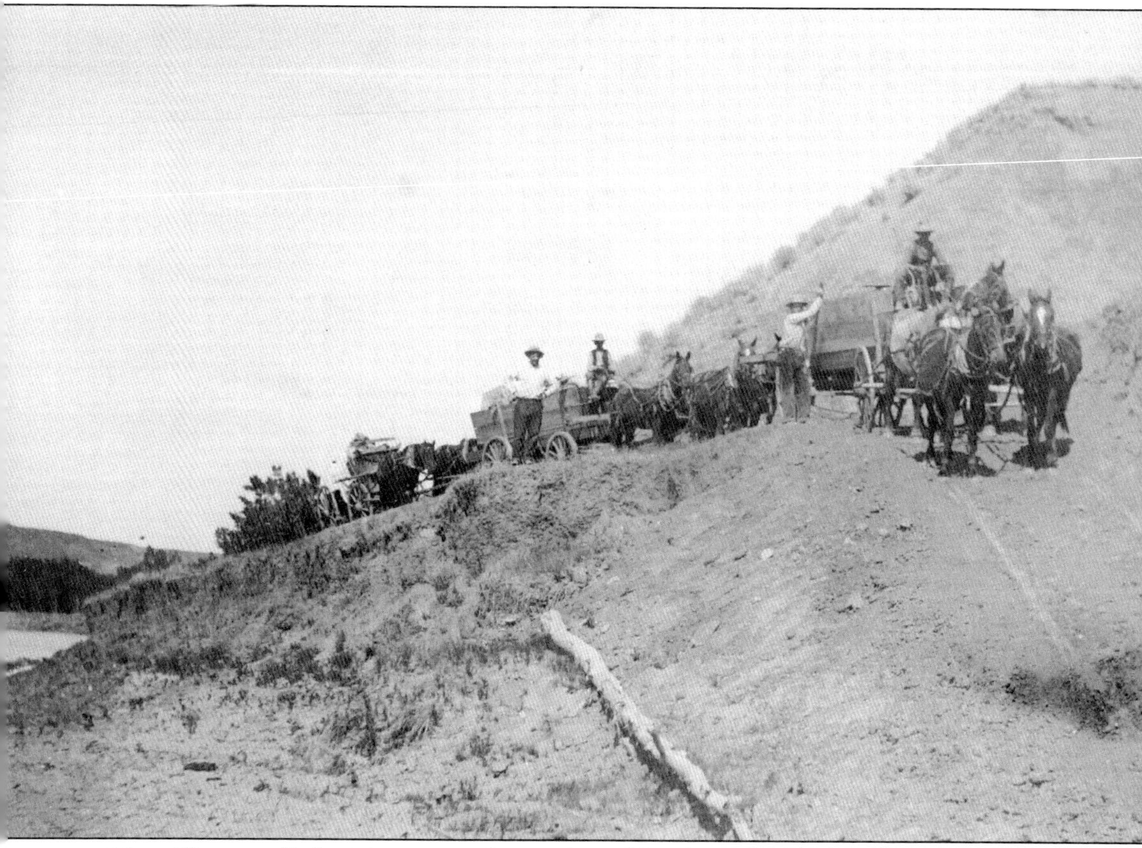

Vermillion supplied mining camps during the gold rush in the Black Hills. J.B. Daily Freight Wagons dispatched a horse-drawn supply "train" from Vermillion to the Black Hills in 1877. (J.E. Spensley Collection, Courtesy of the Clay County Historical Society.)

Three

Vermillion Before the Flood

The founding of Vermillion was due in large part to the Missouri River, which flowed past the old town situated along its banks below the bluff where Broadway still stands. The river approached from the south and followed the course of today's Vermillion River. According to old maps, when the river was high and touched the bluffs, it formed whirlpools. Vermillion was founded as a point of commerce along an important means of transportation.

A.C. Van Meter built the first house of logs in the old town and offered a rope ferry across the river. James McHenry constructed the first store. Not only did it supply the public's material needs, but on Sundays it was the setting for the first church services in Vermillion until a log church could be built. McHenry later built the Vermillion Steam Flouring Mill in the area. The Clay County Bank opened for business in 1871. Its upstairs "Bank Hall" doubled as a theater, public meeting place, and dance venue. Three hotels would ultimately be built—the Adelphi, the St. Nicholas, and the Maynard House. Three sawmills, three drug stores, three hardware stores, and clothing, barber, furniture, harness, and meat shops were available to local residents, along with attorneys, a doctor, livery stables, and two saloons.

Life in the new river town could be rambunctious, as evidenced by an account of Vermillion's first Fourth of July celebration in 1860 written by a Mr. Taylor:

> *We shall not attempt to tell of the incidents or festivities of that day. Some of the scenes would not look well in print. Suffice it to say it was a wild event in the little village, one of those days which were not infrequent in those wild and wooly times. When a drunken rought would go tearing through the streets on the back of an untamed steer or engage in boxing bouts, the first blood for the whiskey.*

The Dakota Southern Railroad reached Vermillion in December of 1872 and later provided service to Elk Point and other localities. When gold was discovered in the Black Hills, Vermillion settlers profited by provisioning the aspiring miners with goods they hauled across the prairie in wagon trains. A contemporary description of J.B. Daily's venture was printed in the *Standard* on February 1, 1877:

> *The Daily train consisted of eight teams and 16 men. The wagons belonging to Mr. Daily, five in number, will be freighted with groceries, provisions and general merchandise of the Black Hills trade. The others are loaded with furniture, household goods, mining tools, etc. to be used in the Hills. The train will take the Fort Pierre route, generally considered to be the best route opened.*

By April 14, the paper would note Black Hillers returning every day "after having found out that life among the Indians and outlaws appears more sublime in the pages of a novel than in the realities of life."

In January of 1875 a great fire burned much of the town's business district. It began in the second floor offices of the probate judge and spread rapidly. Tax books, county records, and about $3,000 in county money were lost. Later there were inevitable charges of arson lodged against Probate Judge Simonsen, but none were proven. Nevertheless, the judge was asked to resign and did so. Residents rebuilt the business district forthwith.

The winter of 1880 and 1881 was particularly difficult, with snow up to ten feet in Clay County. The heavy snows and ice accumulations caused an ice jam on the river to the north. Late in March, the spring thaw caused the Missouri to rise, flooding the town. Residents reported hearing loud grinding and groaning noises as the three-foot deep ice began to dislodge from the frozen river. The bell on the Baptist Church rang out a warning to residents who hurried to safety on top of the bluff. Huge chunks of ice destroyed homes and businesses, while the rising water swept many buildings down the river. Vermillionaires today still tell the story of one determined resident who clung to his home as it was rushed by floodwaters down the river, so that he would be able to dismantle it and reuse the lumber later.

The great flood of 1881 dramatically changed the fortune of the growing river town. More than 100 business structures and homes were lost. The devastated residents, who had endured two major disasters within a decade, decided to rebuild the town on top of the bluff to avoid future catastrophes. A new town began to take shape within weeks, built to some extent from the remnants of the old.

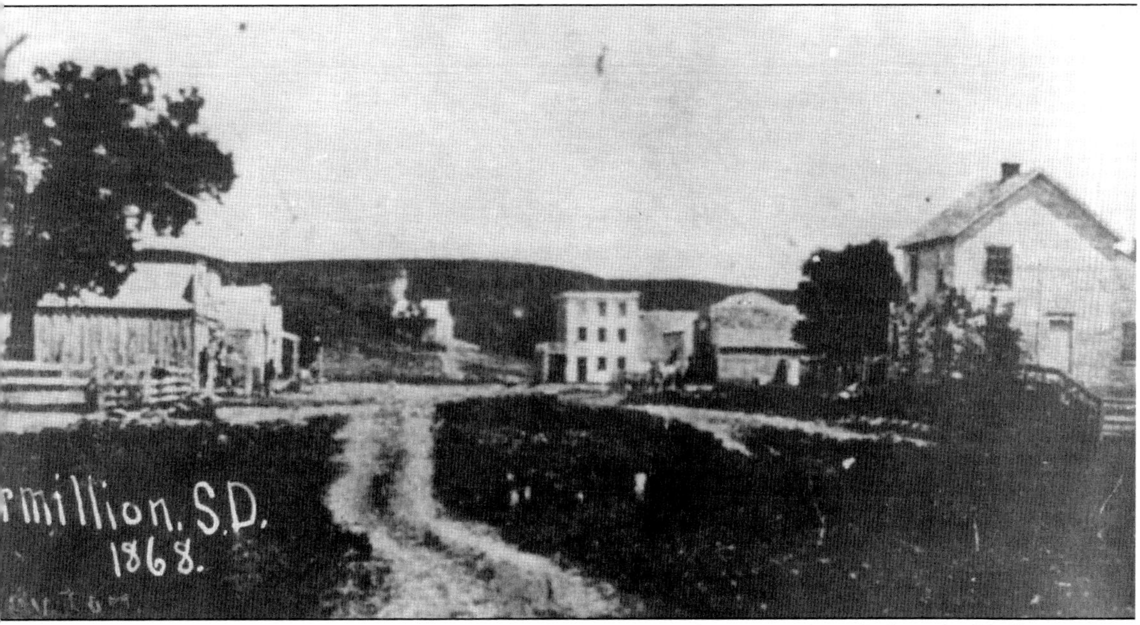

The oldest available photo of Vermillion was taken in 1868 along Broadway below the bluff. Previously a popular camping place for Native Americans, Broadway would serve as the town's main commercial thoroughfare until 1881, when a massive flood destroyed it. On the right foreground is the Jim McHenry house. The tall building at the end of the street is the St. Nicholas Hotel. Boats on the Missouri River stopped just beyond the hotel to drop off supplies and to load produce from local farms. The stagecoach from Sioux City to Fort Randall stopped here regularly. (Courtesy of W.H. Over Museum.)

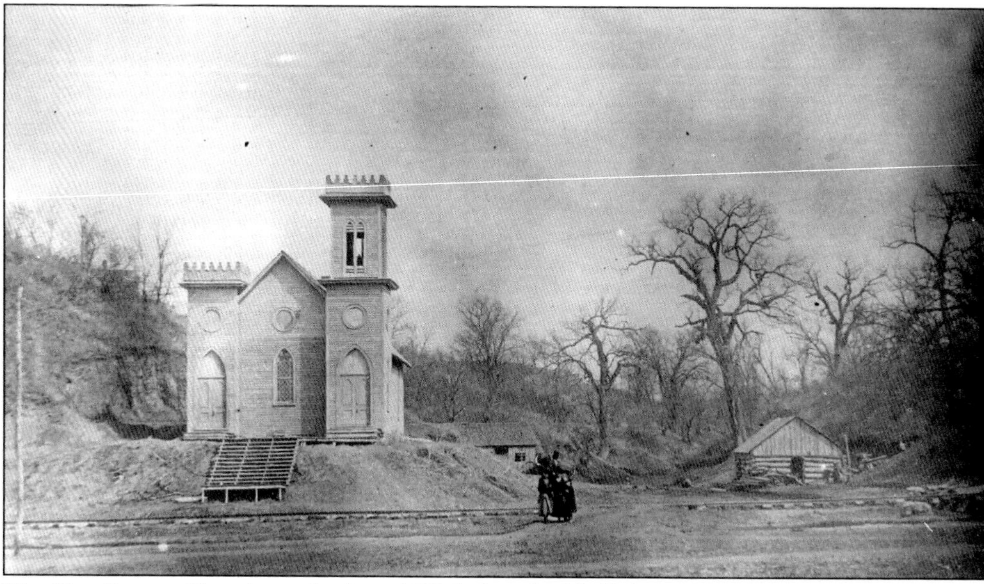

The First Baptist Church was built in 1871 below the bluff along the ravine road, which is now roughly Dakota Street. On the right is the first schoolhouse in Dakota Territory. (Courtesy of the W.H. Over Museum.)

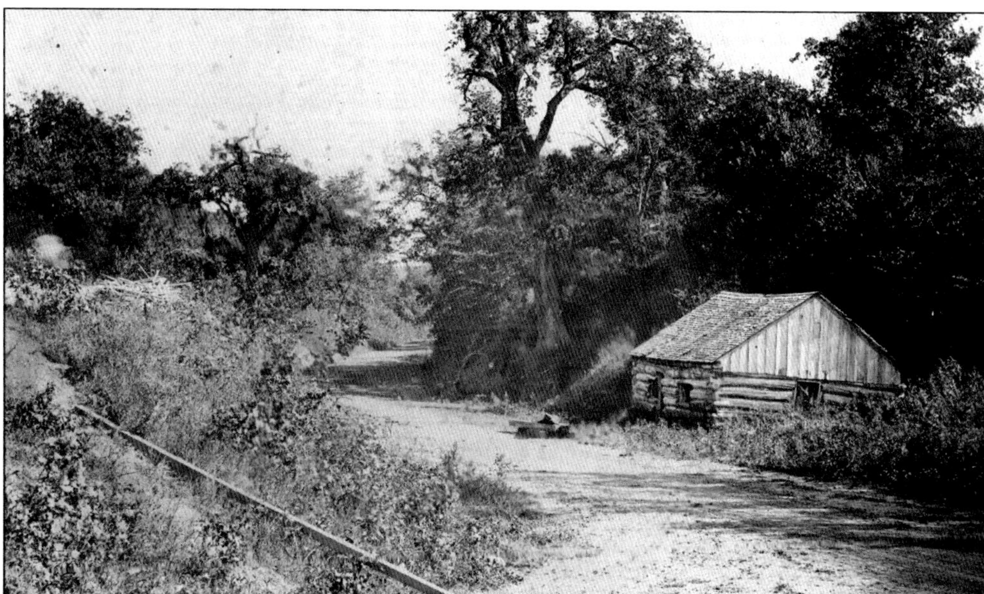

In the fall of 1864, the first schoolhouse in South Dakota was built by Captain Nelson Miner, his Dakota Cavalry Company, and local citizens, and was situated just below the bluff on the east side of what is now Dakota Street. Hugh Compton was unable to leave his job, but he sent along a pail of whiskey and tin cup as his substitute. A local wag said that the substitute was the strongest worker on the job, as "it not only got the logs up. It also got some of the men down." The first schoolmaster was Amos Shaw, a member of the Cavalry who was assigned to the task by Captain Miner. In addition to functioning as a schoolhouse, the structure also served as a meeting place, polling place, and church. (Courtesy of W.H. Over Museum.)

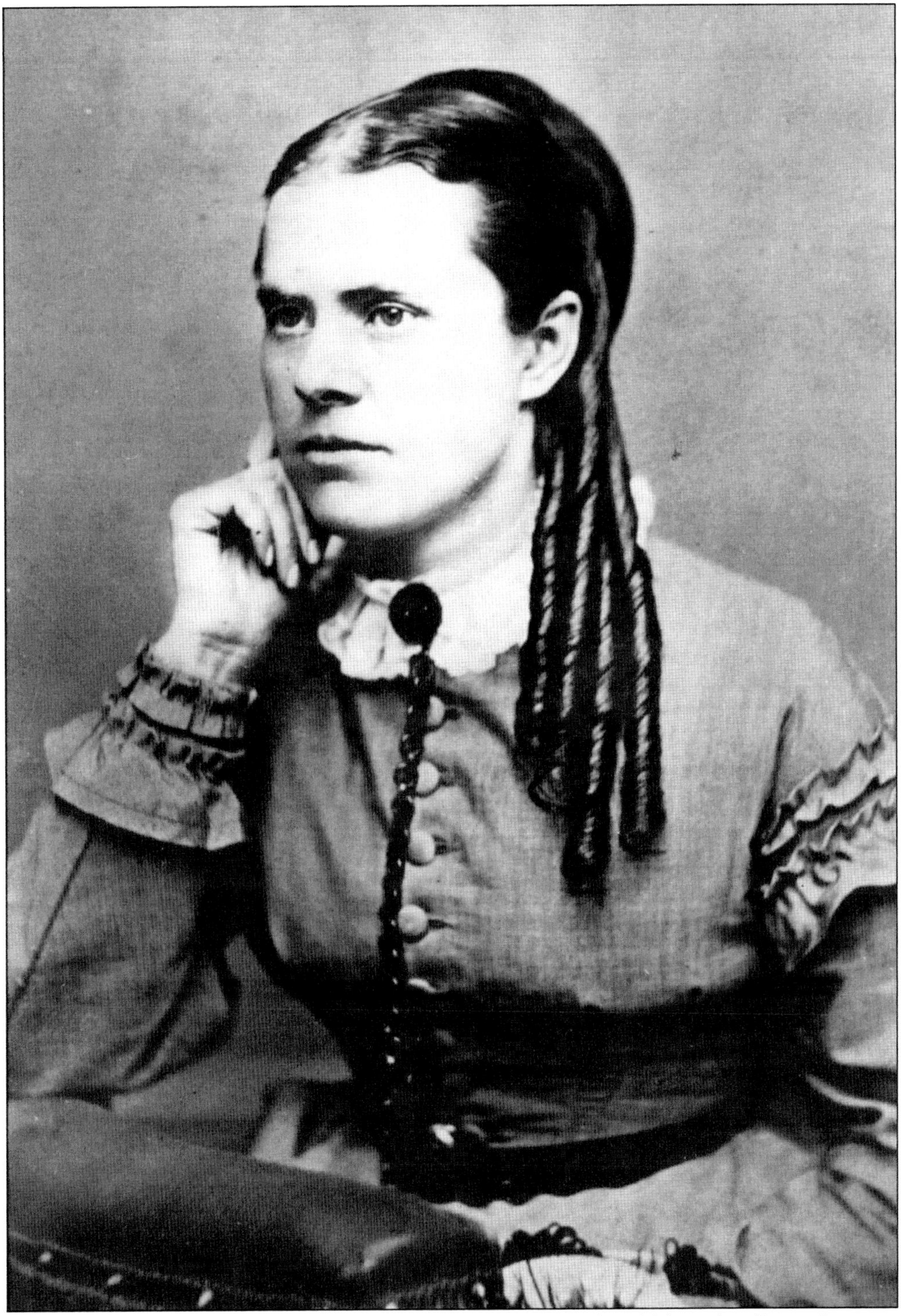

Rachel Ross Austin, wife of Horace Austin, taught school in the old log schoolhouse between 1867 and 1870. Austin Park, the site of Austin School, was donated to the city in memory of Rachel Austin. (Courtesy of the Clay County Historical Society.)

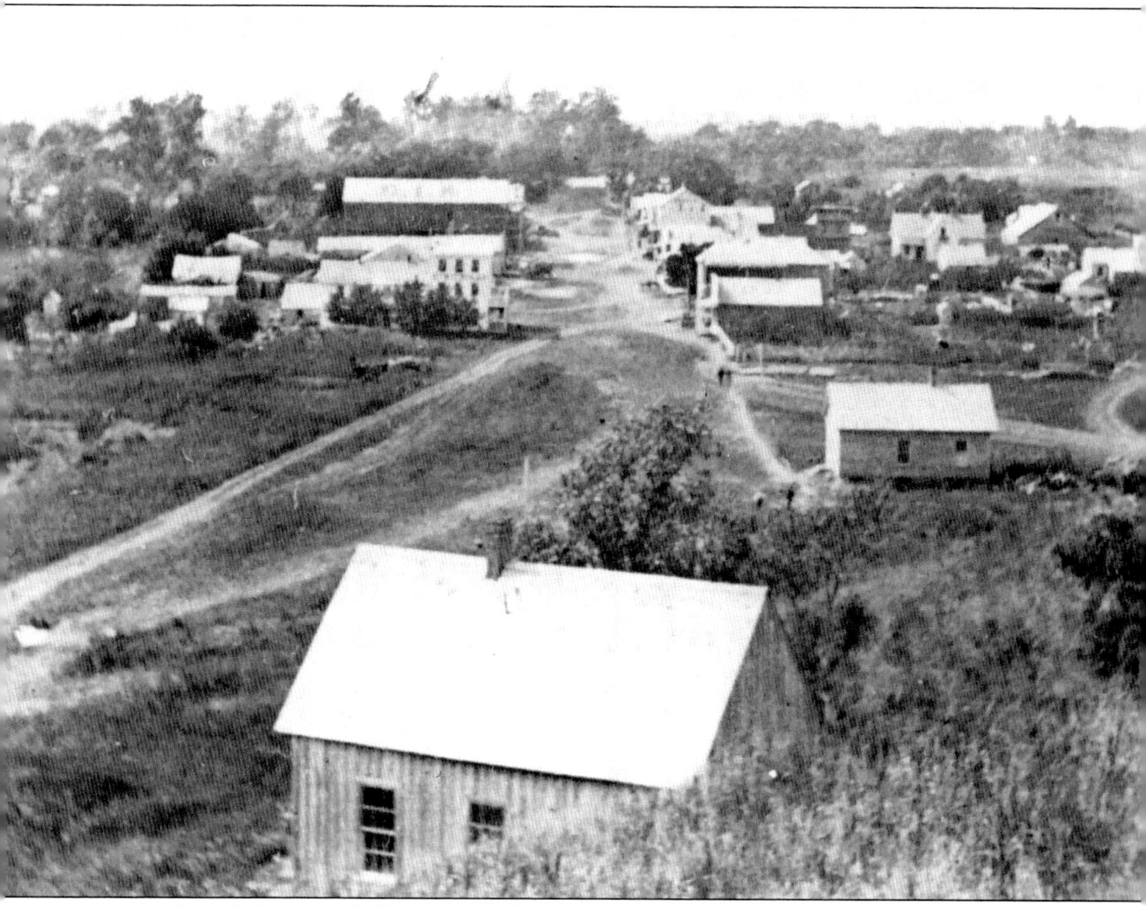

Vermillion, below the bluff, is pictured here as it was in 1872, looking west down Broadway. The first prominent building on the left of the road is the St. Nicholas Hotel. The largest building on the left has "CIK" painted on its roof, an abbreviation for Cash Is King. By the 1870s, the town was thriving, as evidenced by its land office, Episcopal Church, shoe store, Dr. Jonson's Drug Store, Judge Kidder's office and courthouse, and many other businesses. (Courtesy of W.H. Over Museum.)

Around 1880, before the flood, Vermillion had a furniture shop and a harness shop. Plank sidewalks protected pedestrians from the mud and dust. (Courtesy of W.H. Over Museum.)

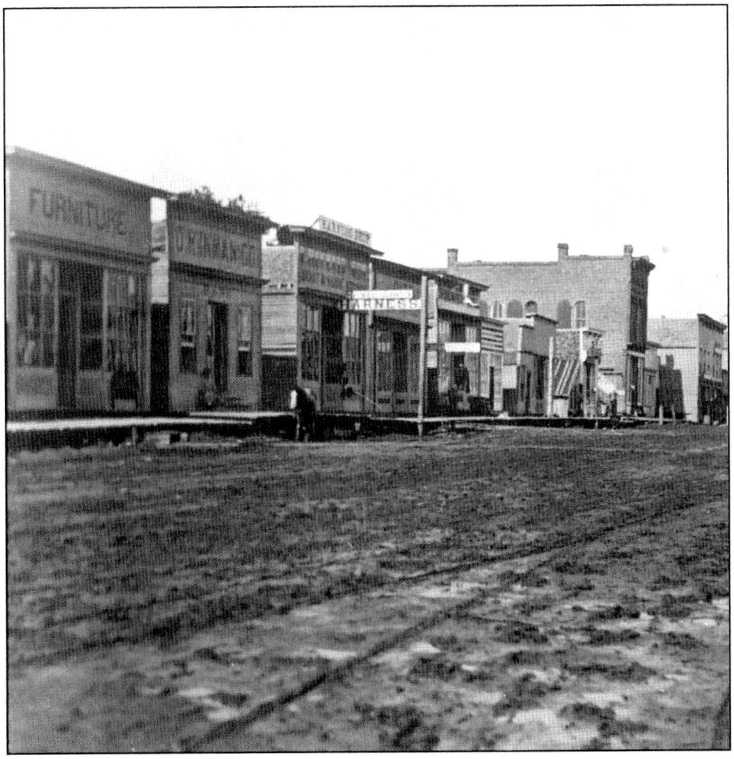

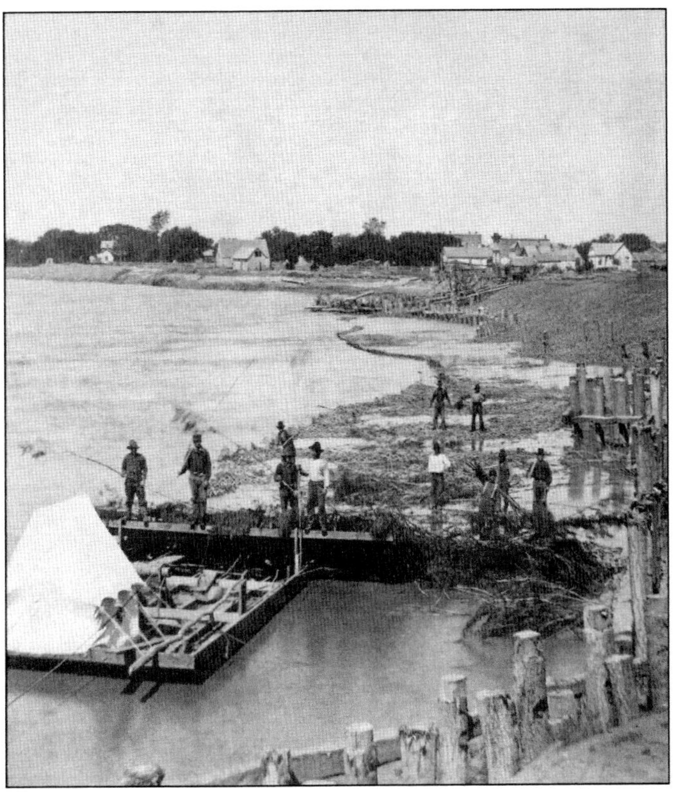

Men fished near the steamboat landing on the banks of the Missouri where it flowed past old Vermillion before the 1881 flood. (Courtesy of W.H. Over Museum.)

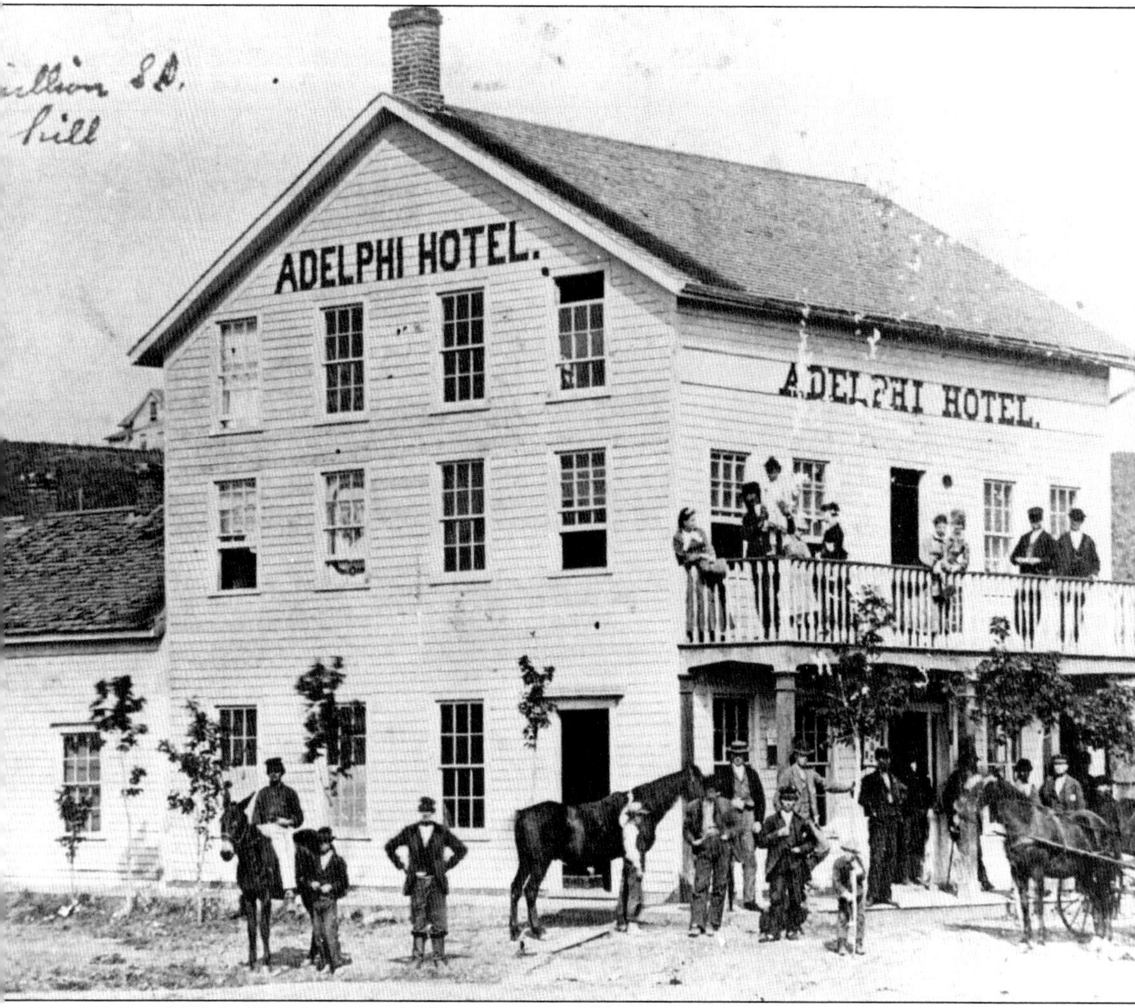

The Adelphi Hotel, below the bluff, is pictured here before the flood destroyed it. (Courtesy of Clay County Historical Society.)

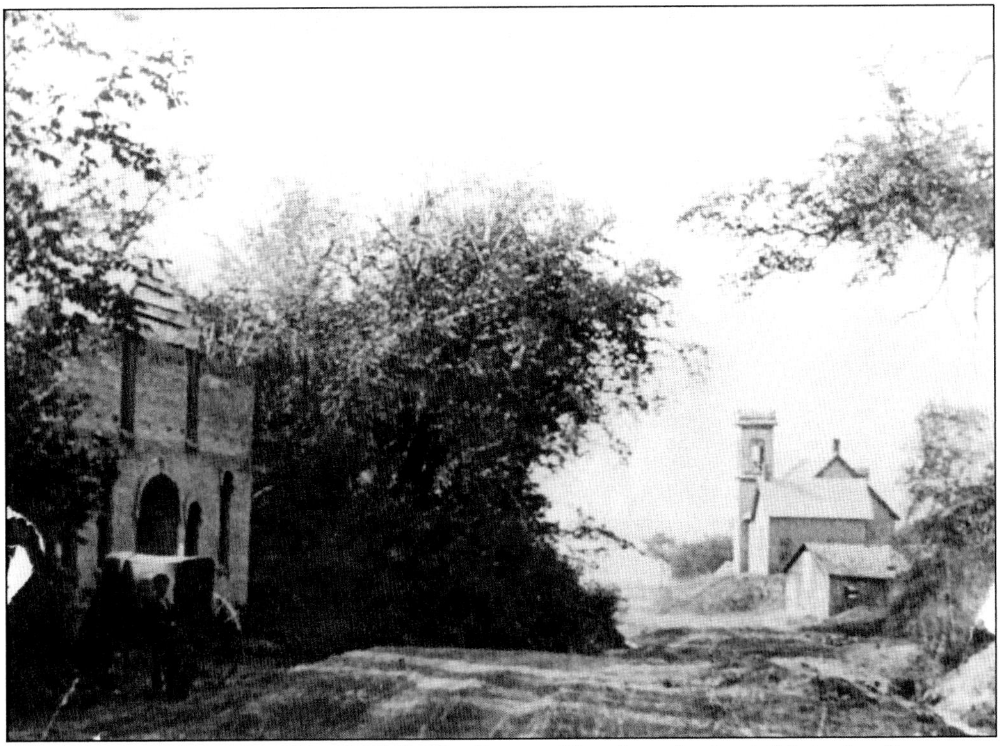

An early brewery is pictured on the left. The Baptist Church is clearly visible in the distance on the right. (Courtesy of W.H. Over Museum.)

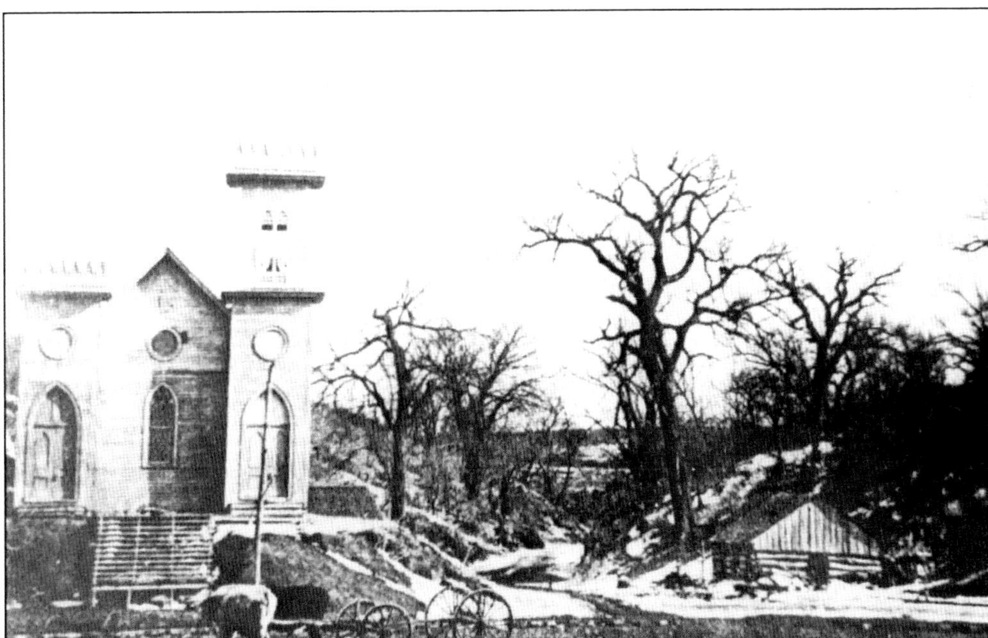

The old Baptist Church is shown here in the snow with the ravine road (Dakota Street) clearly visible in the center. (Courtesy of W.H. Over Museum.)

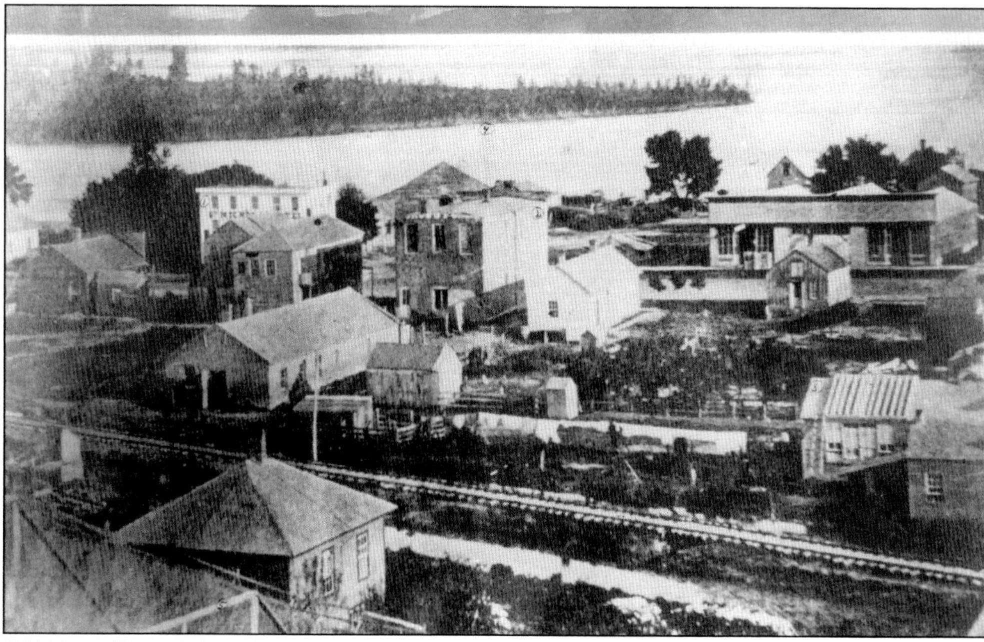

Old Vermillion, below the bluff, with the Missouri River clearly visible in the background and the railroad tracks in the foreground. Old Vermillion was built just below the bluff on the banks of the river. After the flood of 1881, the Missouri River changed course to its present location, miles to the south. (Courtesy of W.H. Over Museum.)

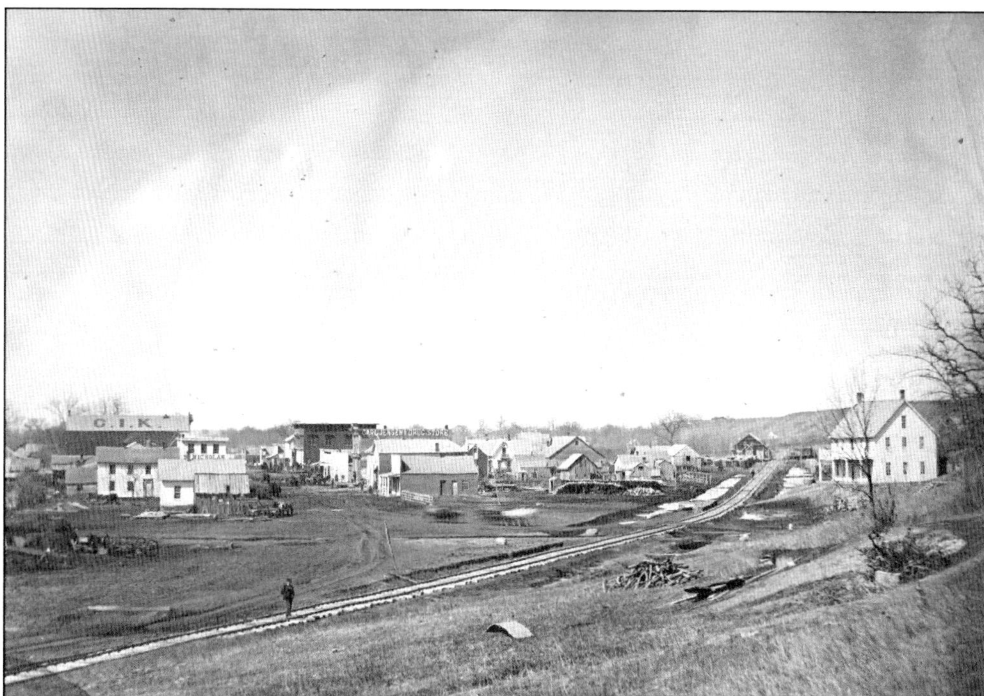

Vermillion is pictured here before the flood and just after the railroad came through. The new tracks are visible in the foreground. (Courtesy of Clay County Historical Society.)

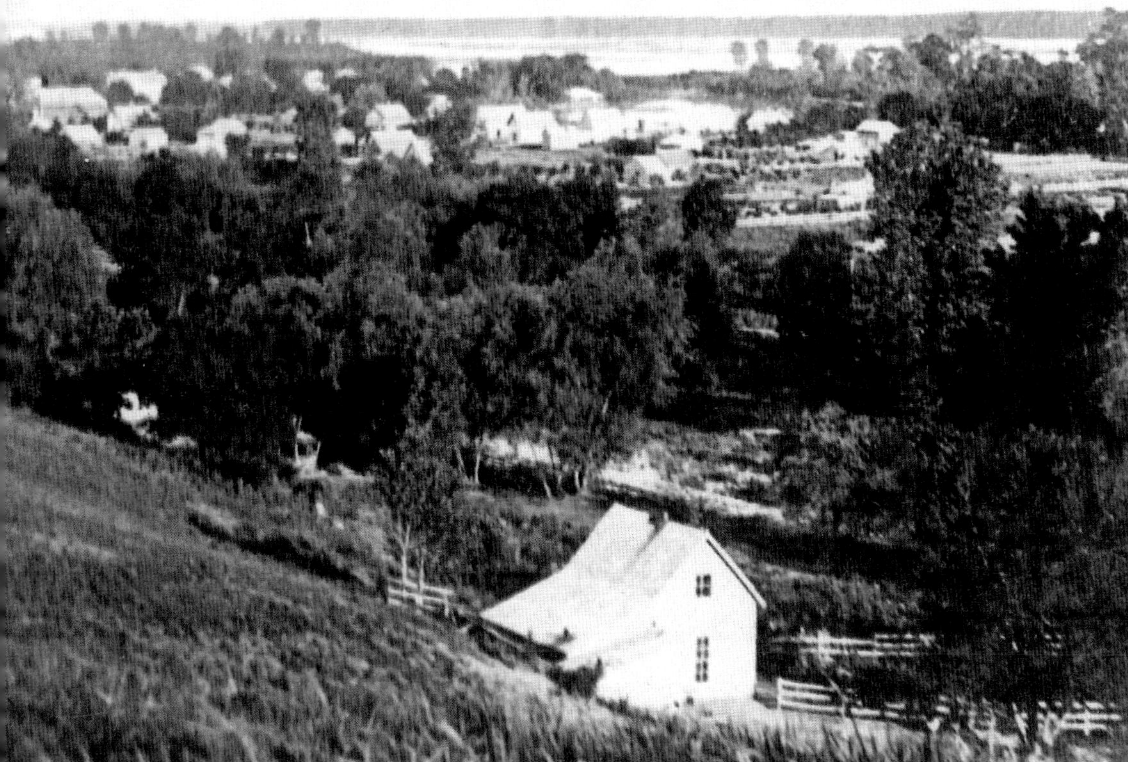

A bird's eye view of Vermillion looking east shows the proximity of the Missouri River in the 1870s. (Courtesy of W.H. Over Museum.)

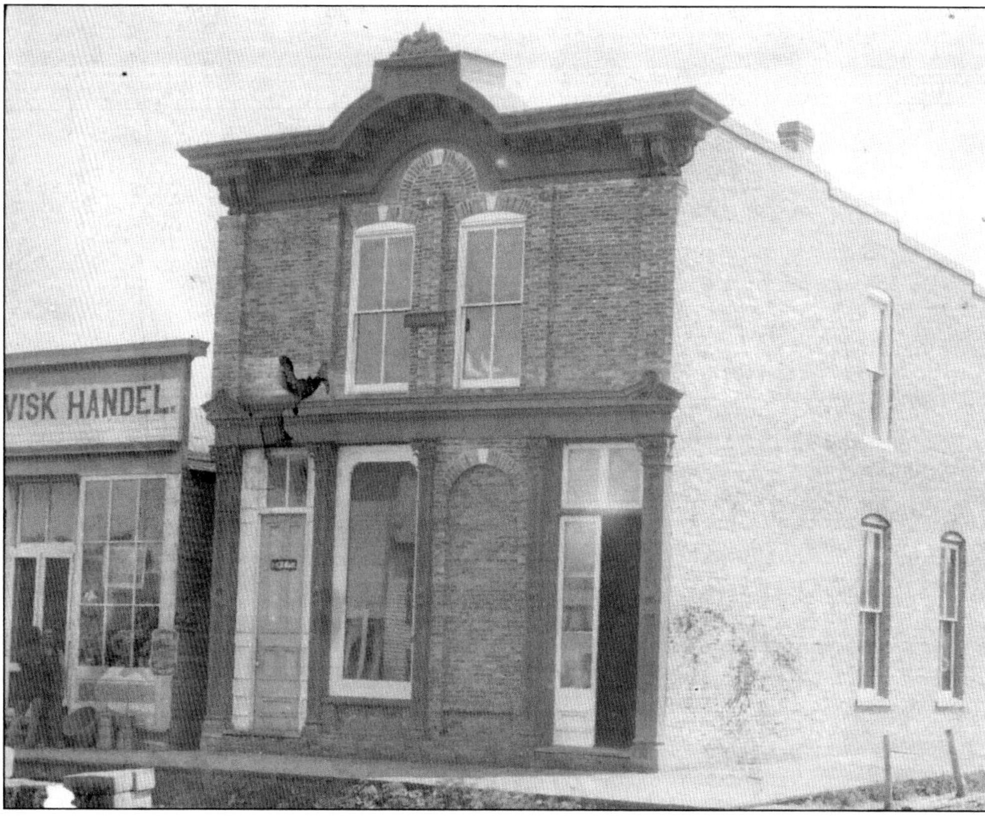

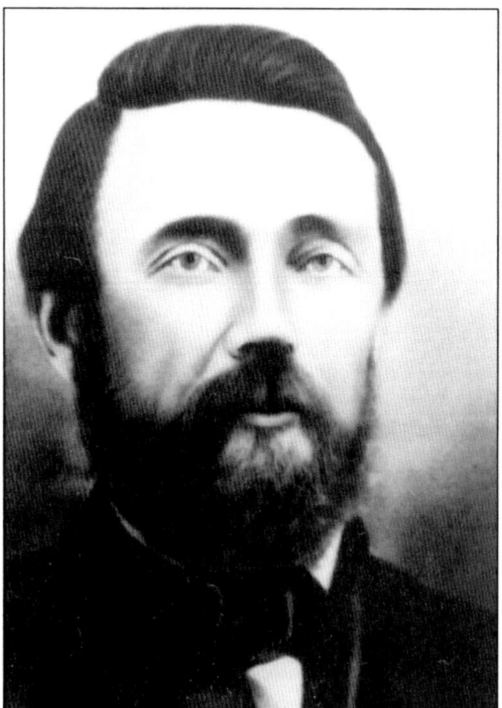

The bank building of D.M. Inman was erected in 1882 and burned down on November 28, 1892. (Courtesy of W.H. Over Museum.)

Captain Nelson Miner was a prominent citizen of early Vermillion who led his Cavalry Company and local citizens in building the first schoolhouse in Dakota Territory. He owned the St. Nicholas Hotel. (Courtesy of Clay County Historical Society.)

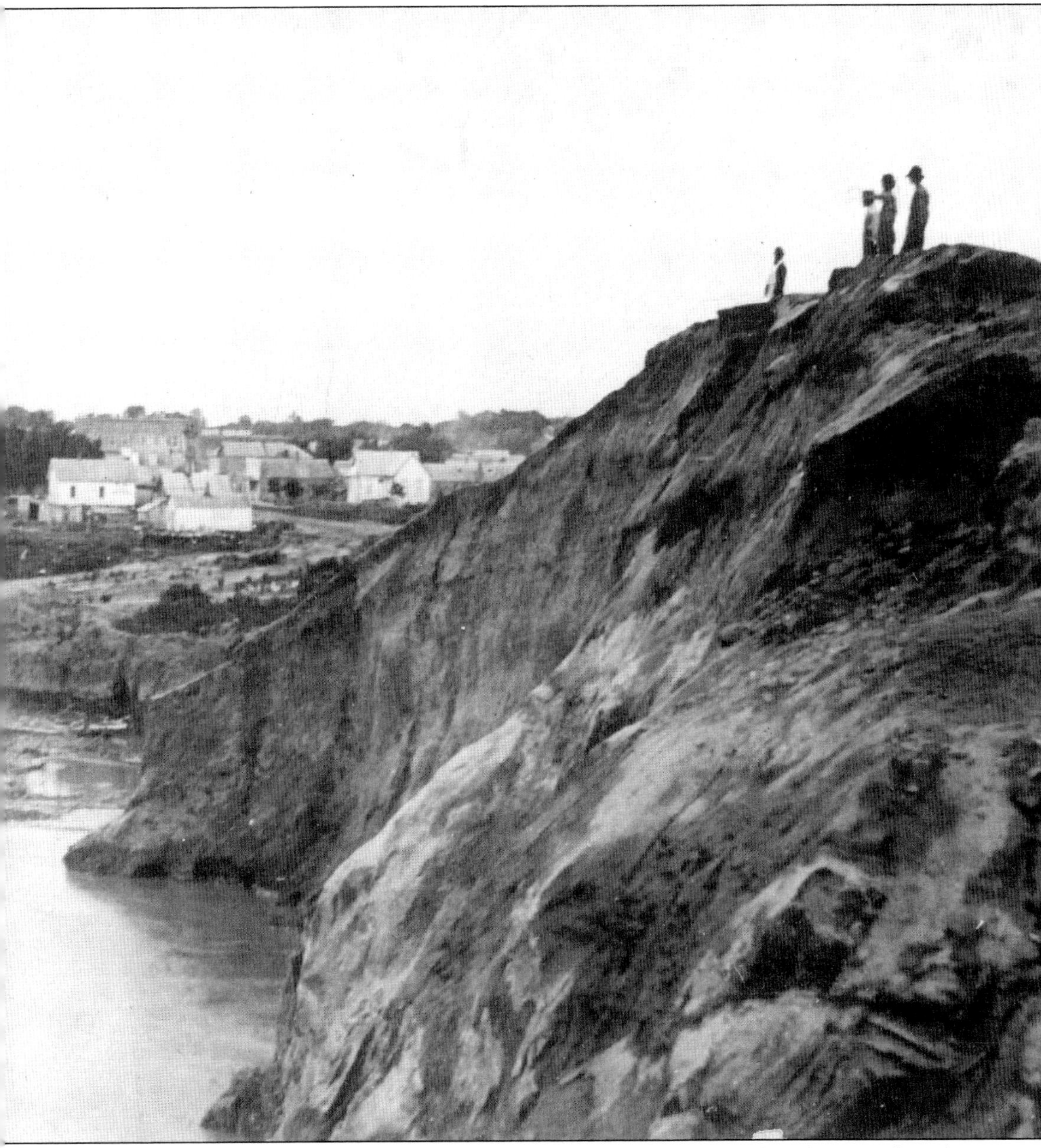

The steep banks of the Missouri River are clearly visible in the foreground as the river flowed past old Vermillion. Years later, the Sletwold Greenhouse would be built on this site. (Courtesy of W.H. Over Museum.)

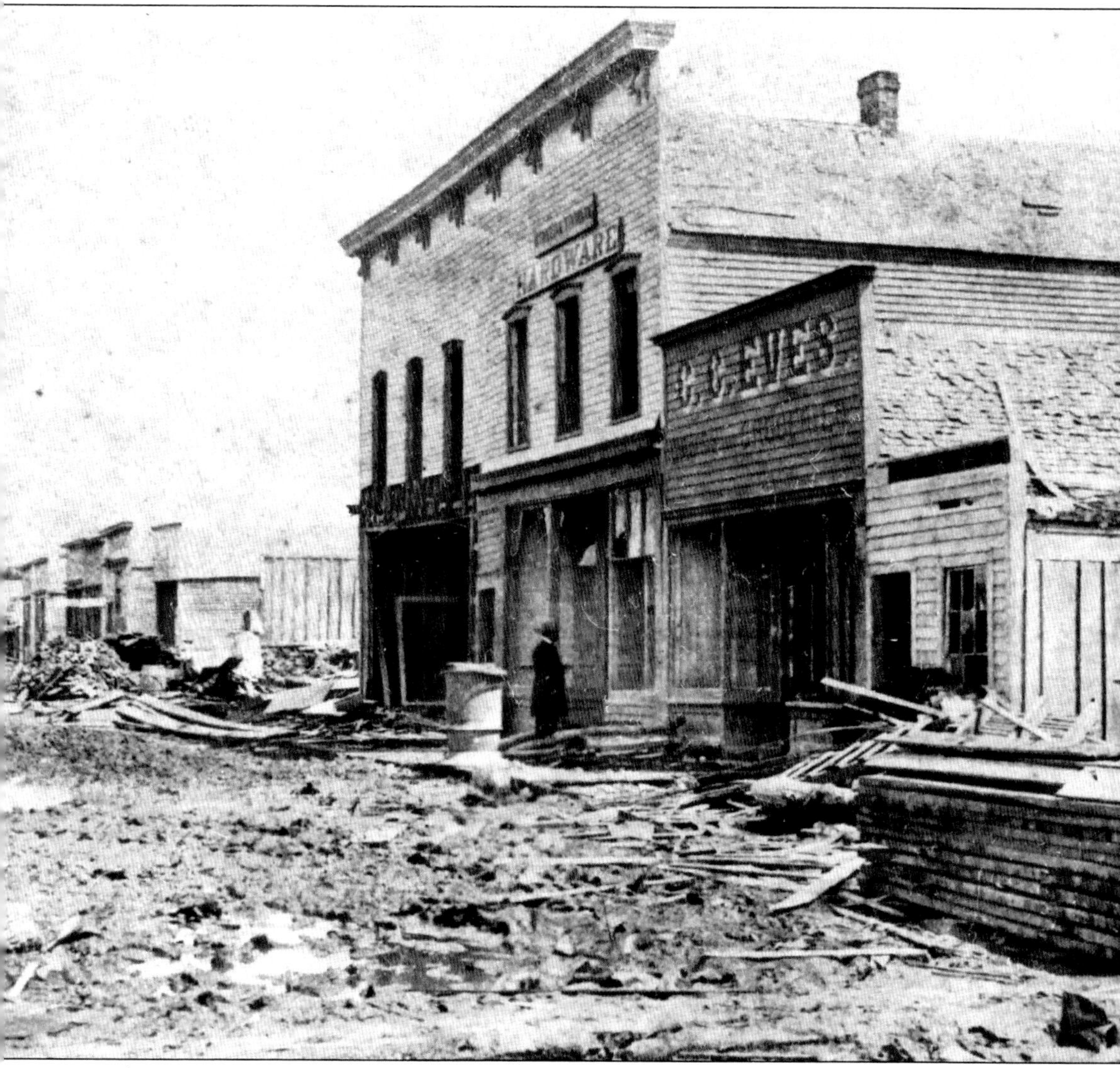

The west side of Broadway was severely damaged by the 1881 flood. (From the Morrow Collection, courtesy of the W.H. Over Museum.)

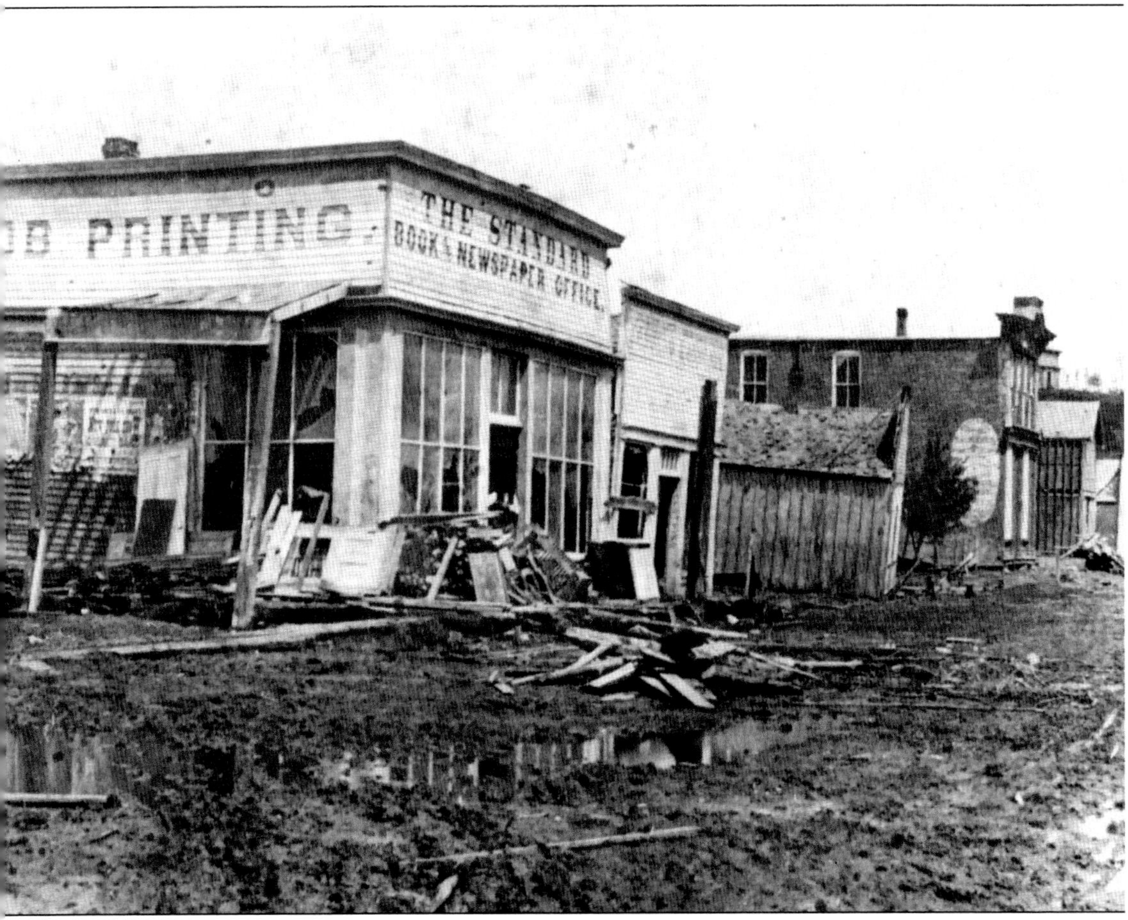

The Standard Printing Company is shown here in May of 1881, months after the flood that devastated the town of Vermillion. (Courtesy of the W.H. Over Museum.)

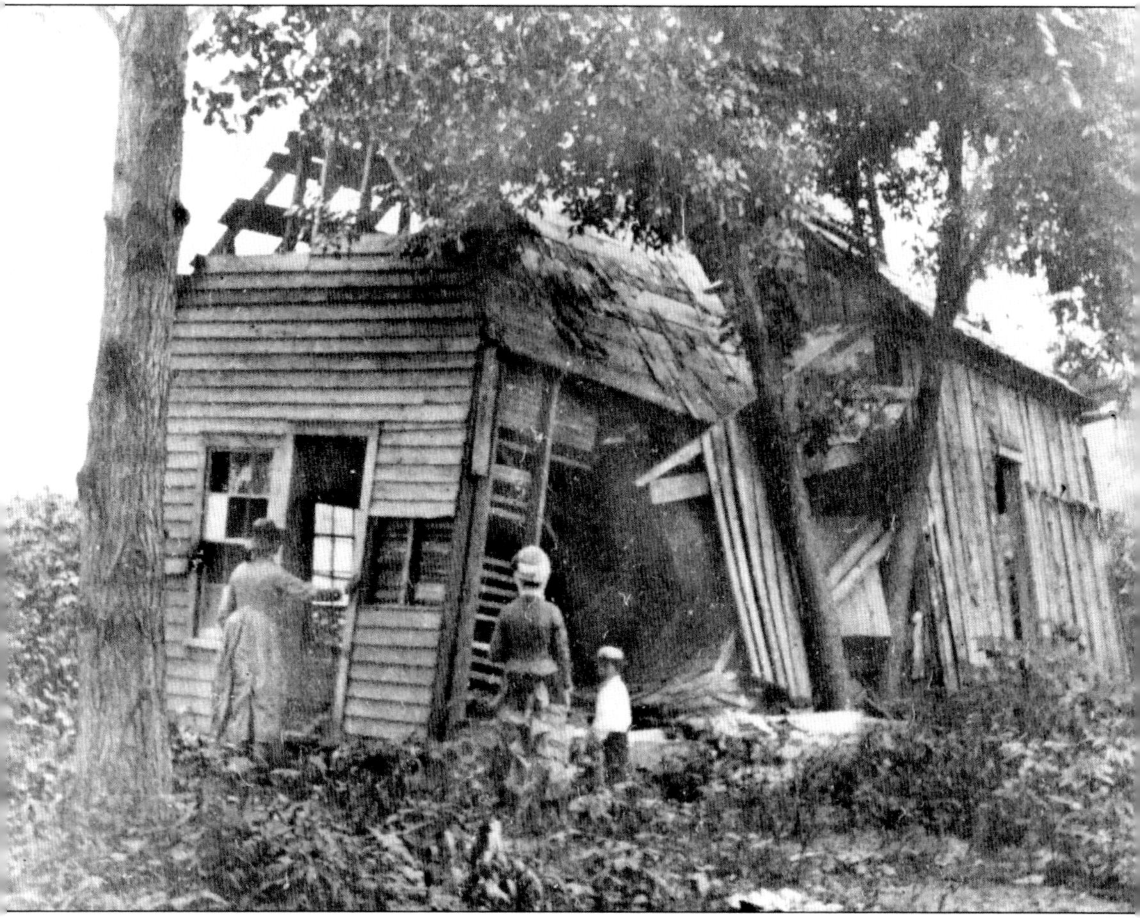

The W.G. Bowers family returned to their home, which had been devastated by the flood of 1881. (From the Morrow Collection, courtesy of the W.H. Over Museum.)

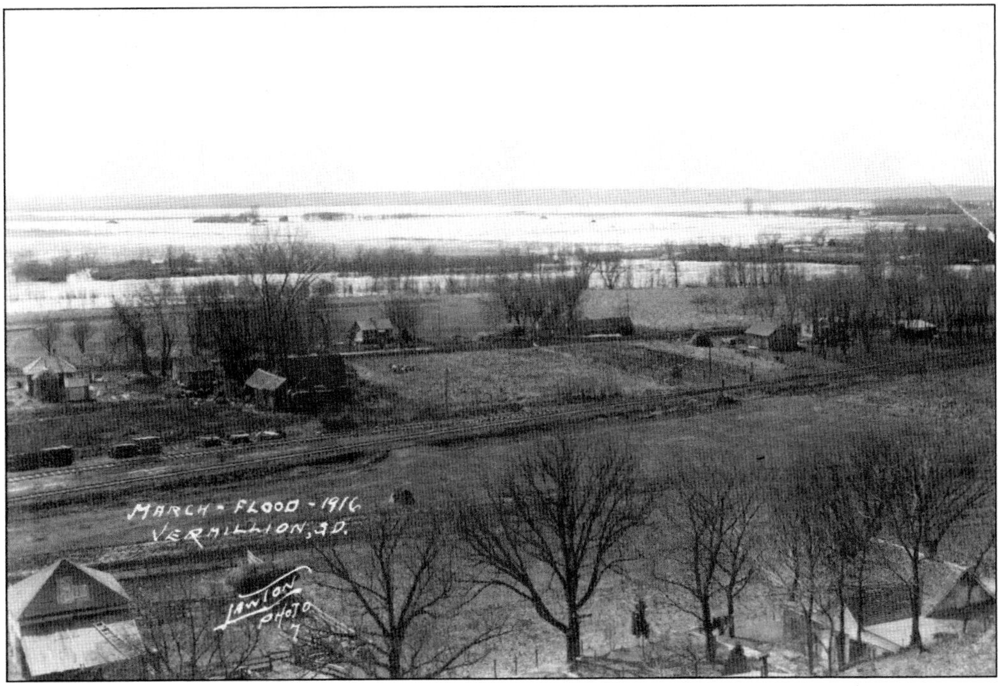

The flood of 1881 was by no means the last flood to bedevil Vermillion. In 1916, the waters rose to inundate surrounding farms and homes once again.

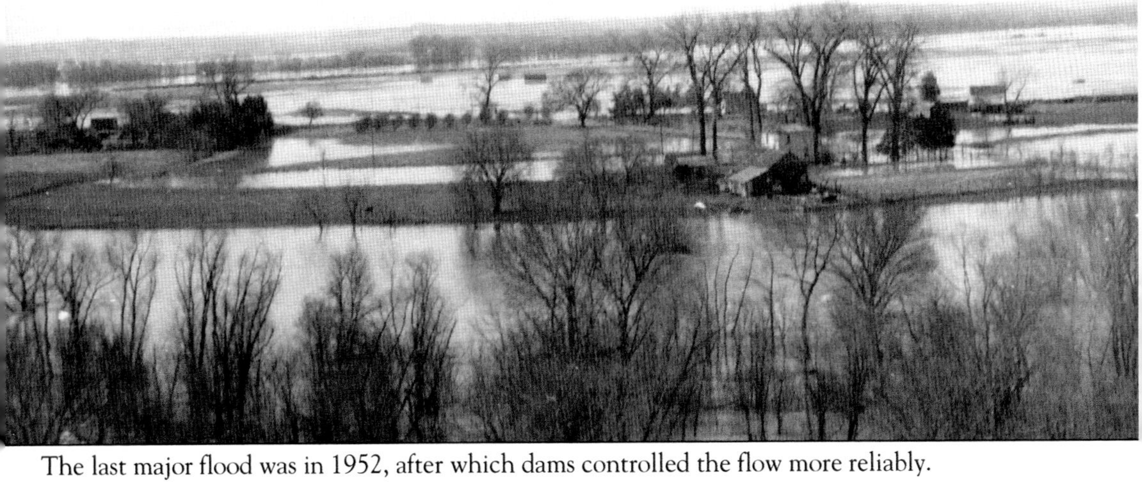
The last major flood was in 1952, after which dams controlled the flow more reliably.

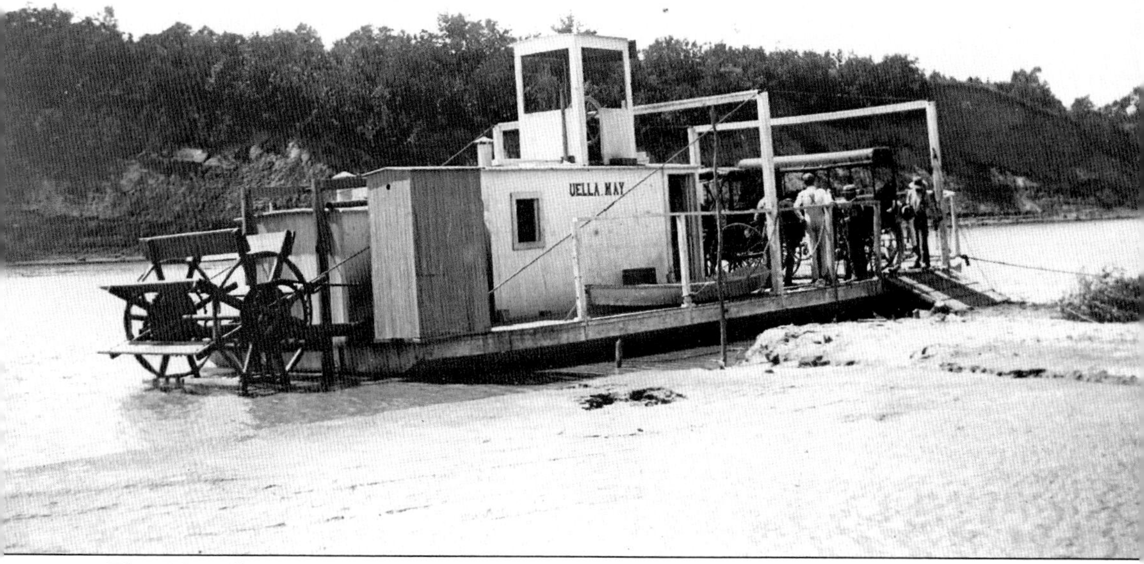

The Vermillion Ferry, *Della May*, plied the waters of the river. (Courtesy of W.H. Over Museum.)

Four

Historic Downtown Vermillion

The new town began to take shape within weeks of the great flood. Materials from old buildings were hauled up the bluff to supply parts for the new town. A few of the stores were repaired and moved up the hill. Vine Street was renamed Main in consideration of its new status as the town's main artery. A courthouse was constructed early in 1882 at the site of the present post office. Judge Kidder loaned space in the building to the University of South Dakota's first students. Shortly afterward, University Hall was constructed on the present campus. The University would shortly become a major engine of growth for Vermillion.

Disaster struck again in the form of a major fire in 1890 that burned two blocks of businesses on Main Street, with losses estimated at $100,000. In its wake, the city council adopted an ordinance requiring that buildings be made of brick and mortar or other fireproof materials.

By the turn of the century, Vermillion was a thriving community with small manufactories, the nationally chartered Bank of Vermillion, livery stables, and a Main Street with markets and stores to fulfill the needs of local residents. Andrew Carnegie donated $18,000 in 1903 to build a community library. Clay County constructed a 16-mile canal, called "Little Panama," at a cost of $116,000 to connect the Volin area with Vermillion. By 1910, Vermillion had 2,183 residents, many of whom took up residence along the wide tree-lined streets to the east of the downtown area. Mrs. Inman bought an electric car and presumably obeyed the town's 25 mile an hour speed limit. The Waldorf Livery Service began to offer "automobile service at reasonable rates." A sign of the times, the last livery barn closed in 1917 and five years later the last hitching post was removed from the business district.

The 1920s boom did not reach Vermillion until mid-decade when the University of South Dakota decided not to move to Sioux Falls. The decade was one of local prosperity during which downtown Vermillion thrived as a market center for the surrounding area. By the 1940s, the streetscape began to change, incorporating modern lights, new sidewalks and storefronts, and many new service stations for the growing number of automobiles in town.

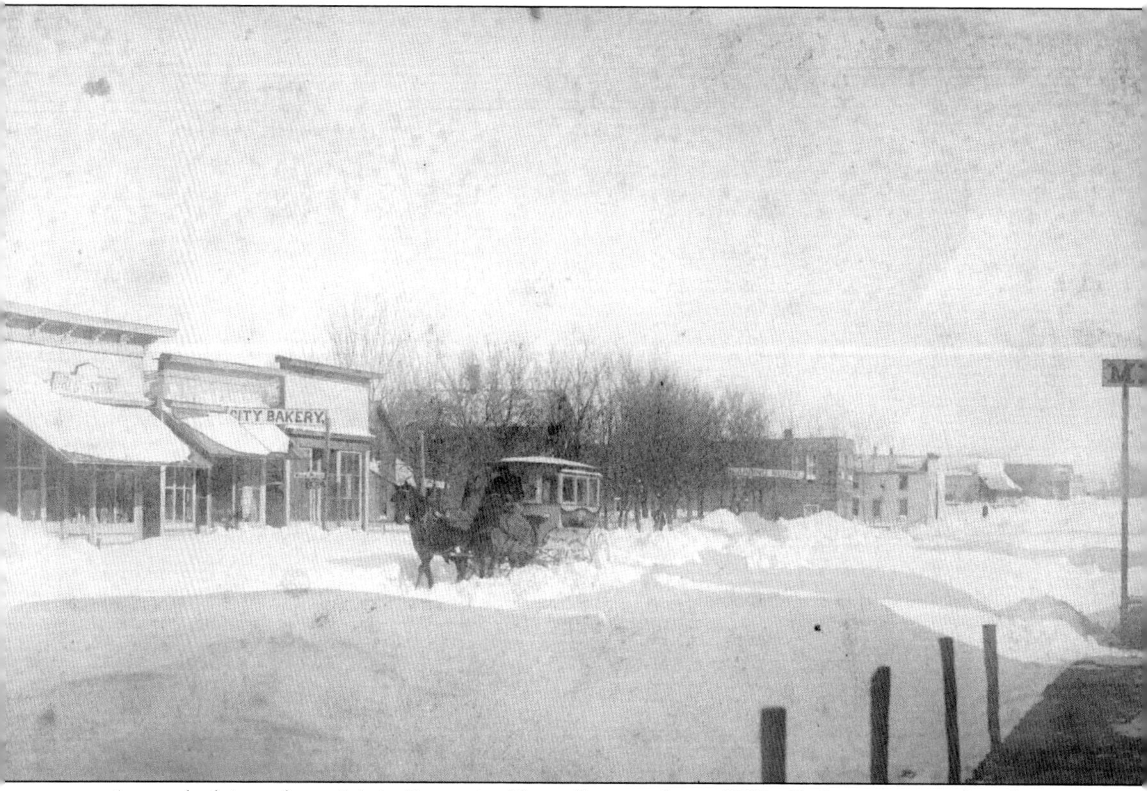

A coach drives down Main Street in Vermillion early in 1882. Only one year after the great flood, the new town was already well-established. (Courtesy of W.H. Over Museum.)

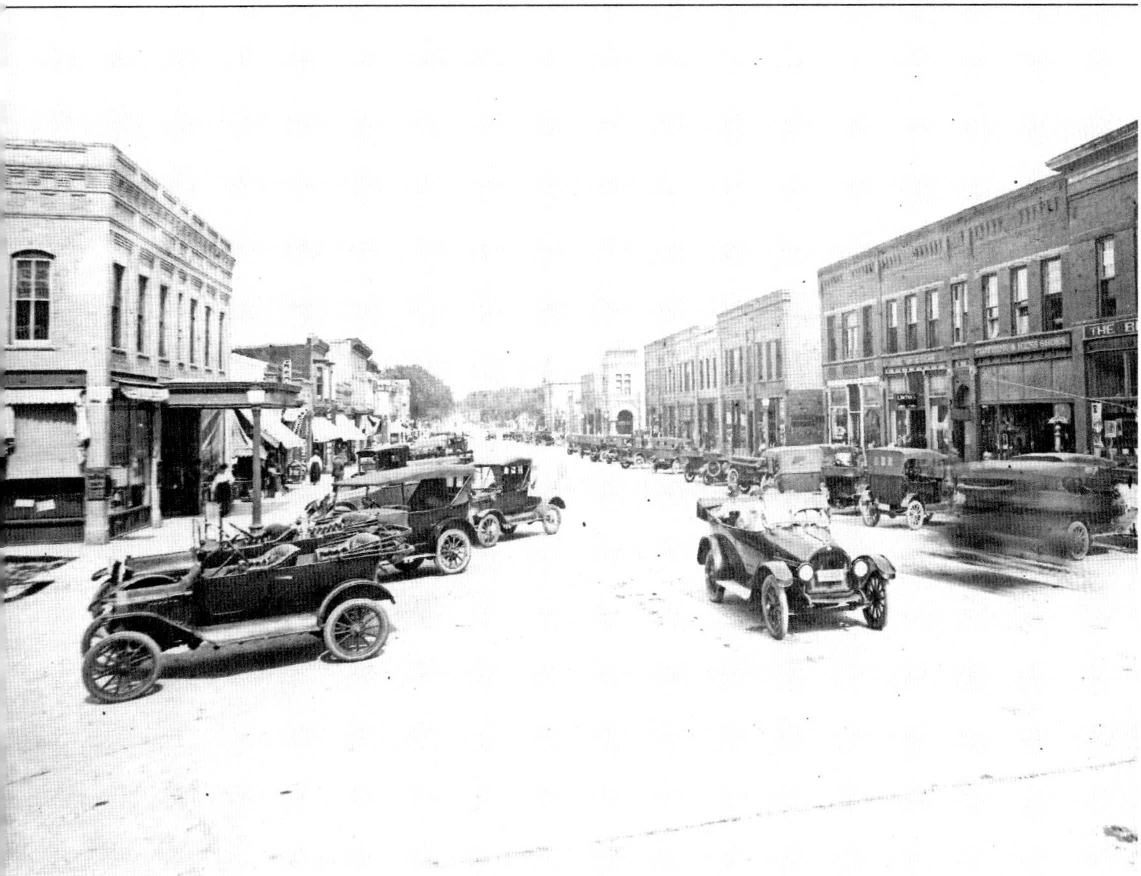

During its early days, downtown Vermillion bustled with activity. Awnings opened out over stores to protect shoppers and merchants from the bright midday sun. Motorcars rapidly replaced horses as a mode of local transportation. (Courtesy of W.H. Over Museum.)

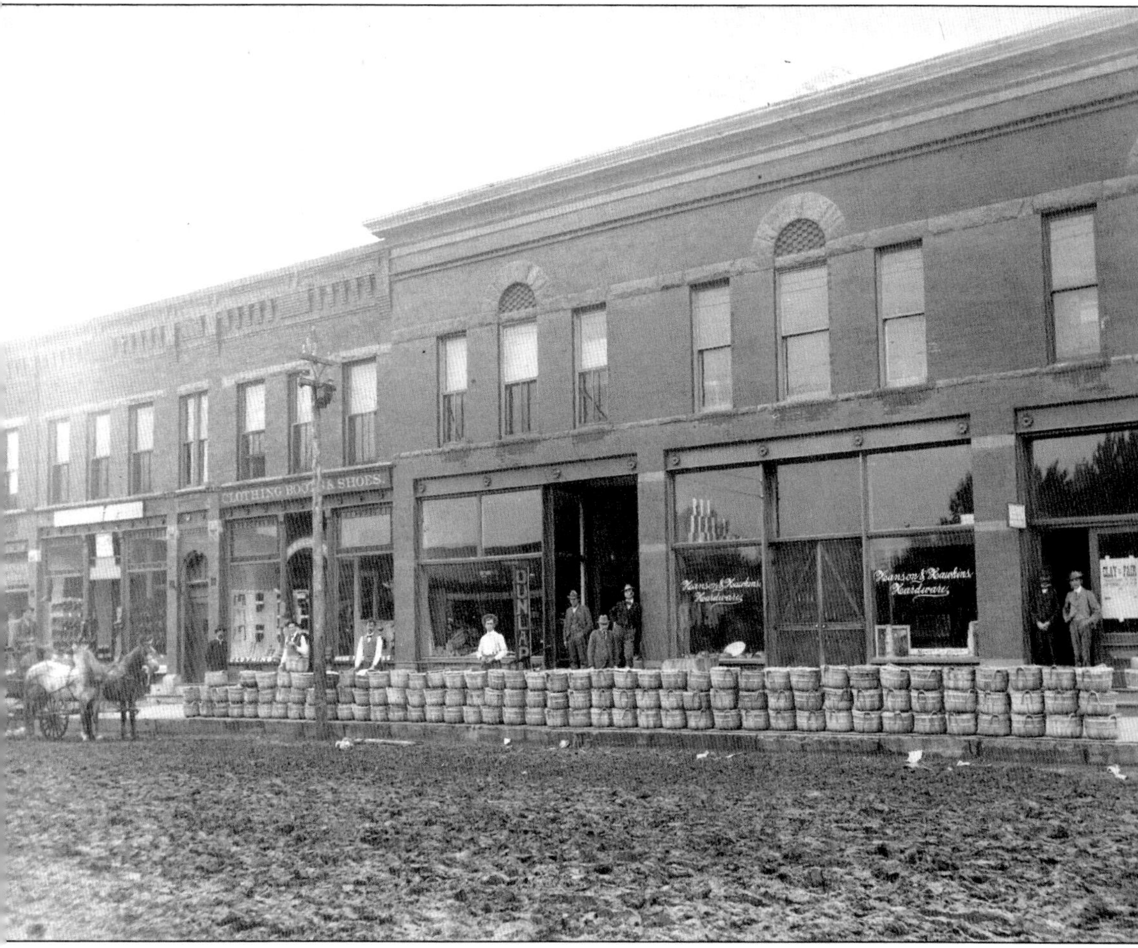

Fruit baskets are stacked along the sidewalk on Main Street, presumably as a barrier to the mud, which must have presented difficulties to ladies in long skirts. (Courtesy of Clay County Historical Society.)

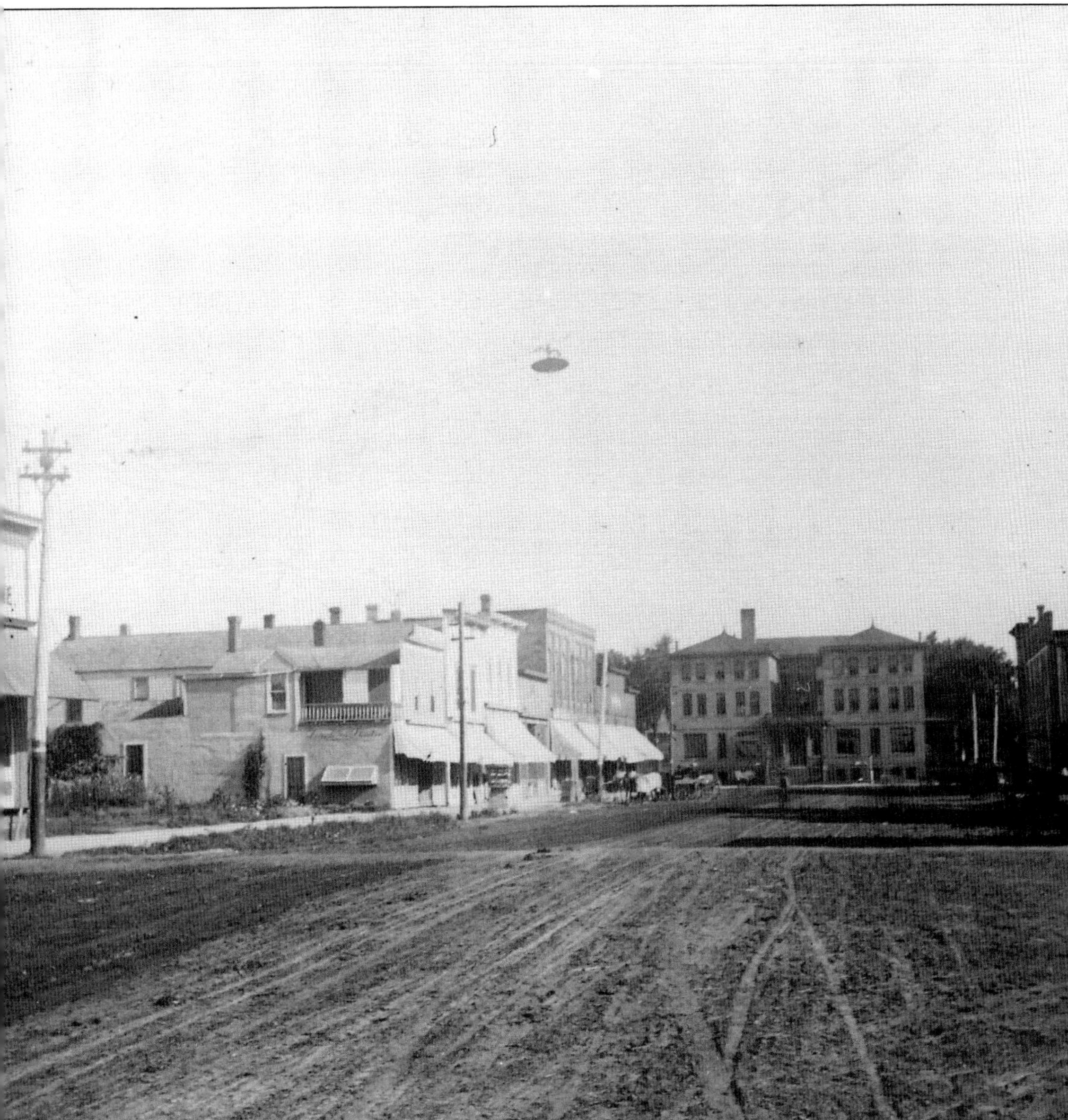

Market Street in Vermillion frames the Waldorf Hotel on Main Street, which is shown in the center of this photograph. At one time, Market Street had aspired to be Vermillion's major commercial thoroughfare. However, as the story is told, a Main Street partisan built a residence blocking any extension of Market Street on the north side of Main, thereby preventing Market from becoming a through street. Main Street merchants declared victory, and the downtown area grew predominantly along Main. (Courtesy of W.H. Over Museum.)

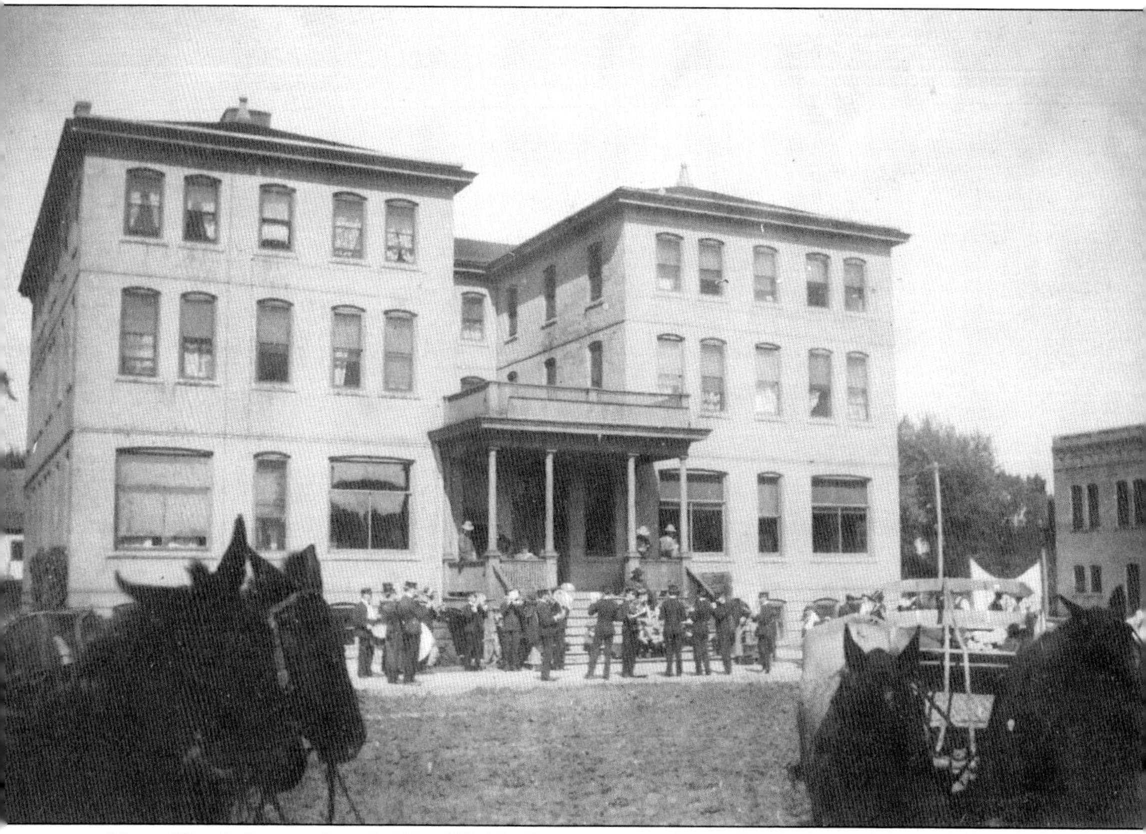

Vermillion's largest hotel, The Waldorf, was situated on the corner of Main Street nearest Market. In later years, it became the Burke Hotel until it was torn down to make way for Livestock State Bank and later CorTrust Bank. (Courtesy of W.H. Over Museum.)

Old City Hall was built on Main Street. (Courtesy of W.H. Over Museum.)

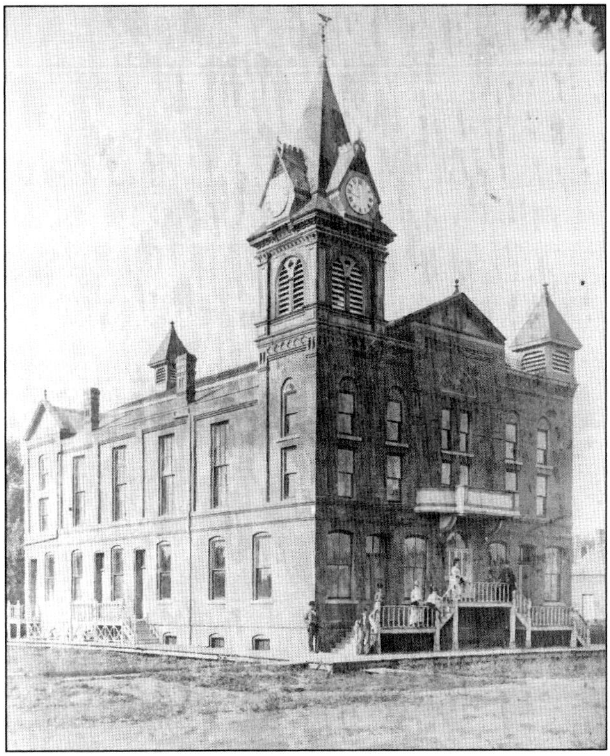

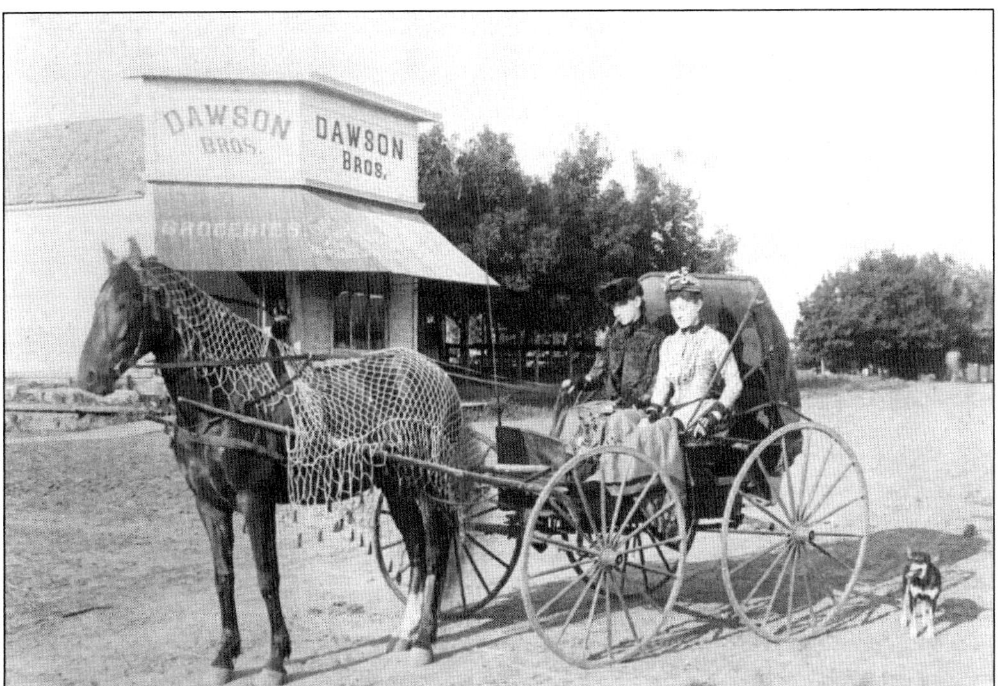

Mrs. Chris Scott and her sister, Mrs. Hansen, pause in their horse and buggy in front of Dawson Brothers Grocery Store at the intersection of Main Street and North Dakota Street. (Photo courtesy of W.H. Over Museum.)

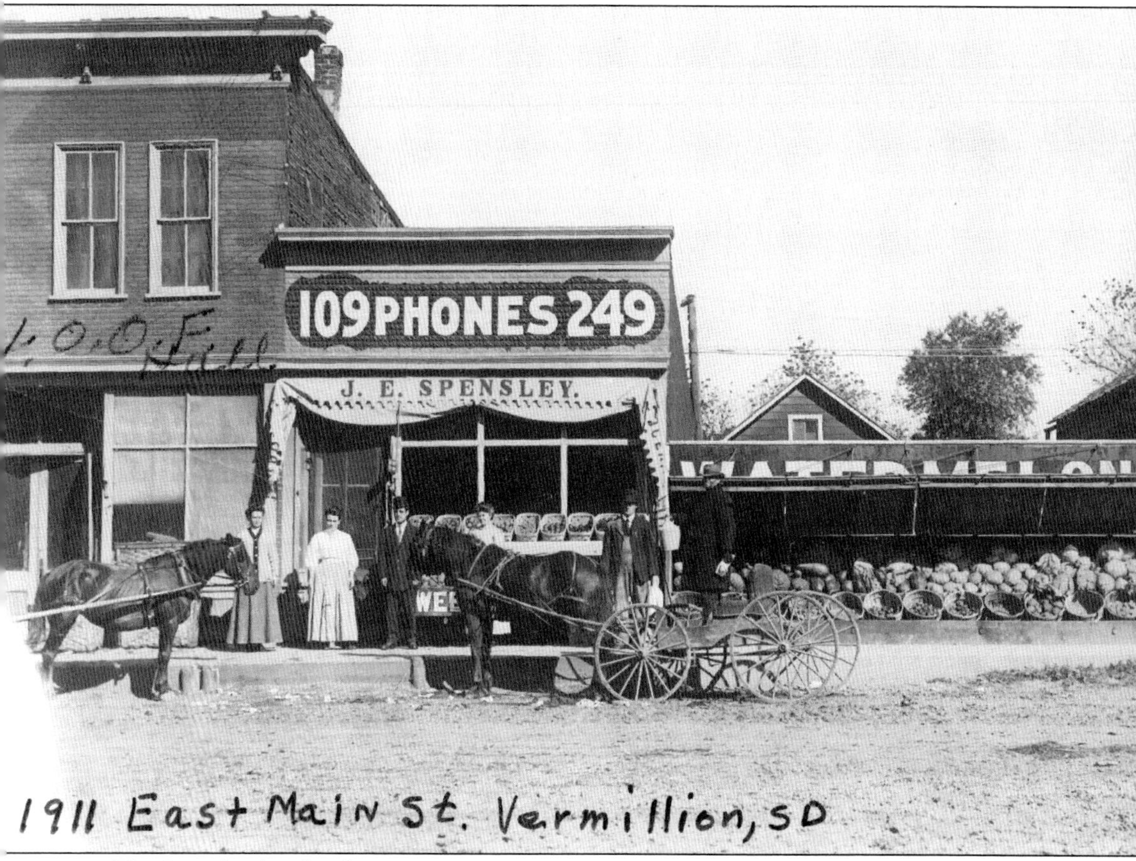

The Spensley family's first grocery store, pictured here on the north side of Main Street, burned down in 1911. (Courtesy of W.H. Over Museum.)

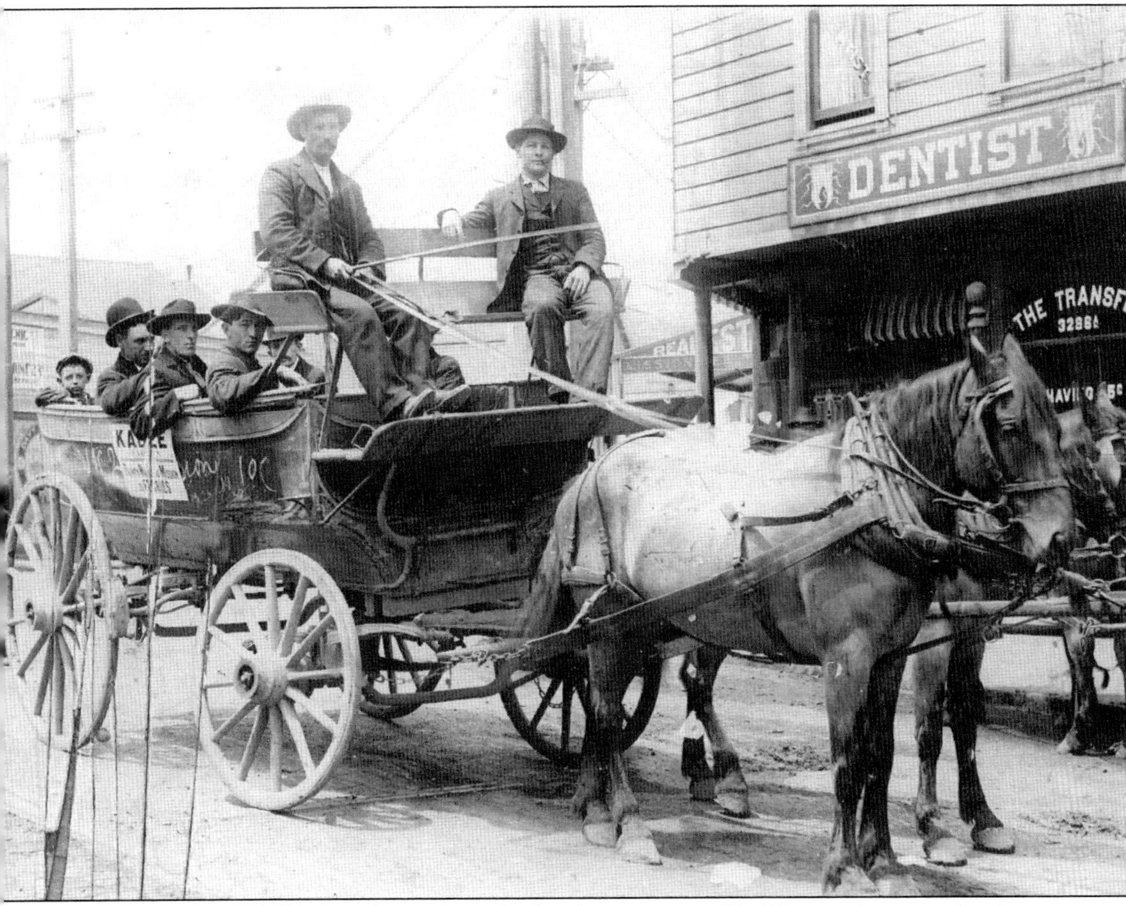

This open coach, pulled by two horses, was the local taxi service. Dr. Maxim, the town dentist, practiced at 110 East Main Street. (Courtesy of W.H. Over Museum.)

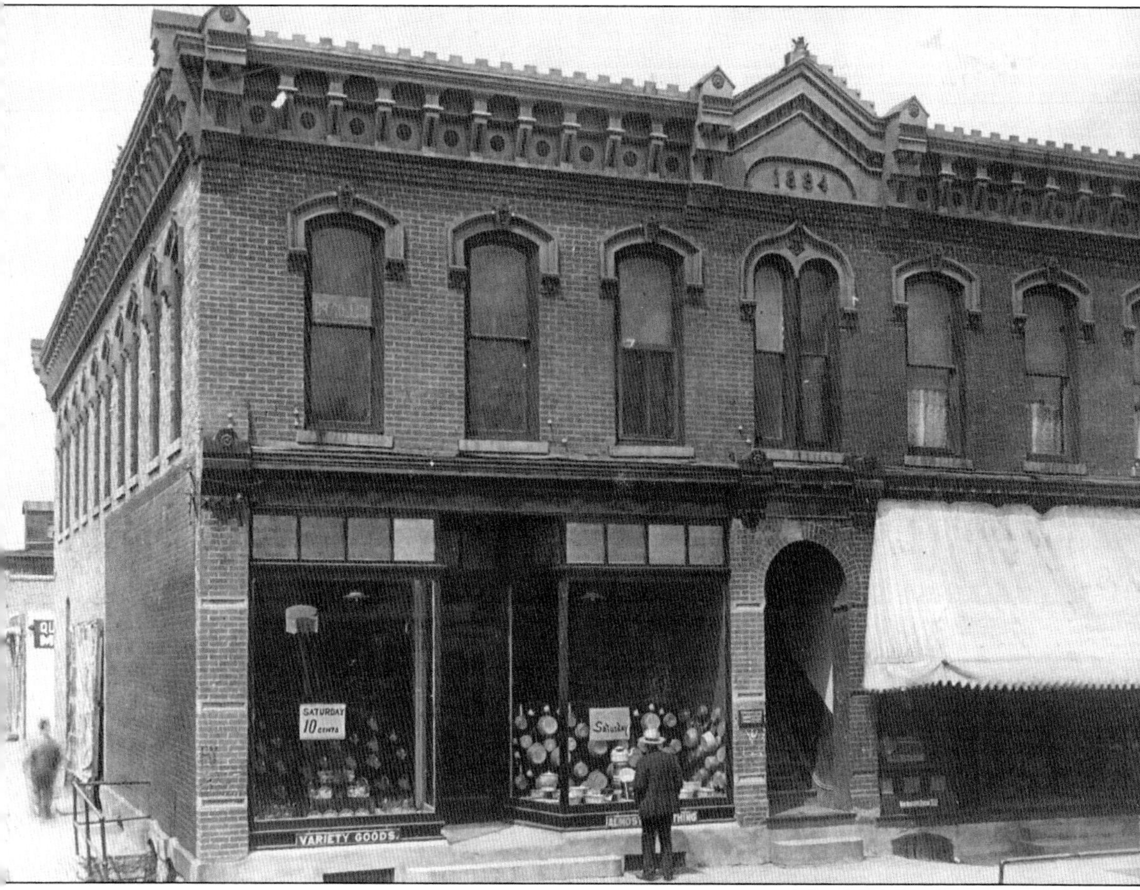

This commercial building stood on the corner of Main and Center Streets. It was built by McVicker in 1884 and housed a variety store on the first floor. Dr. Collisi had his offices on the second floor. Later, Dr. Burdick would install a water fountain on this corner. (Courtesy of W.H. Over Museum.)

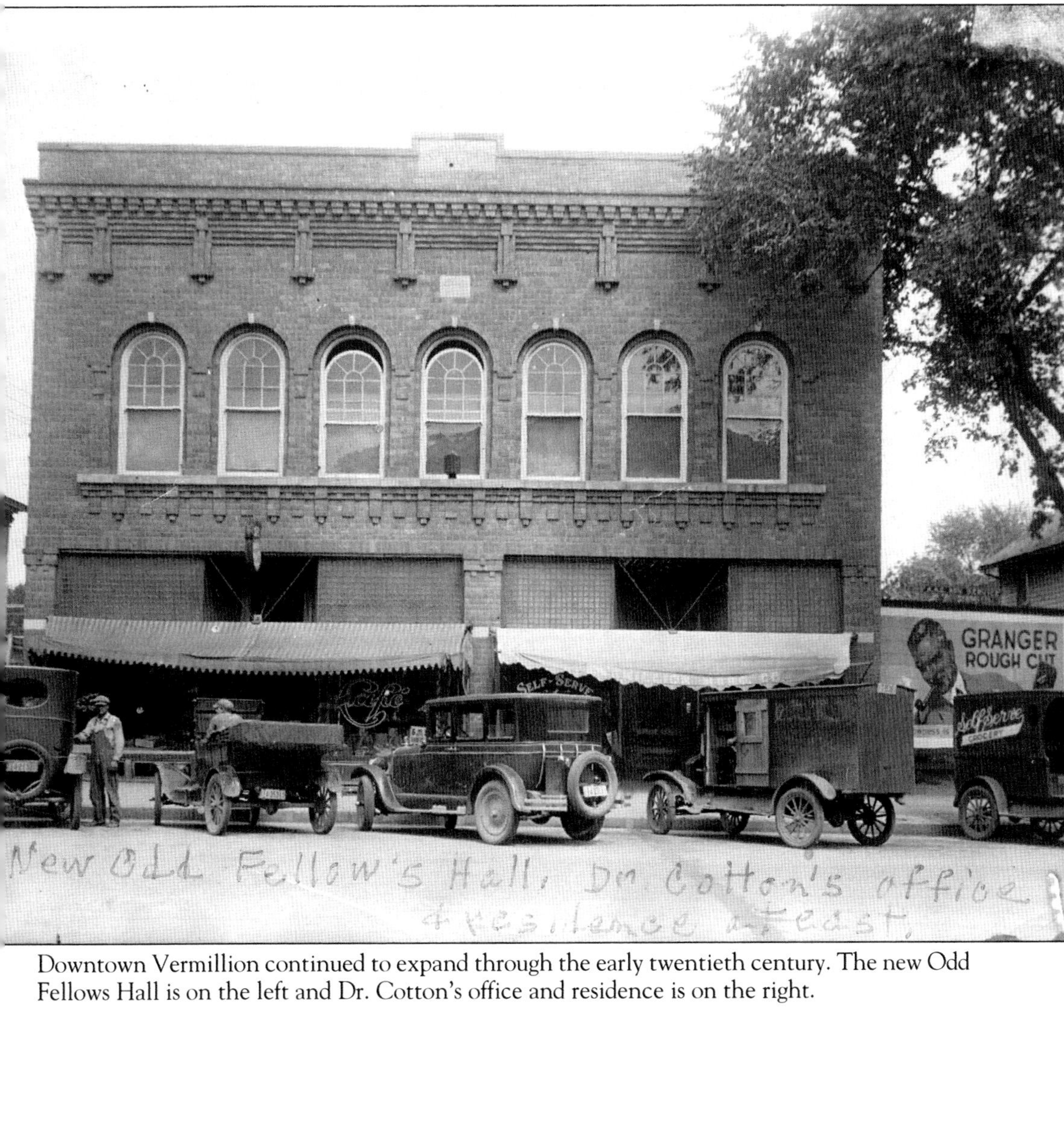

Downtown Vermillion continued to expand through the early twentieth century. The new Odd Fellows Hall is on the left and Dr. Cotton's office and residence is on the right.

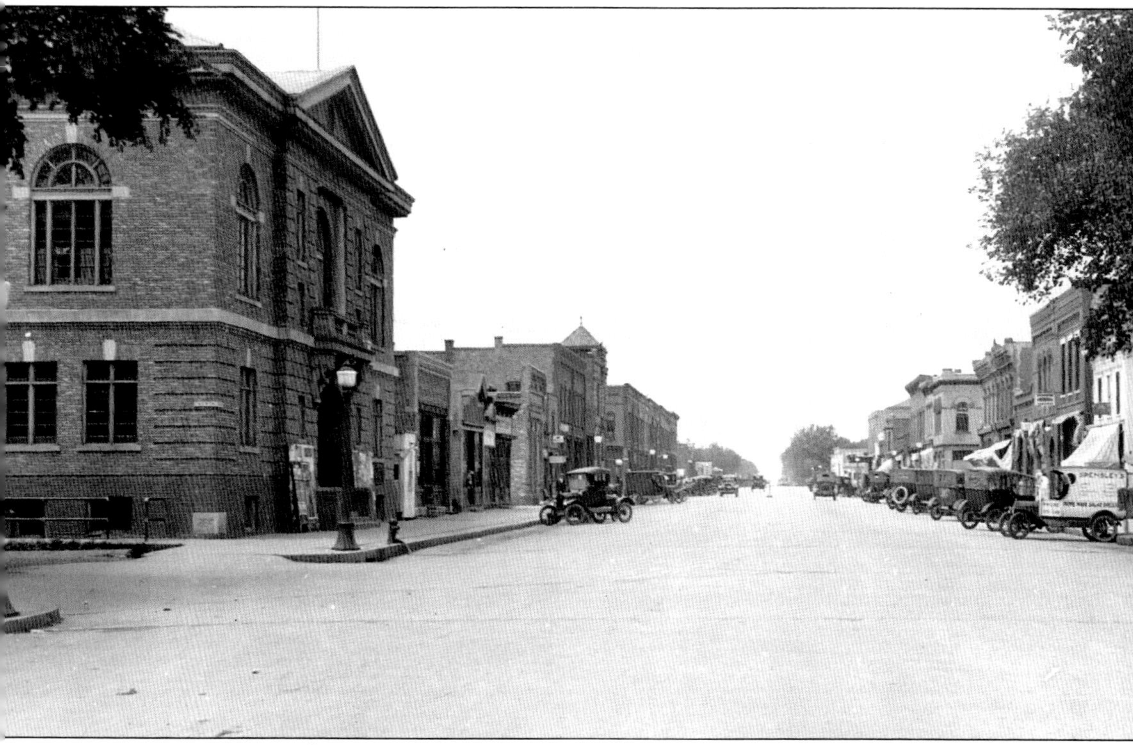

Main Street Vermillion became a thriving downtown commercial district.

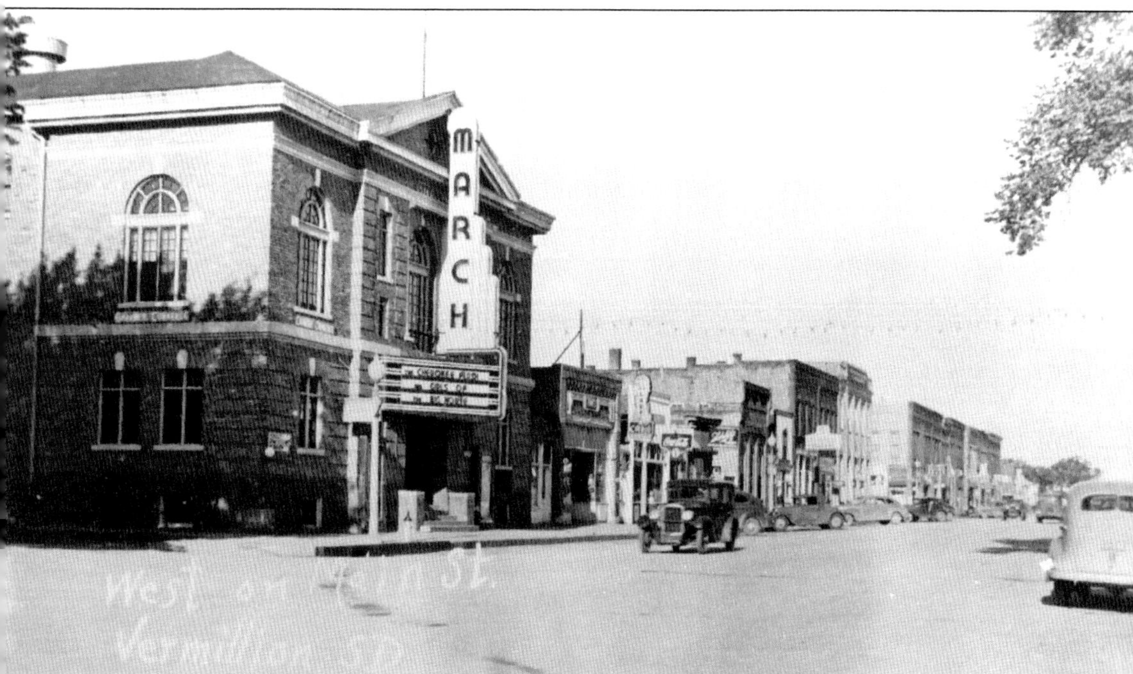

The March Theater was a prominent downtown landmark with its neoclassical façade and period marquee.

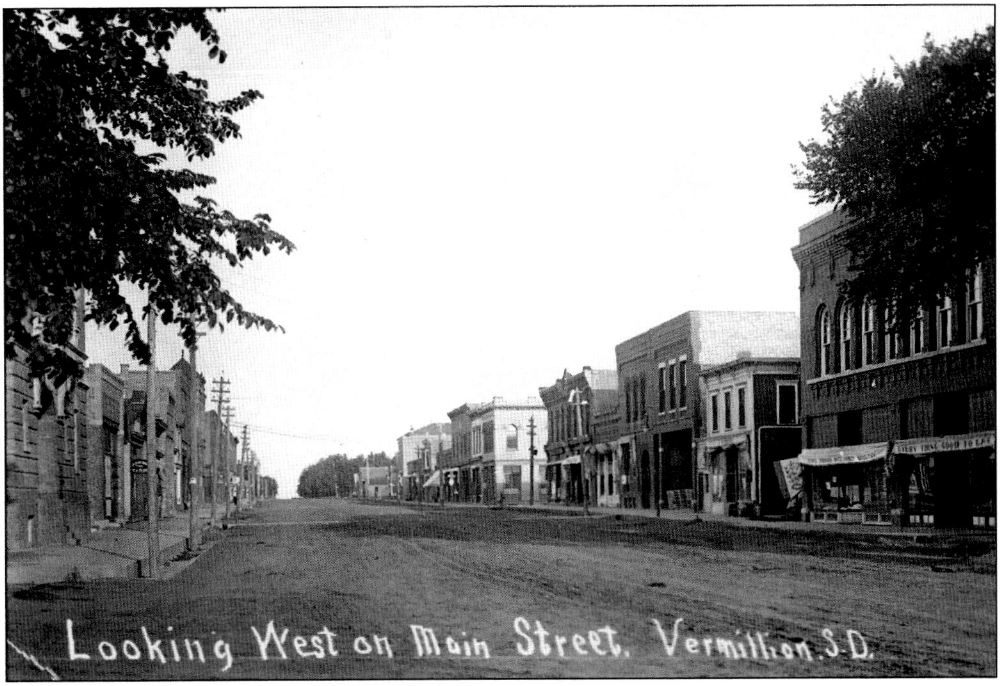

This is a view of Main Street looking west.

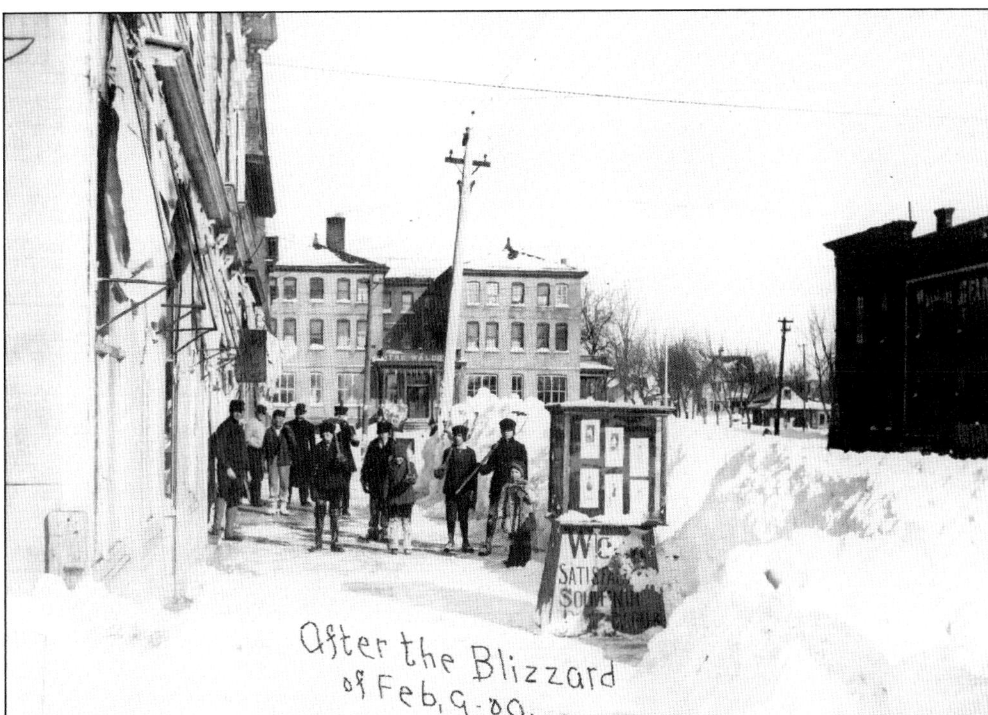

Market Street, facing the Waldorf Hotel, is piled with snow in the aftermath of the blizzard of February 9, 1909.

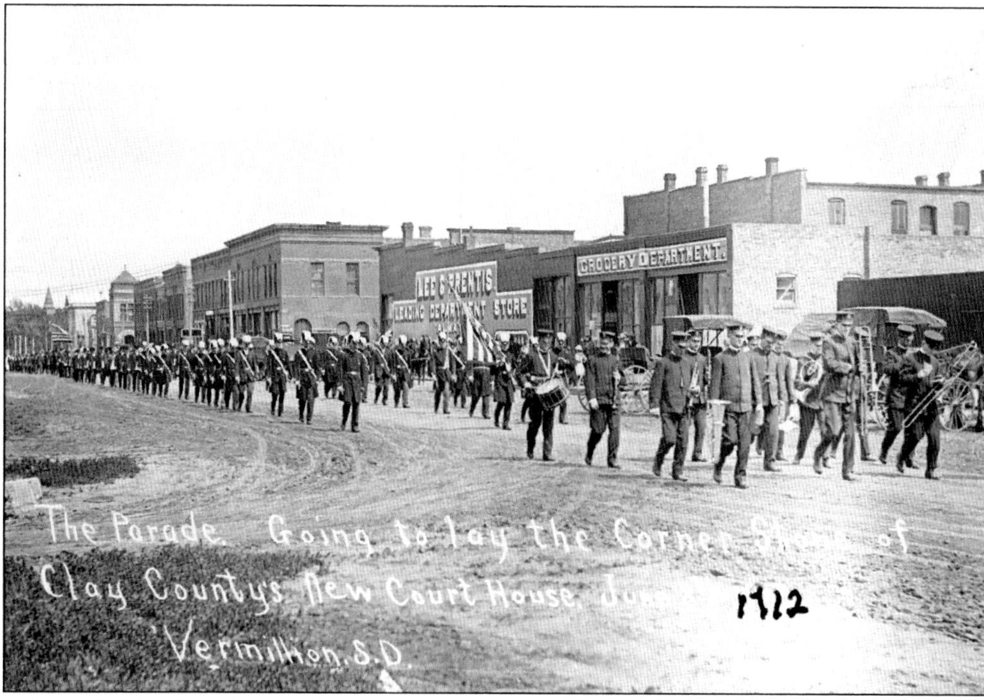

In June of 1912, Clay County began construction of a new courthouse. This June parade through downtown Vermillion led the way to lay the cornerstone.

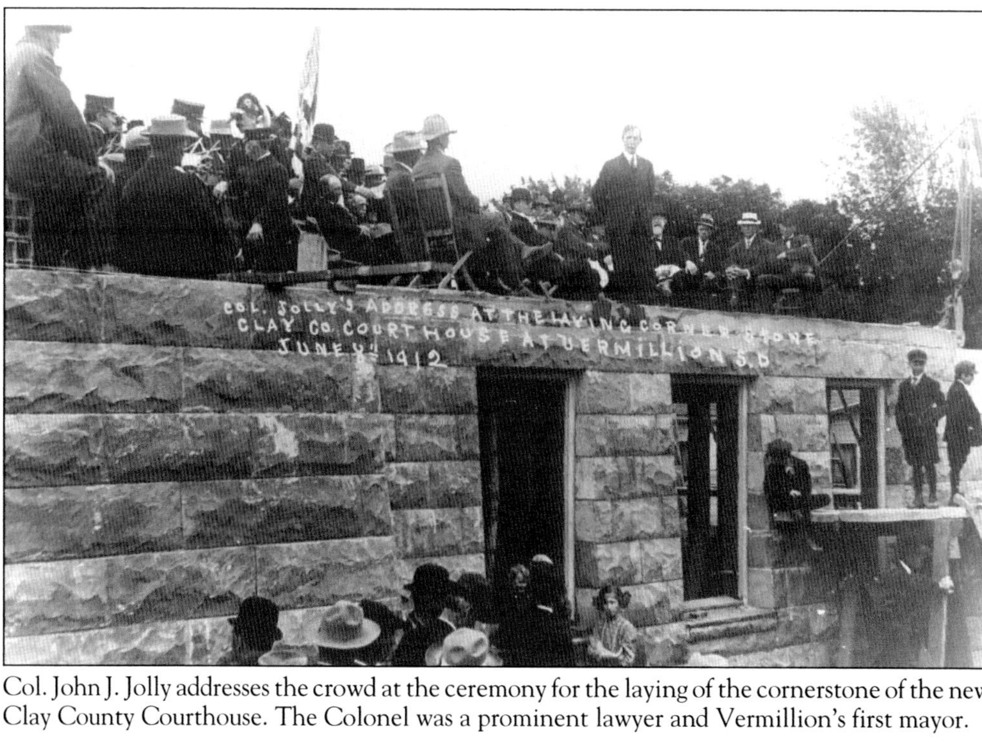

Col. John J. Jolly addresses the crowd at the ceremony for the laying of the cornerstone of the new Clay County Courthouse. The Colonel was a prominent lawyer and Vermillion's first mayor.

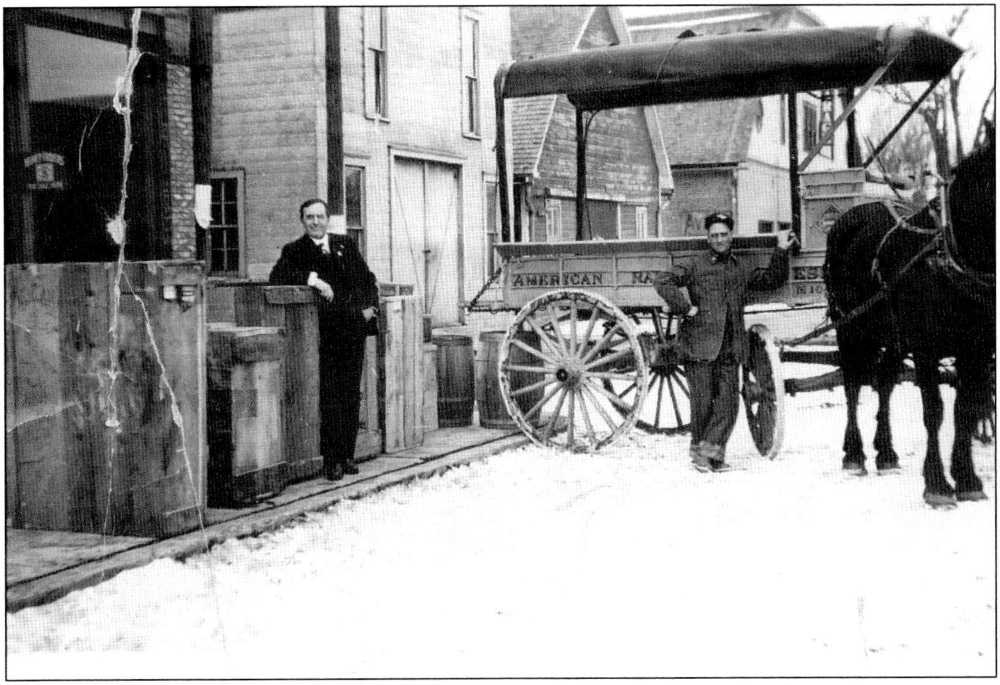

On Center Street in 1918, a gentleman and Richard Chamberlain, a local cart driver, pose in front of a shop. The old livery stables are visible at the end of the block.

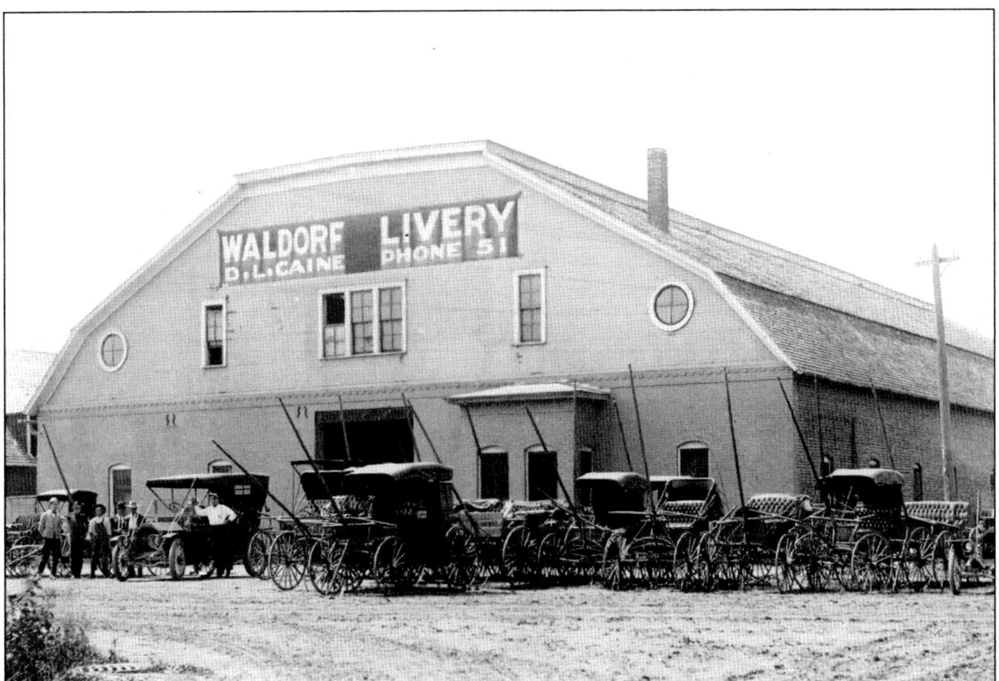

Richard Grange built the Grange Livery Stable, located at 29 Center Street, in 1902. Initially, the stable rented horses and buggies. Later, as the Waldorf Livery Stables, the business was faced with rapidly-declining demand for horse rentals and began to rent motor cars.

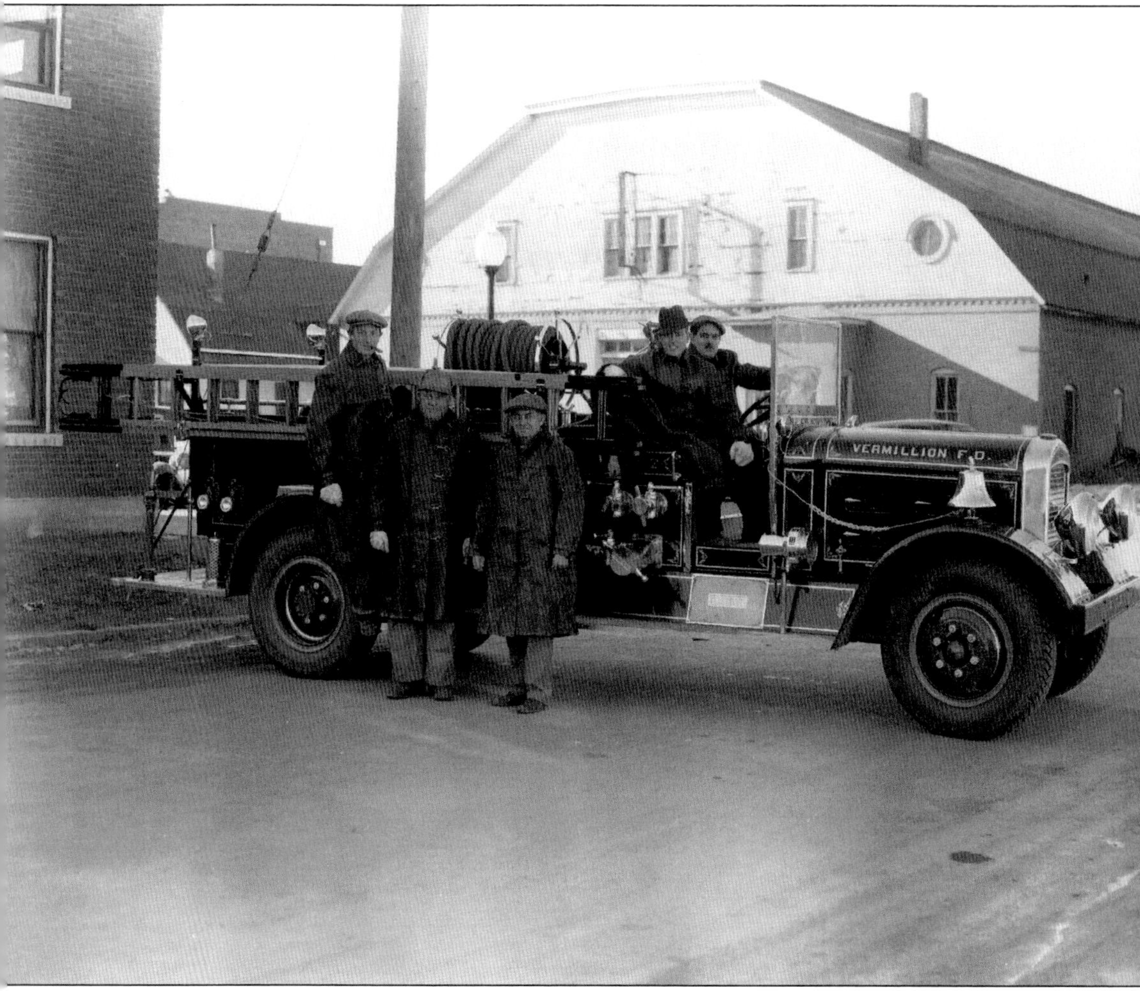

Vermillion Fire Truck No. 2 was built in Luverne, Minnesota in 1936 and purchased by the city in 1938. Robert Gobell is seated at the wheel next to Herman Berke. (Courtesy of the W.H. Over Museum.)

Five

UNIVERSITY OF SOUTH DAKOTA

The Territorial Legislature established the University of Dakota in 1862, though it failed to provide funding. Concerned that the legislature's later establishment of a land grant university in Brookings might lead to the loss of its own institution, Vermillion residents took matters into their own hands and decided to establish the university themselves. A board of trustees was established and a $10,000 bond issue voted to provide support. Judge Kidder offered rooms in his courthouse where the first classes were held in 1882. Initial construction included West Hall, which served as a men's dormitory; University Hall, which held the main classrooms and offices; and East Hall which served as a women's dormitory. To discourage local farmers from herding cows and hauling hay across campus, as was not uncommon, a fence was erected, walkways established, and shade trees planted during the 1890s.

Town and gown have always been intimately connected in Vermillion. During the early years, town leadership decided to clean up the city's river town drinking and gambling for the sake of the students. The Territorial Legislature passed a law banning the sale of intoxicating liquor within three miles of Dakota University. Enforcement, however, proved to be elusive. Saloons moved to an island area that was claimed by both Nebraska and South Dakota, not far from today's airport. Saloon owners used the confusion to avoid enforcement action, pleading in each state's court that they resided in the other state. Not until the late 1890s was the problem resolved, when a court awarded the land to South Dakota.

As enrollment at the University grew, new divisions were created including the Colleges of Law and Music (1901), and Engineering and Medicine (1907). Additional buildings were built to accommodate the new programs: Science Hall (1902), Armory Hall (1905), Law (1908), Library (1911), and Chemistry (1915.) The new law building, built in 1908, was a replica of Ohio State University's law building. Much later, the schools of Business Administration and Education were established (1927), followed by the Graduate School (1929), and a College of Fine Arts (1931.)

The *Volante* produced its first edition in November 1887. It was initially a literary journal and later became the student newspaper.

In the fall of 1893, a massive fire nearly destroyed University Hall. Classes were temporarily reassigned to East Hall, West Hall, and local churches while the University pondered its options. A local fund drive raised $10,000 and a county bond issue secured the balance of $30,000 required to rebuild.

Sorority row began on Plum Street in the 1920s when Dean Julian and Peter Olson sold their lots to Kappa Alpha Theta and Alpha Xi Delta at cost. The lots were sold for the purpose of sorority housing at about the time that Mr. Prentis deeded land to the city for Prentis Park.

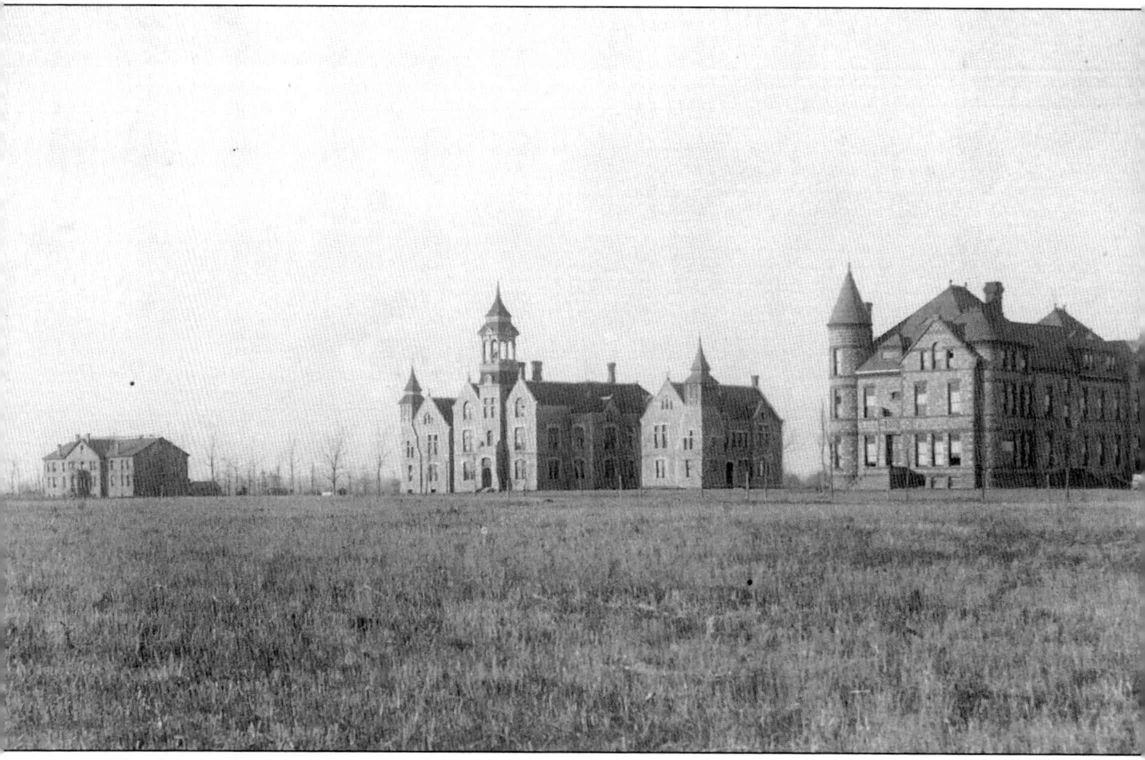

The heart of the University of South Dakota's campus in 1891 featured (from left to right) West Hall, University Hall, and East Hall. University Hall burned and was later rebuilt as Old Main. Only East Hall remains. (Courtesy of USD Archive.)

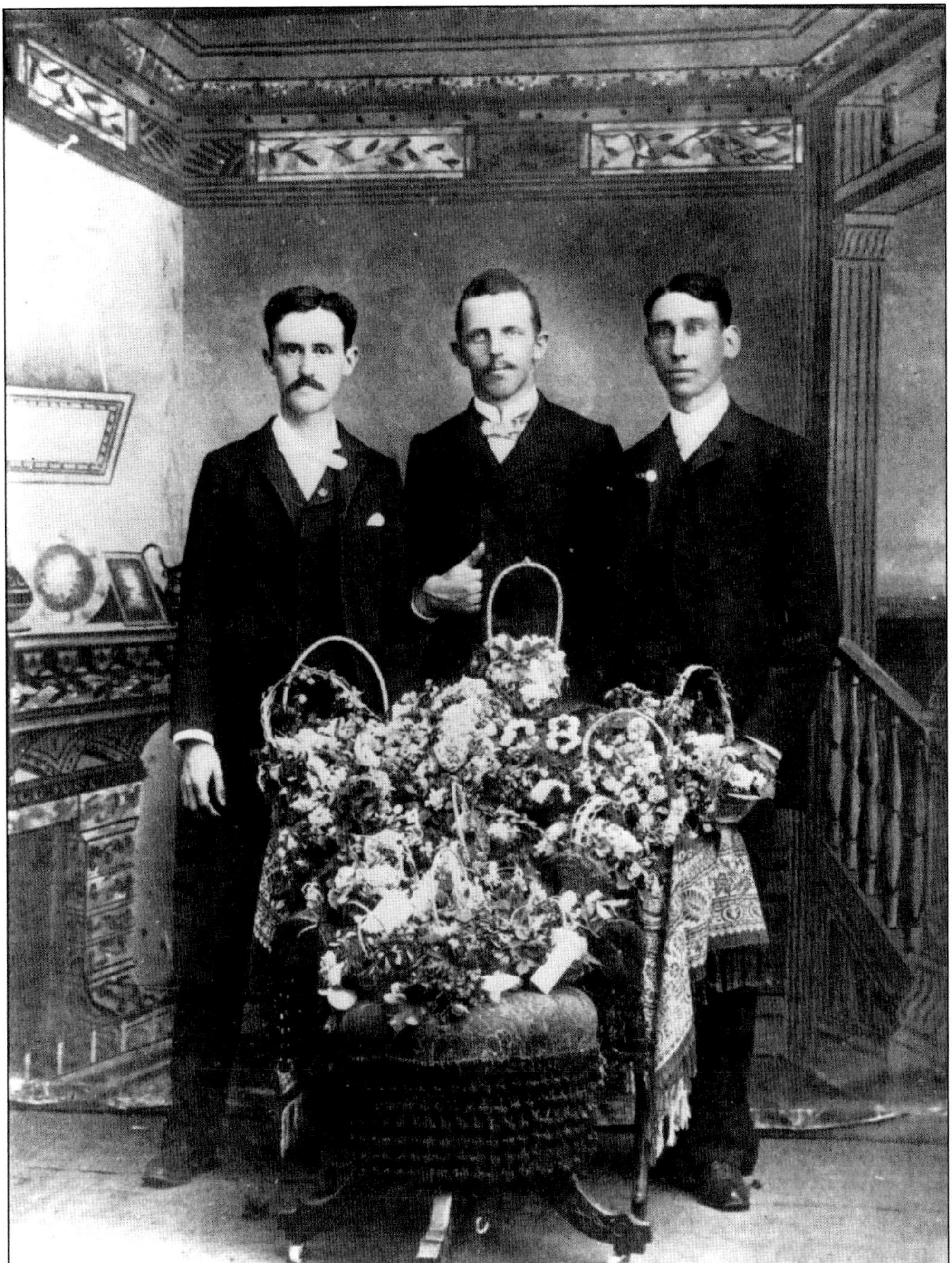

Members of USD's first graduating class celebrate with a trip to the local photographer's office. From left to right, they are H.S. Houston, C.W. Brinstad, and C.B. Antisdel. (Courtesy of USD Archive.)

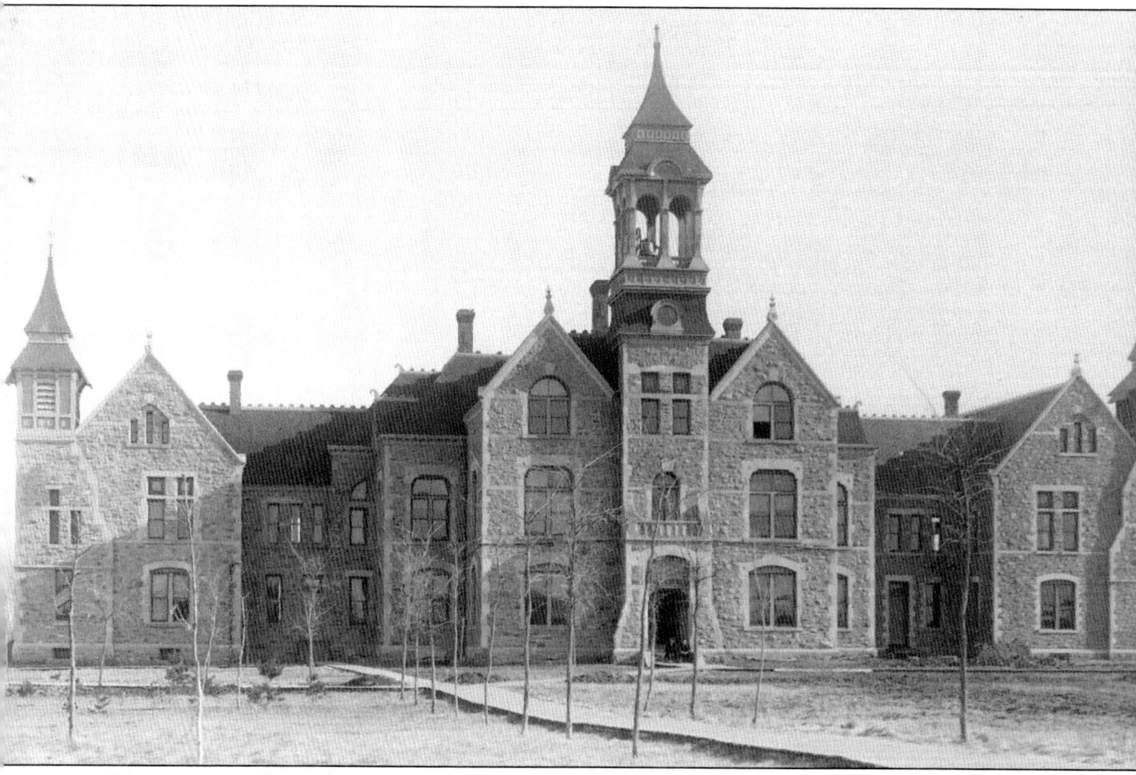

University Hall was built in 1891 on the site where Old Main is now situated. (Courtesy of USD Archive.)

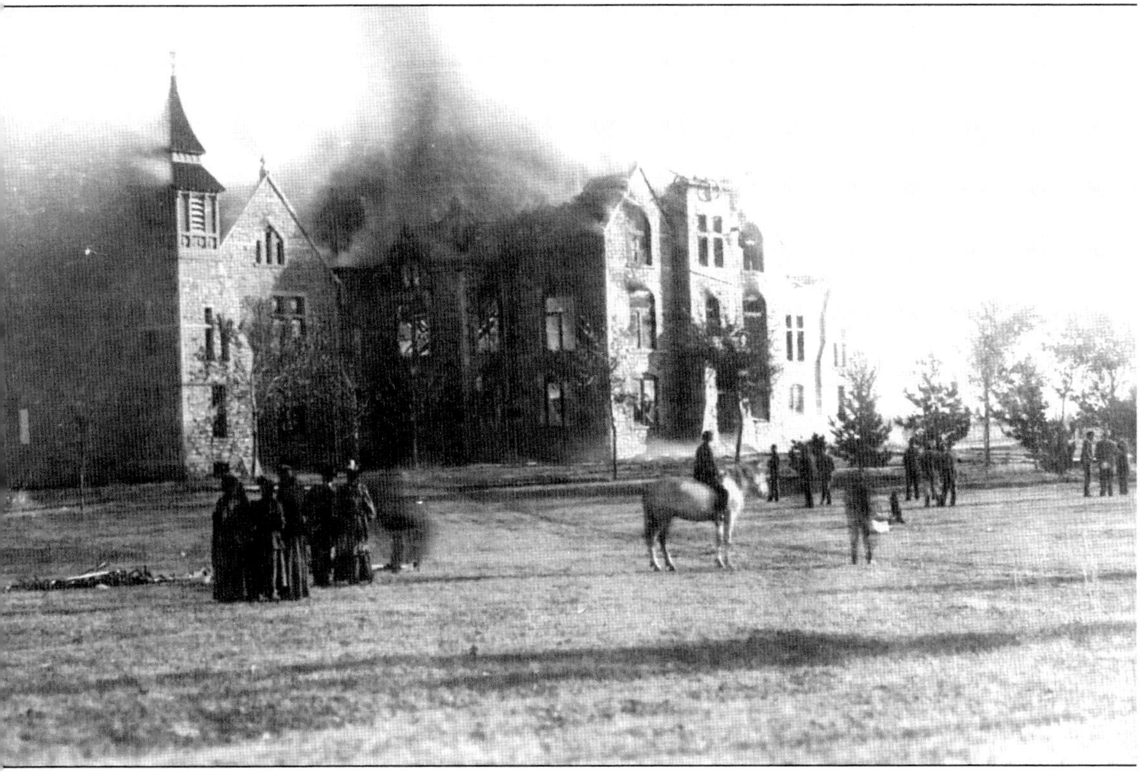

A fierce fire destroyed University Hall in 1893. (Courtesy of USD Archive.)

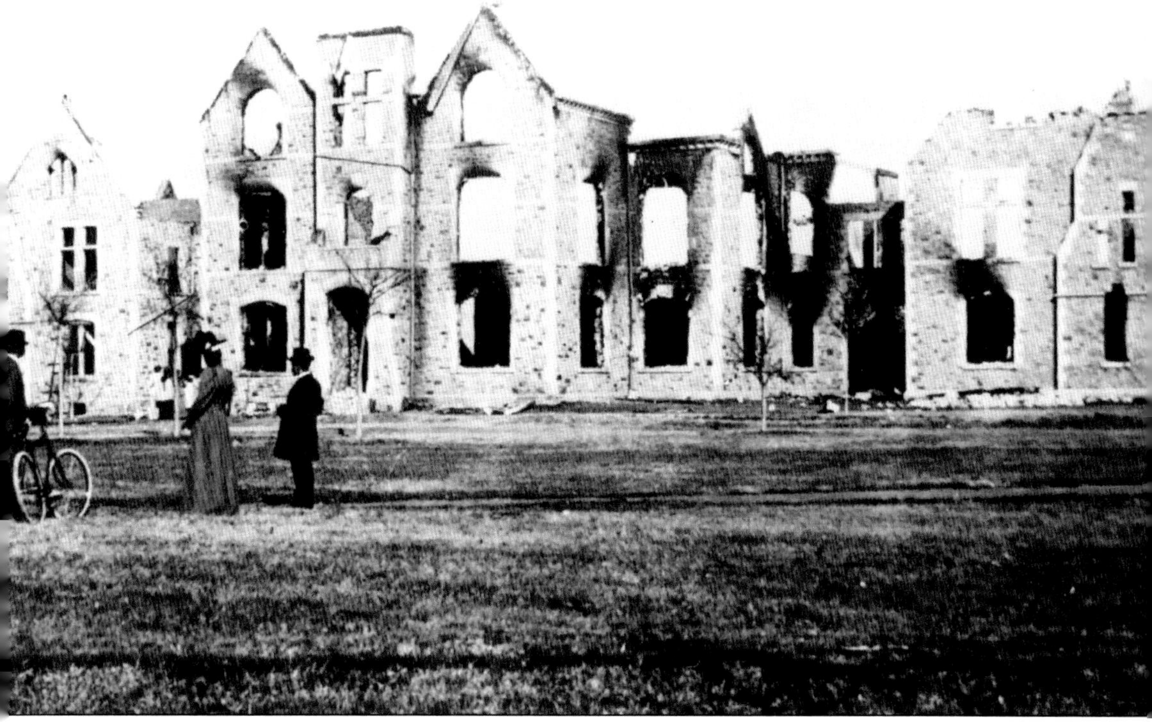

In the aftermath of the fire, University Hall could not be salvaged. It was rebuilt as Old Main in 1900. (Courtesy of USD Archive.)

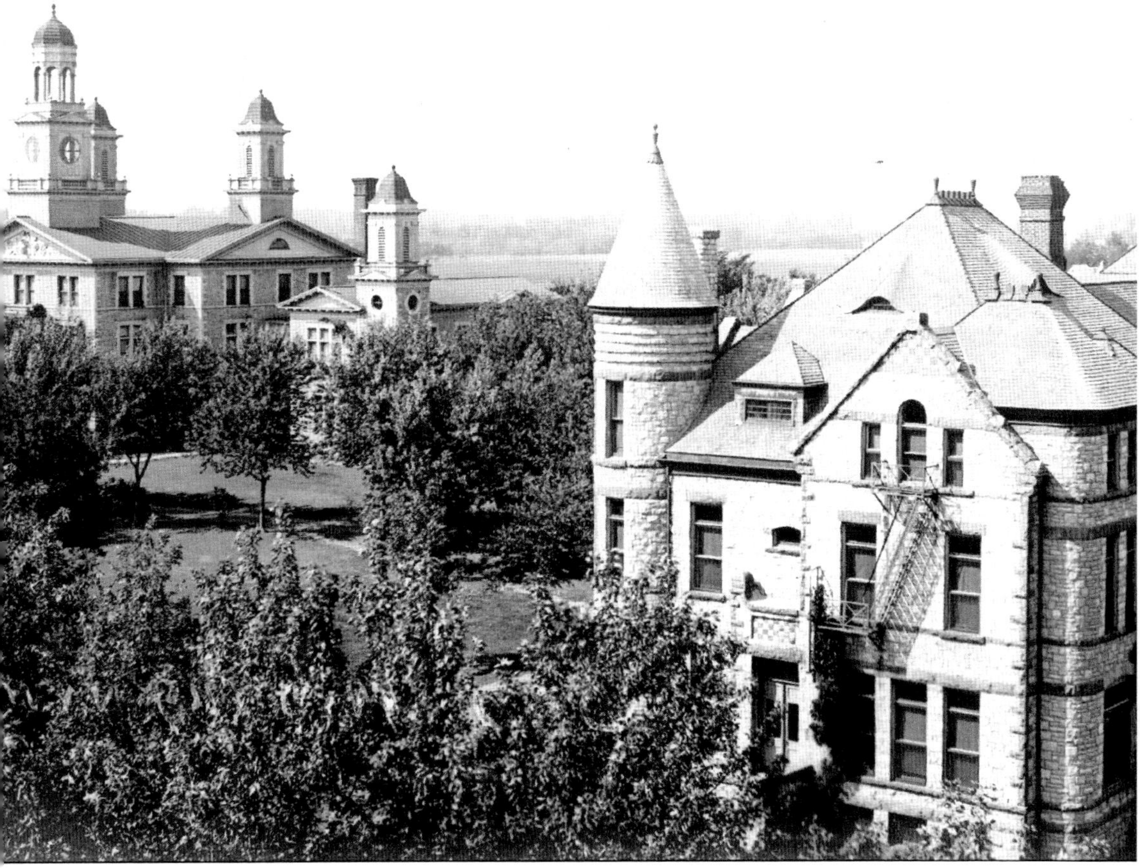

This is a view of Old Main (left) and East Hall (right) from a window in the old Law School, which now houses the College of Arts and Sciences. (Courtesy of USD Archive.)

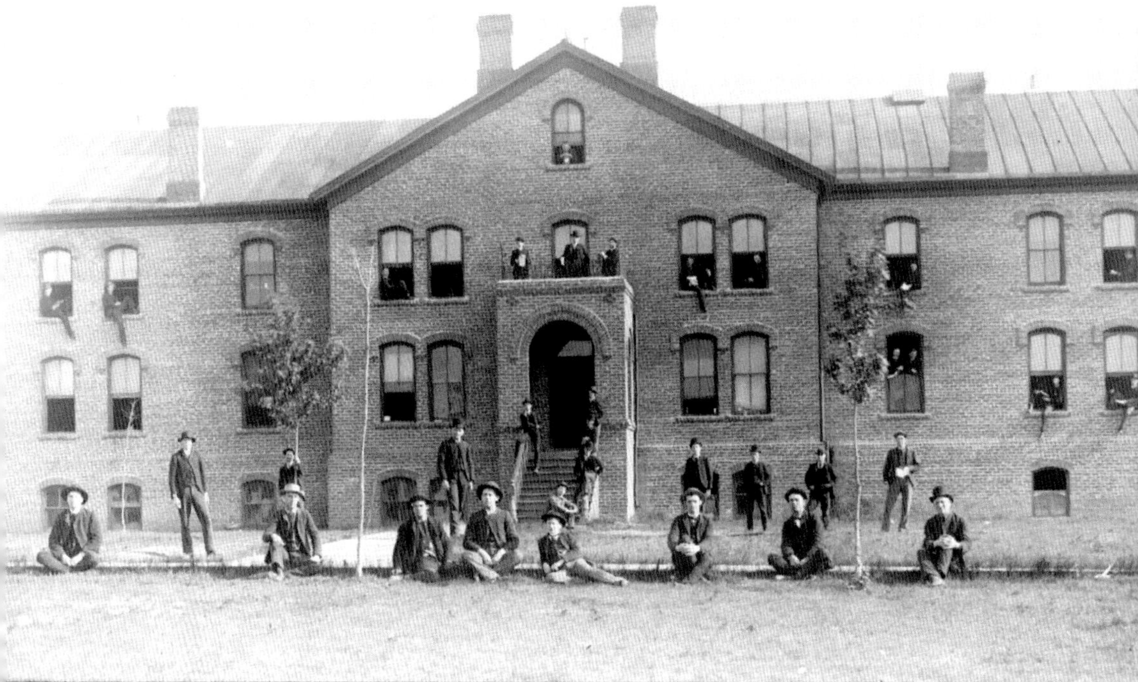

The residents of West Hall pose in front of the building. West Hall was a men's dormitory; it has since been demolished. Two Vermillion residents who were USD students reduced West Hall to ashes in 1905. Feeling guilty, they confessed to the crime at a Methodist revival meeting and later served time in the penitentiary for their misdeed. (Courtesy of USD Archive.)

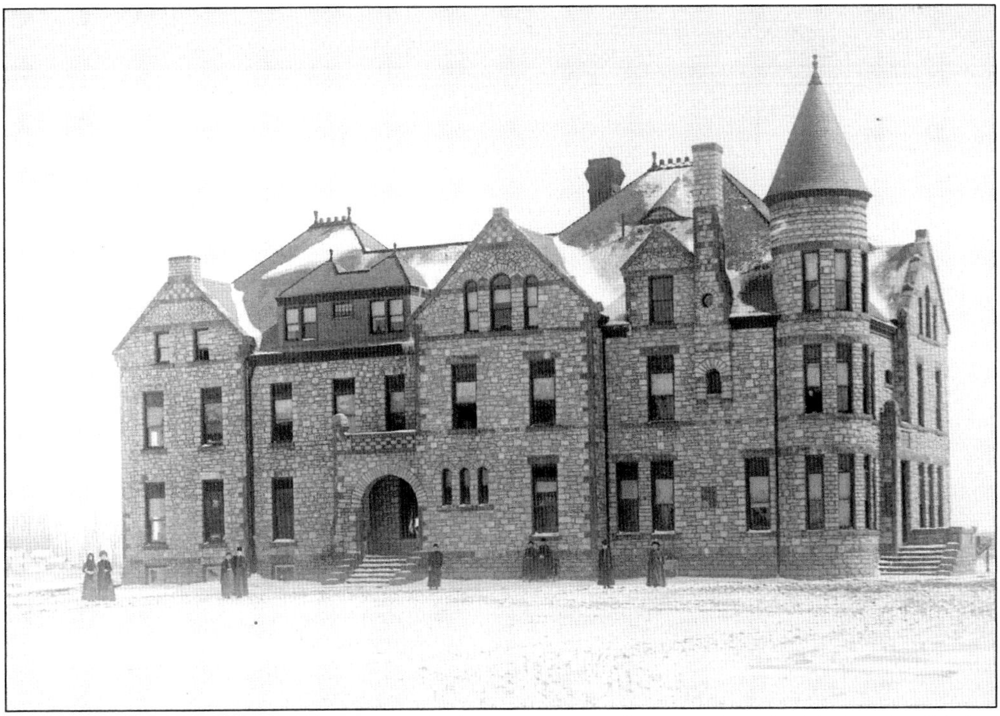

East Hall was built in 1887 as a women's dormitory and also served as the University Dining Hall. (Courtesy of USD Archive.)

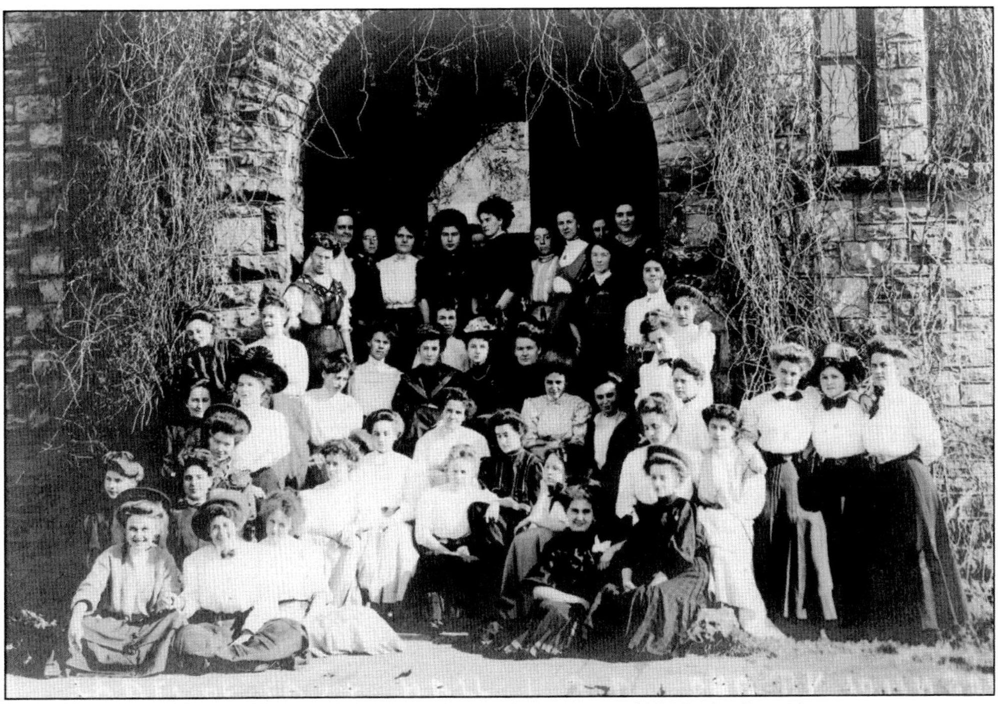

Early residents of East Hall pose at its entrance. (Courtesy of USD Archive.)

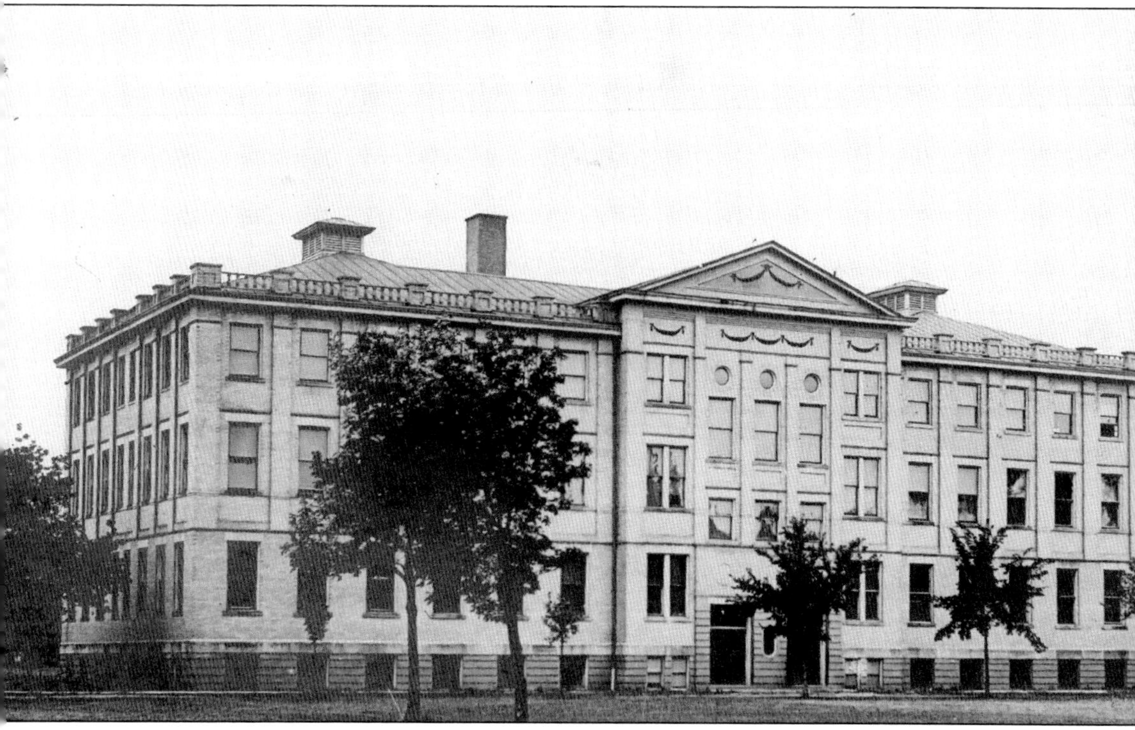

The Science Hall at USD also housed a University High School. (Courtesy of USD Archive.)

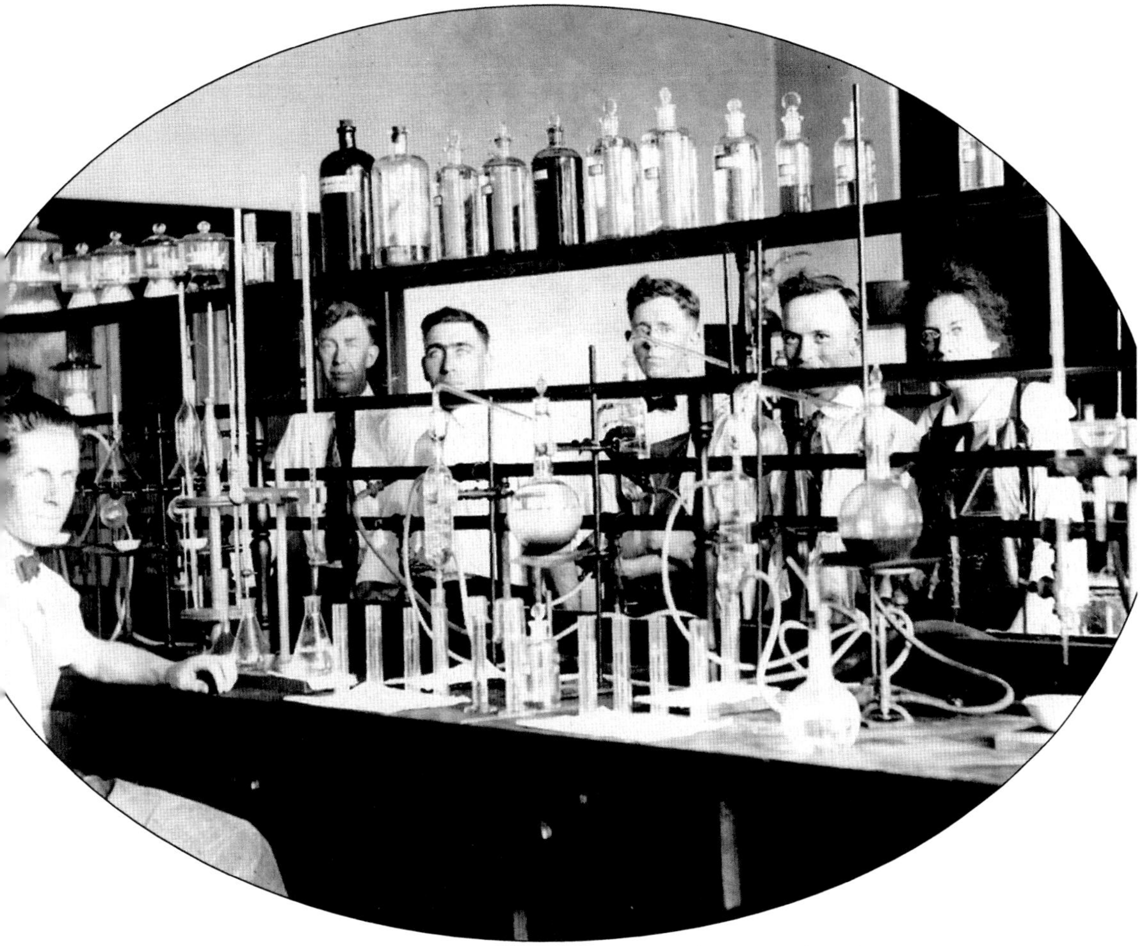

This chemistry lab was located in Haines in 1910. (Courtesy of USD Archive.)

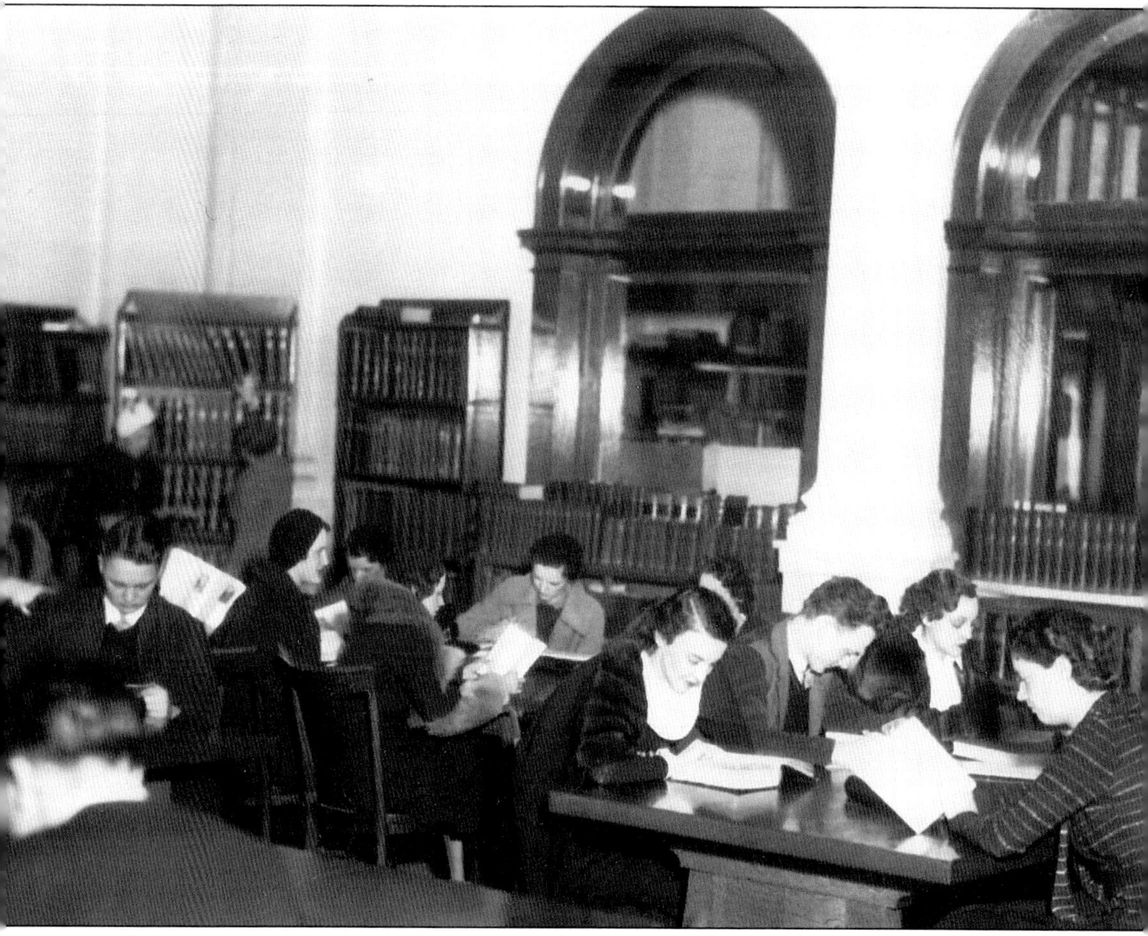

USD was one of the few universities in the nation to be awarded a Carnegie Library. The reading room pictured here is now the concert hall of the Shrine to Music Museum. (Courtesy of USD Archive.)

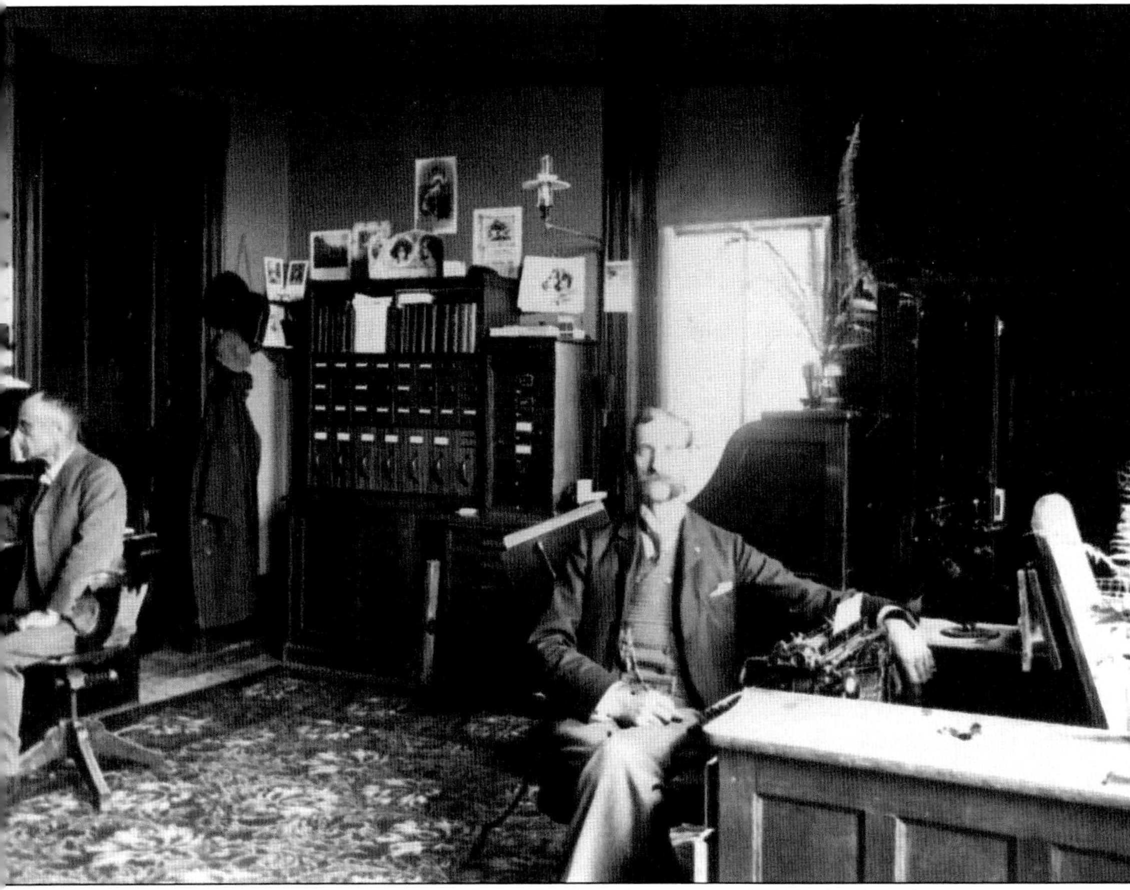

University offices were more spacious in the early days. (Courtesy of USD Archive.)

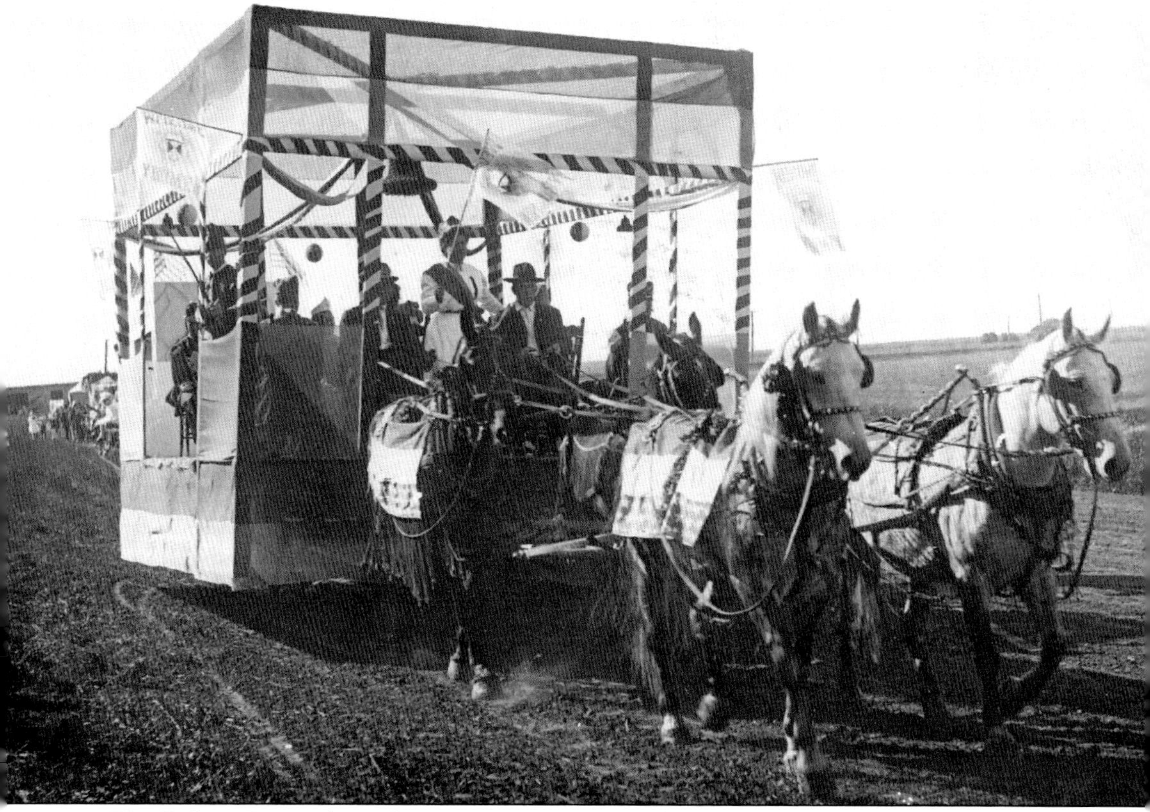

The Dakota Day tradition began in 1914. A team of horses pull this early Dakota Day parade float. (Courtesy of USD Archive.)

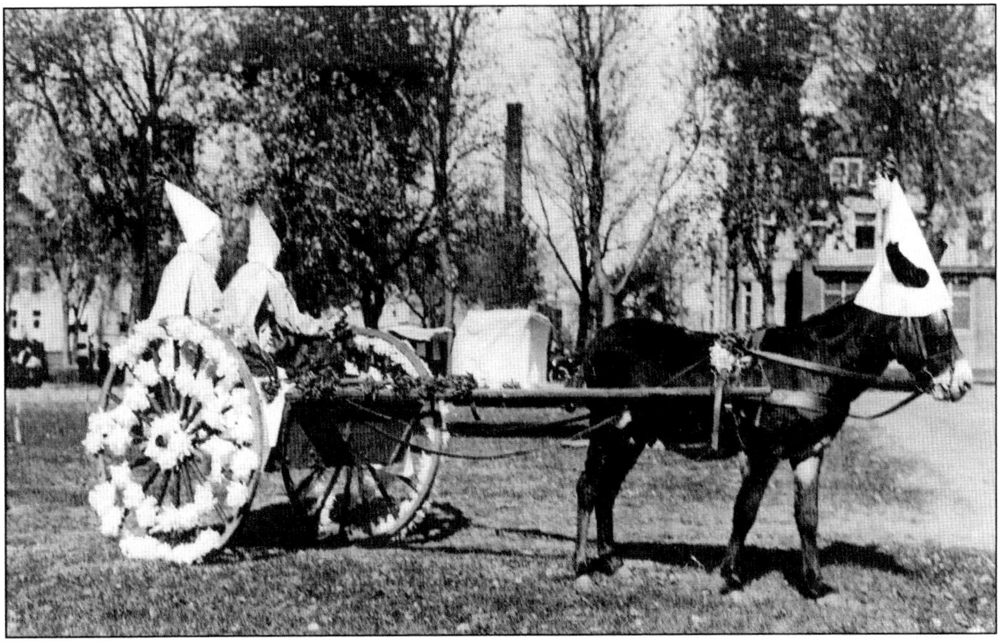

USD students clown around on a donkey cart as they prepare to participate in the 1915 Dakota Day parade. (Courtesy of USD Archive.)

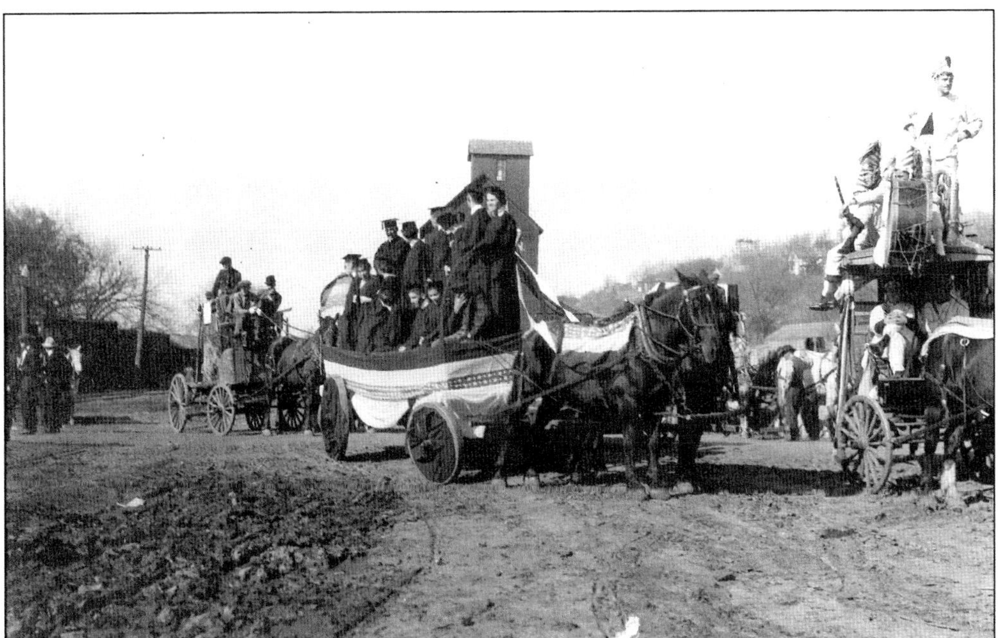

Most floats in the 1915 Dakota Day parade were horse-drawn. (Courtesy of USD Archive.)

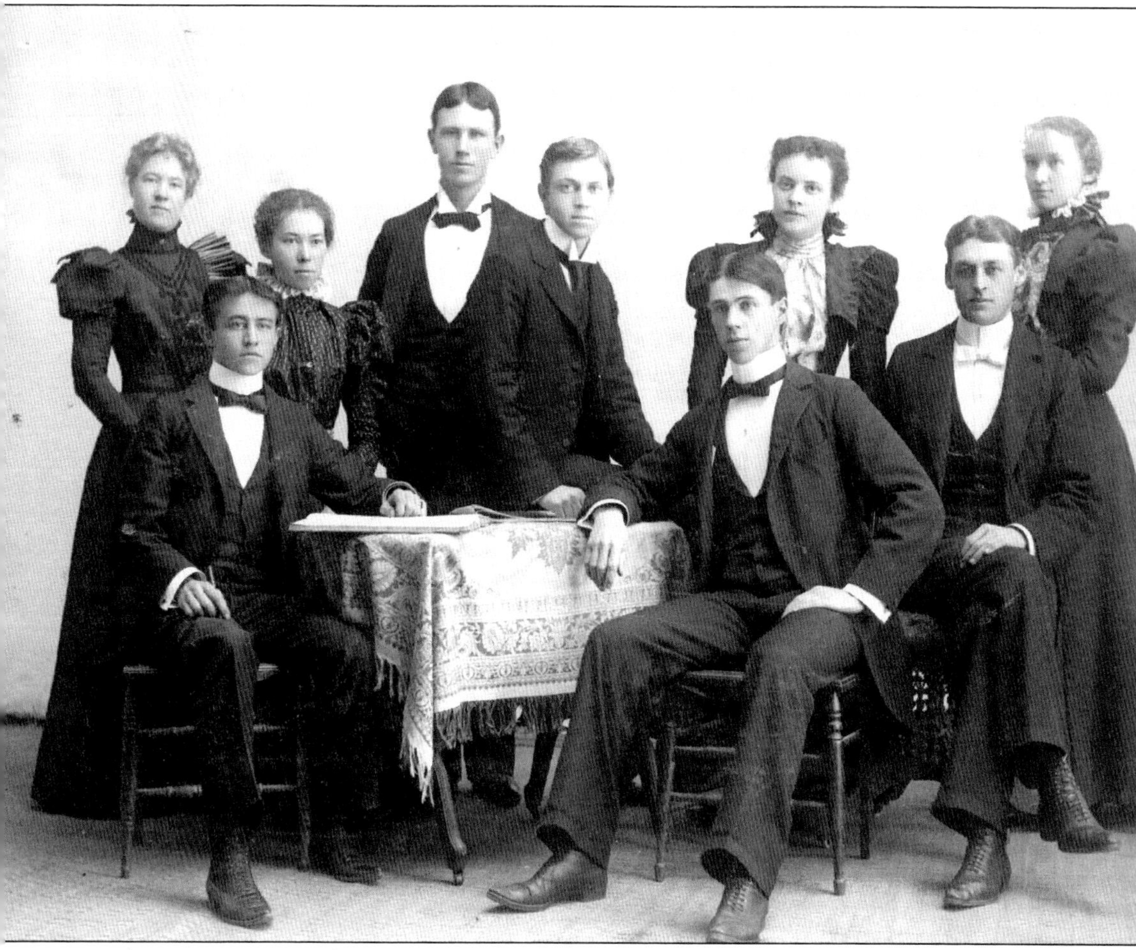

The University's student newspaper, the *Volante*, published its first edition in November of 1887, for the purpose of acting as "the representative of all the students of the University" and to "voice their desires, champion their interests and earnestly endeavor to advance all movements that can in any way conduce to their welfare." The 1895 *Volante* staff posed for this photograph. (Courtesy of USD Archive.)

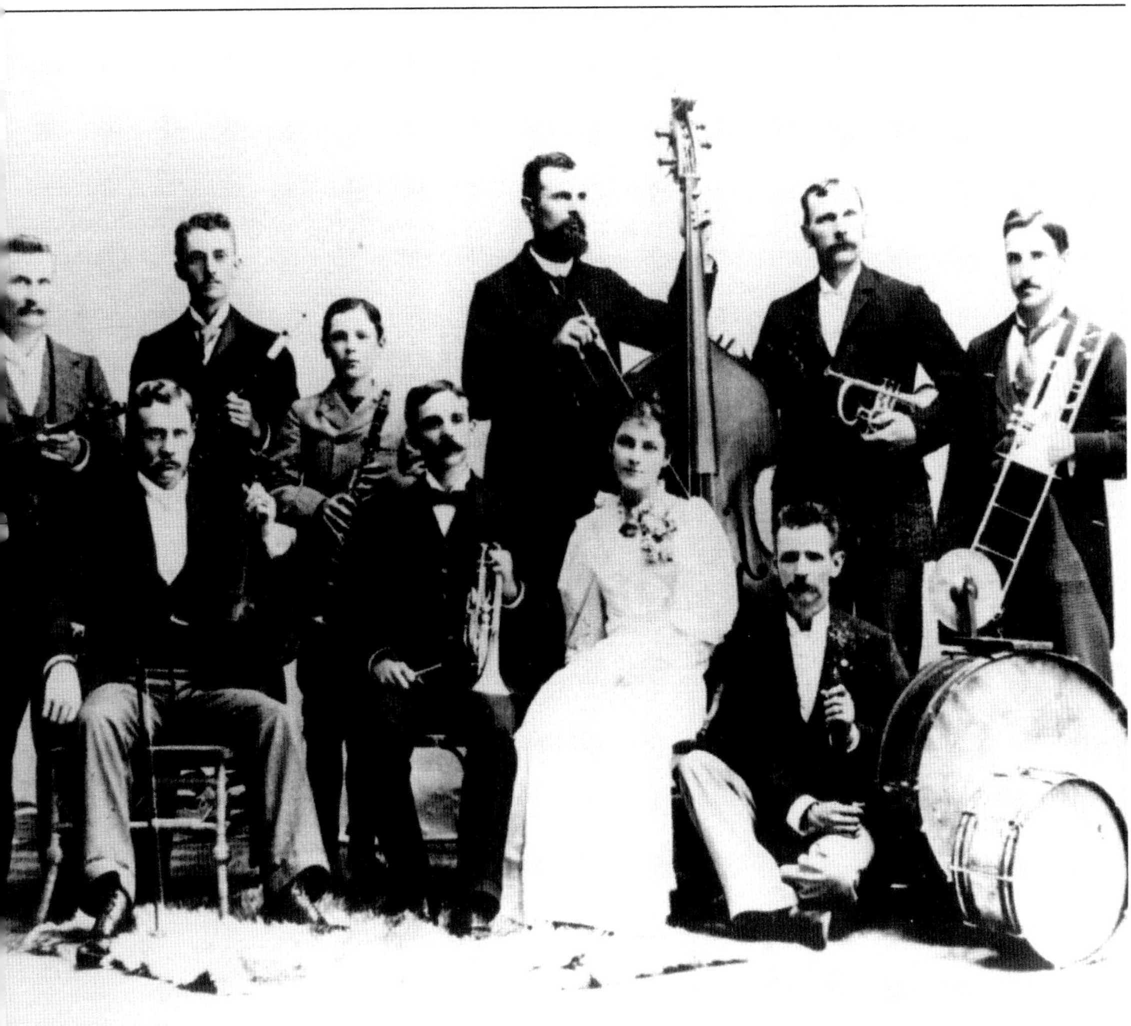

The Vermillion and University Orchestra gave concerts throughout Clay County. Its members are pictured from the left in the front row: Dick Stinson, viola; G.W. Collins, conductor and cornet; Ruth Brady Hallam, piano and organ; and an unknown professor. In the back row are Mr. Matson, violin; Conrad Collins, E.E. Collins, bass; Fred Heglin, and an unidentified man. Fred Heglin had found an organ in the 1881 flood, put it back in working order, and taught himself to play it. (Courtesy of W.H. Over Museum.)

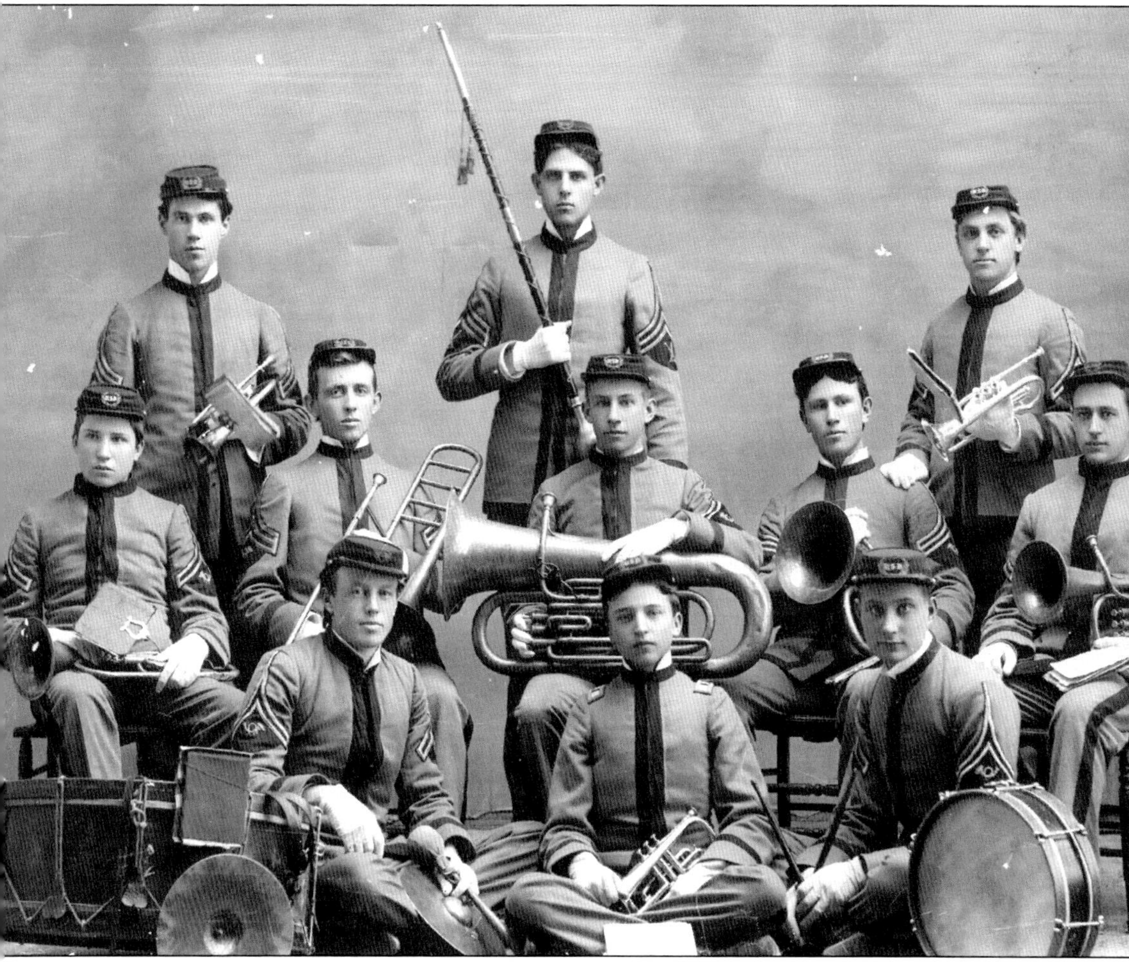

The USD Band entertained the campus in 1899. (Courtesy of USD Archive.)

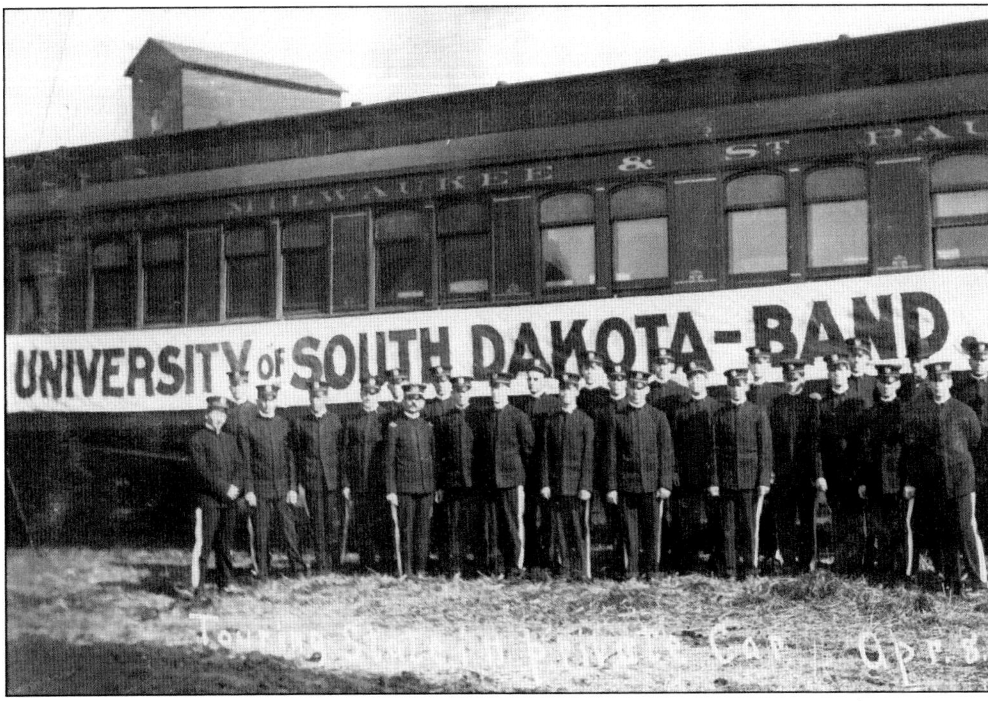

USD Band members pose at the train station in 1908 as they prepare to tour the state on a Milwaukee and St. Paul Railroad car. (Courtesy of USD Archive.)

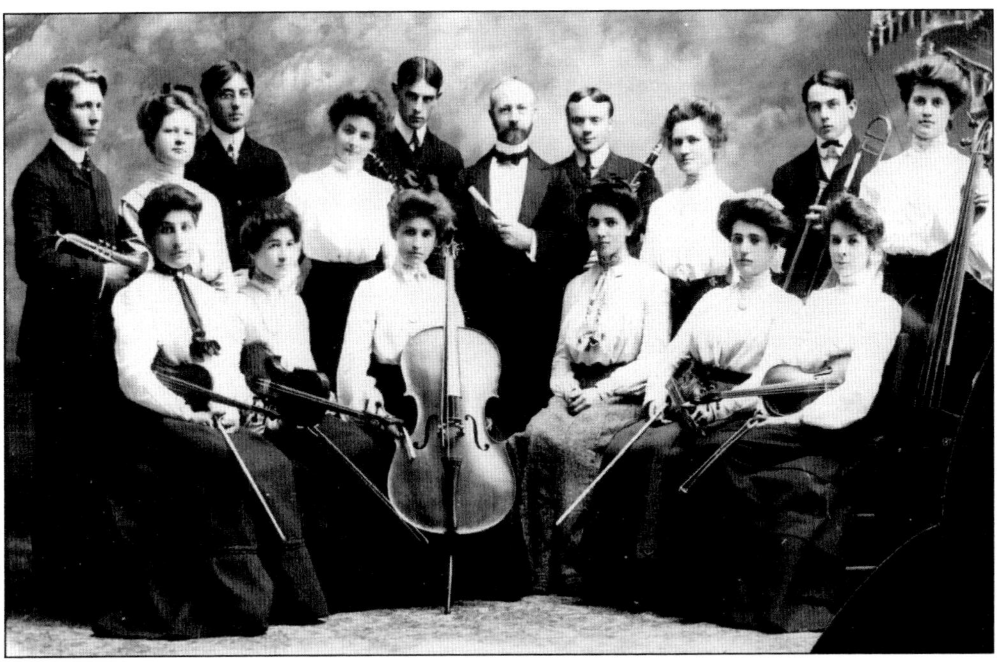
In 1905, USD had an orchestra as well as a band. (Courtesy of USD Archive.)

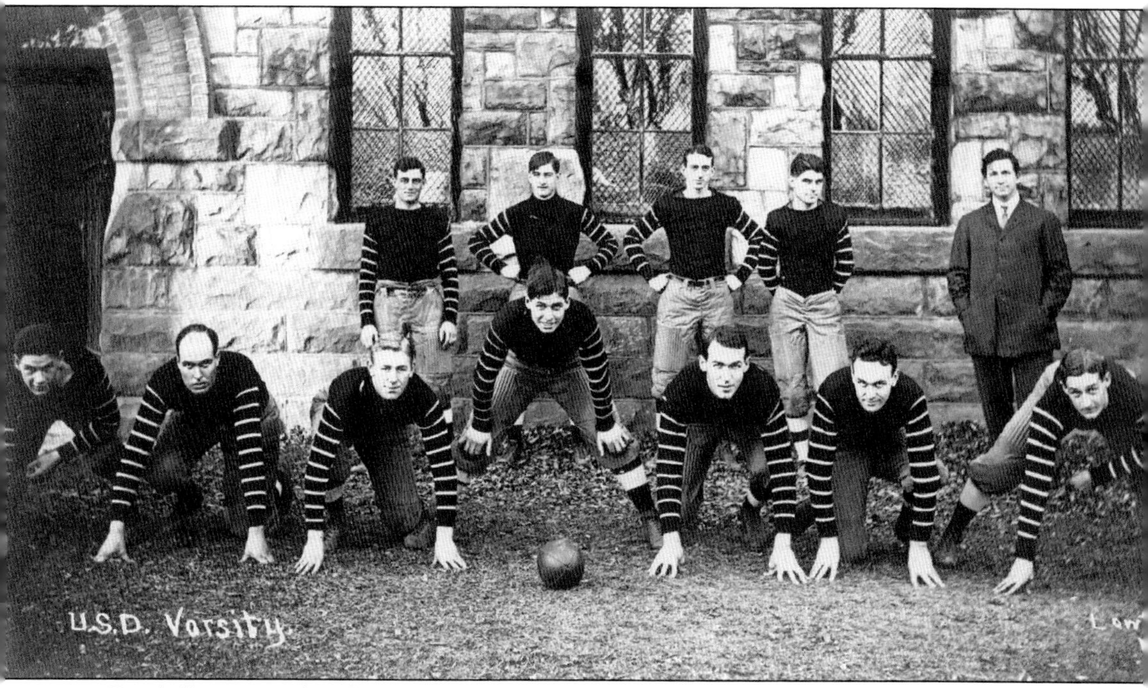

Football was introduced in 1900, and from 1900 through 1913, USD won 60 games, lost 27, and tied 4. The University of South Dakota's proud football team posed in uniform in 1911 outside the gymnasium. (Courtesy of USD Archive.)

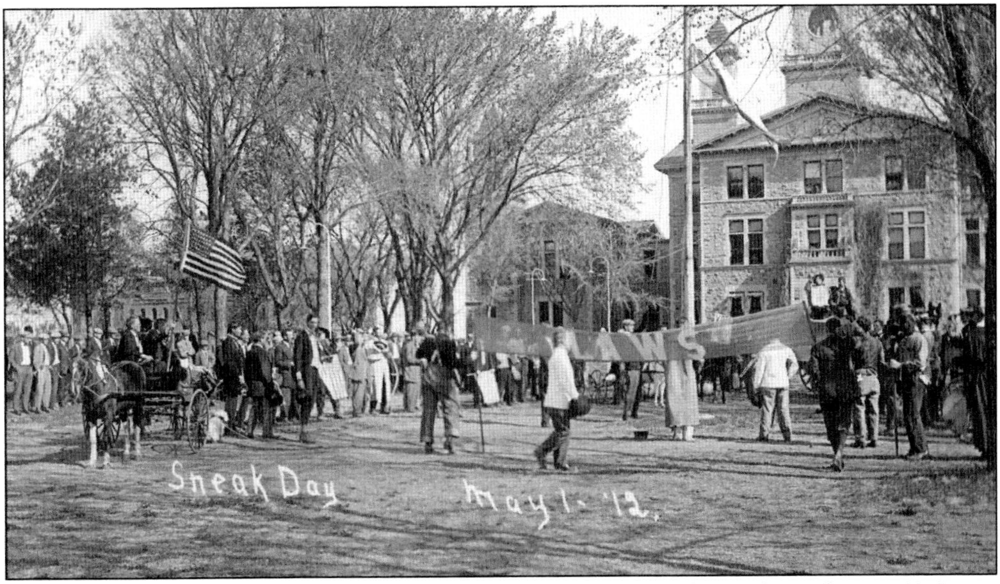

At one time, the Law School celebrated "Sneak Day" each May with parades and general hilarity. While the precise details of the annual event have been lost in the haze of time, the above provides a general idea of the tenor of the celebration c. 1912. (Courtesy of USD Archive.)

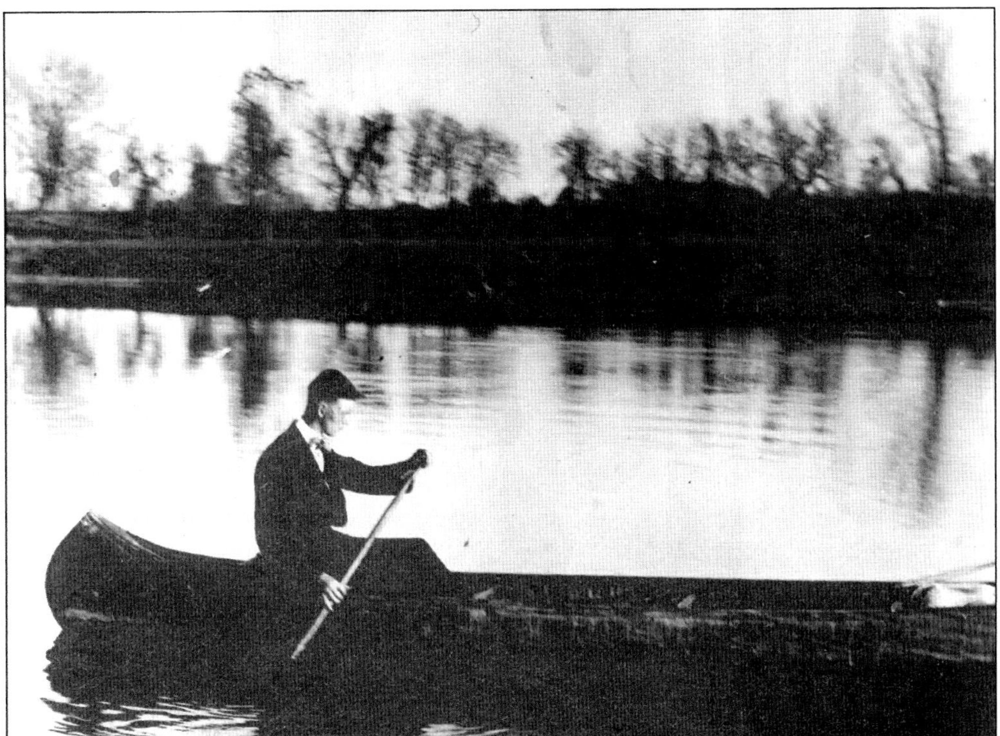

A young man wearing his freshman beanie paddles his canoe on the Missouri. (Courtesy of USD Archive.)

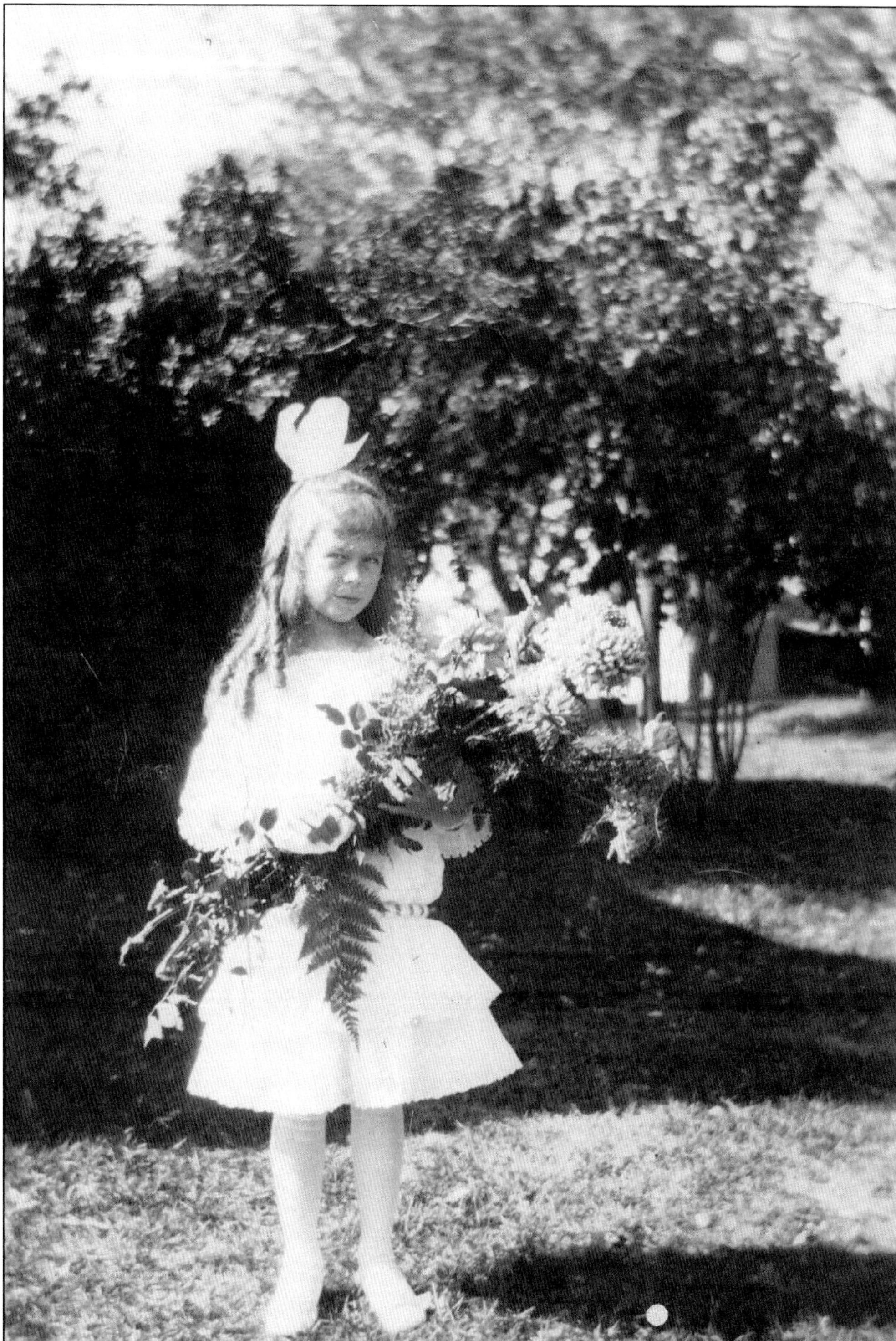

Grace Beede, for whom Beede Hall is named, posed for this informal portrait. (Courtesy of W.H. Over Museum.)

Six

Social Life

In its first years, Vermillion's social life was simple, if a bit on the rowdy side as befitted a river boat town on the frontier. The Old Settlers organization held dances at the local hall. Church socials were packed to capacity. The Sons of Temperance held a "popcorn social." The Vermillion Dramatic Association put on five-act dramas for residents and the Vermillion band gave free concerts on the lawn of the Jolley's home. Minstrel shows, a magic lantern show, ice skating, singing, dancing, and traveling shows and concerts provided entertainment for early residents.

The temperance movement blossomed in Clay County during the last quarter of the century with the support of local clergy. Temperance societies grew and created conflict between the pro- and anti-liquor forces until prohibition rendered the local question moot. The Red Ribbon movement began in Clay County with a lecture by the Reverend John H. Lozier who convinced some 320 attendees to sign a pledge to abjure intoxicating beverages for life. The wearing of a red ribbon was a sign of that pledge. A local organization formed in an effort to spread the campaign to every township and to publicize the names of those who had signed the pledge. They also organized a temperance singing band to perform popular temperance songs.

Perhaps the most prominent temperance organization was the Women's Christian Temperance Union (W.C.T.U.). Members met on Sunday evenings for services and published a weekly column in local newspapers. They occasionally visited local saloons where they prayed for the "unfortunates" that were there. Prominent advocates of the movement visited Vermillion including Frances Willard, president of the national W.C.T.U., and Carrie Nation, a militant advocate of national reputation from Kansas. Local opinion polarized and voters were often faced with saloon and anti-saloon tickets. When the question appeared on the South Dakota ballot as a constitutional amendment on prohibition, Clay County's voters passed the measure by a margin of more than two to one. Vermillion itself was a dry town from the 1885 "three-mile" law until the repeal of prohibition in 1933.

A second organization that made a strong impact on Clay County was the Chautauqua Movement, which began in 1874 in western New York, originally for the purpose of educating Sunday school teachers. Over time, Chautauquas became a popular adult education vehicle that offered public lectures, home reading courses, and a forum for group discussions on areas of cultural and intellectual interest. In 1885, the first Chautauqua reading club was formed in Vermillion. Members paid $7 for books and a magazine outlining the reading program. Topics of study were as various as the French Revolution and astronomy. Chautauqua assemblies began to form in South Dakota in 1891 when a number of Clay County residents attended a training session for leaders. University musicians and lecturers were popular performers at the assemblies.

Tent Chautauquas, or the "people's university," became popular just after the turn of the century. Vermillion notables formed a committee to contract with a group to provide a series of cultural and educational events during July of 1913. Area residents filled the tent to capacity night after night, and others had to stand outside—so popular did the series prove to be. Chautauquas continued in Vermillion through the early 1920s. William Jennings Bryan lectured there twice, once on patriotism and women's suffrage and a second time on religion and Darwinism. Wakonda held its own Chautauquas from 1915 to 1920.

As a University town, Vermillion's social life was enriched by the skills and interests of its resident faculty. The Vermillion city band held weekly concerts during the summer on Main Street near the Waldorf Hotel. An Opera House was constructed on the corner of Court and Main Streets and opera was a popular form of entertainment. Later, the old Opera House was sold to the March Theatre. In 1937, a band shell and outdoor theater were constructed in Prentis Park under a W.P.A. grant, and band concerts were regular events in the life of the community.

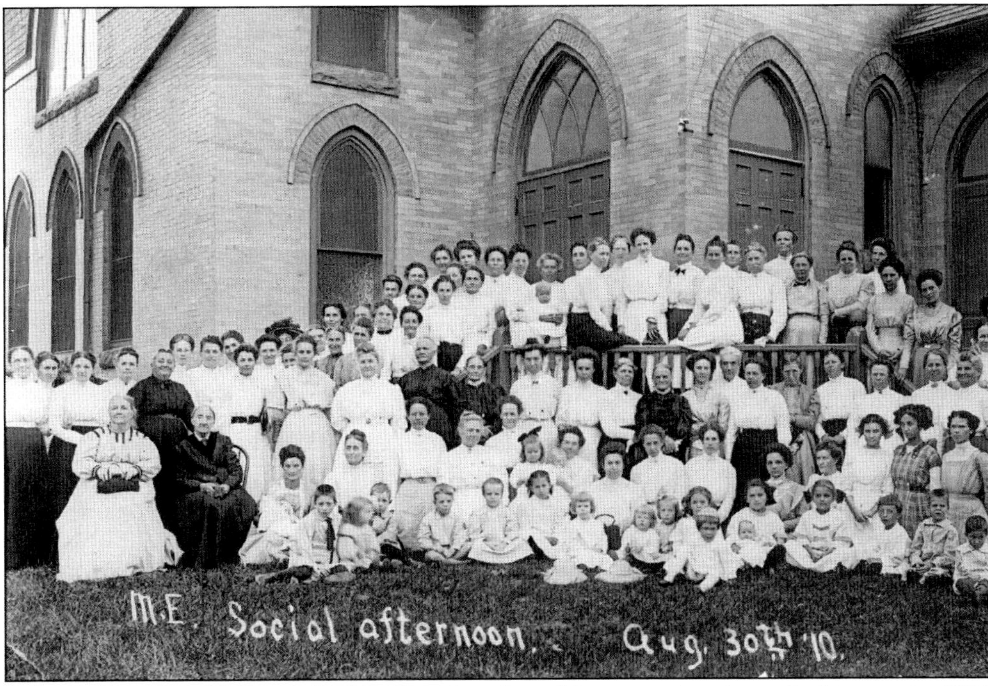

Members of Vermillion's Methodist Church gathered for a social at the end of August in 1910. (Courtesy of W.H. Over Museum.)

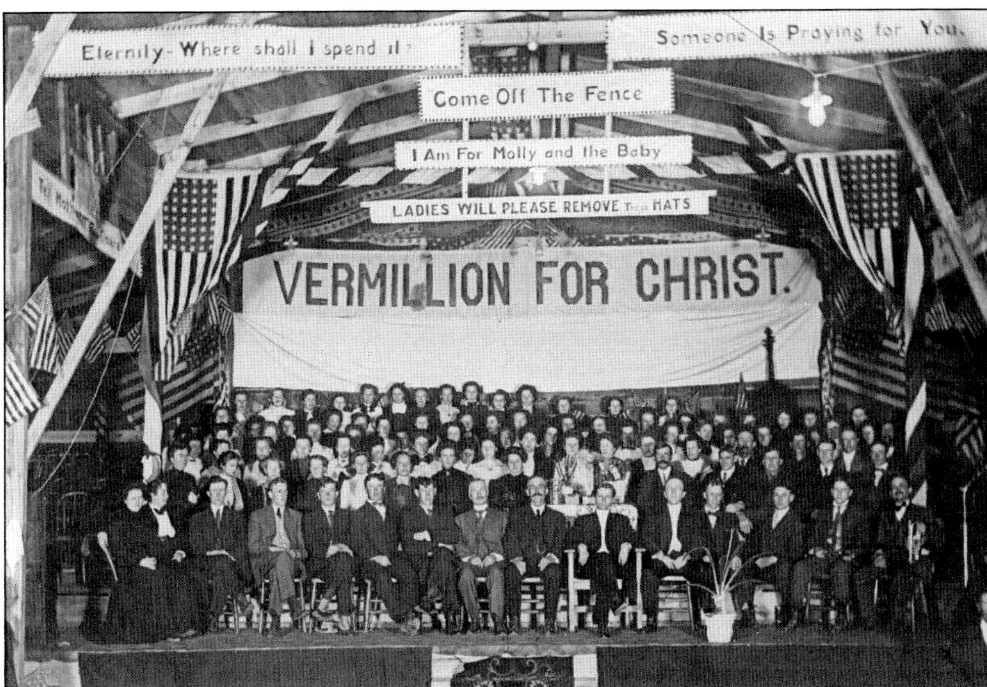

A religious revival meeting was held in Vermillion in 1910. In addition to messages about salvation, stage banners included a reminder to the ladies to remove their hats. (Courtesy of W.H. Over Museum.)

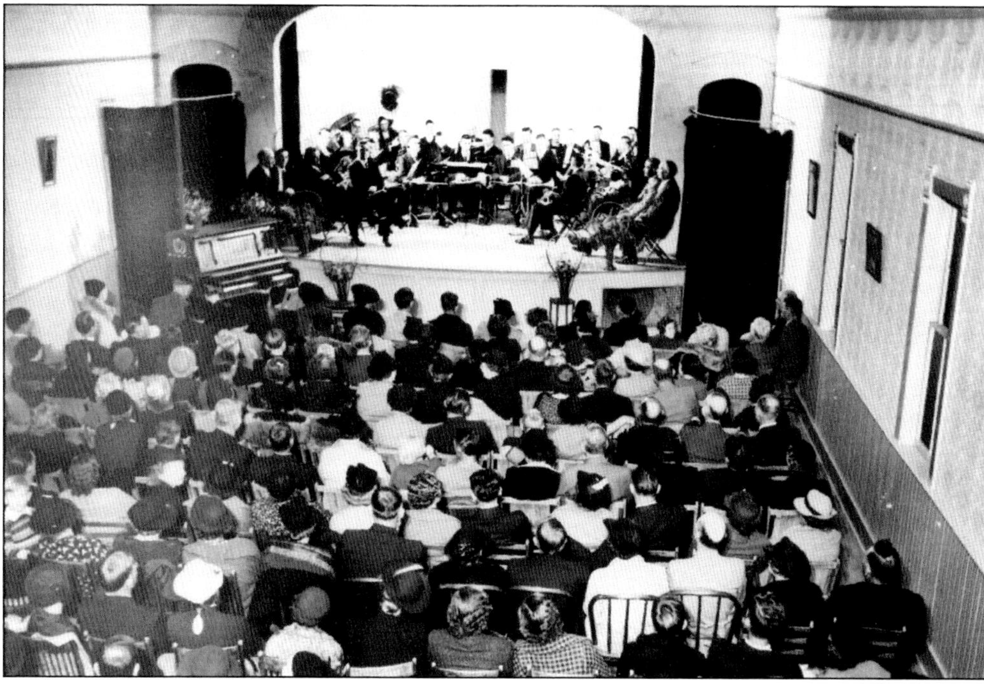

This photo shows a musical production at Garfield Township Hall. (Courtesy of W.H. Over Museum.)

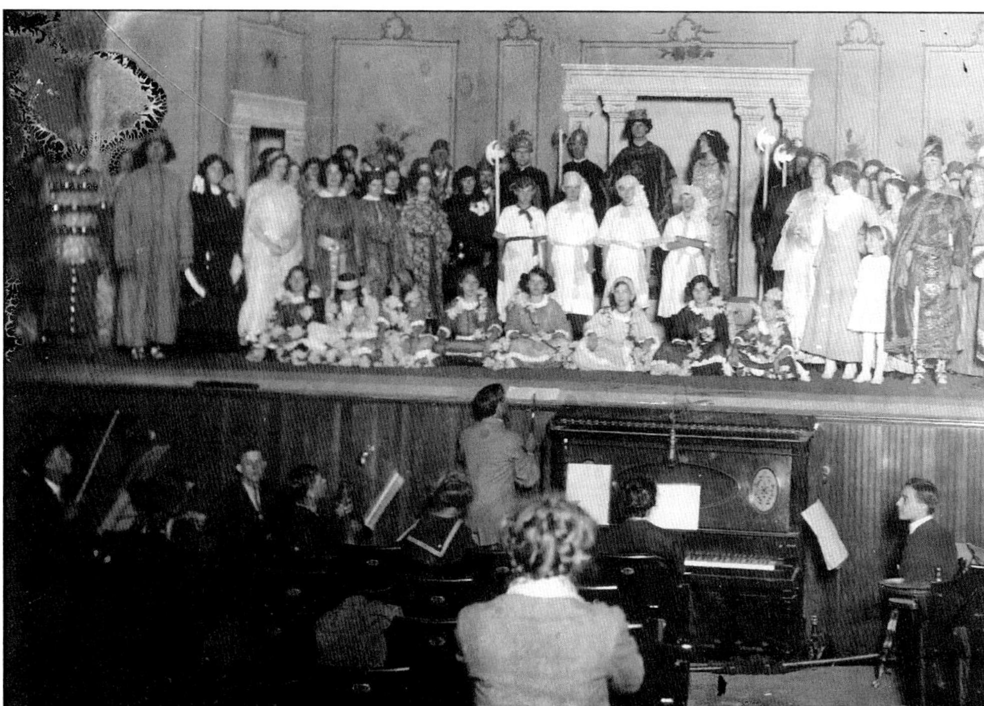

In Vermillion, amateur opera was a popular form of local entertainment. This production was given in 1901, complete with elaborate costumes and stage sets. (Courtesy of USD Archive.)

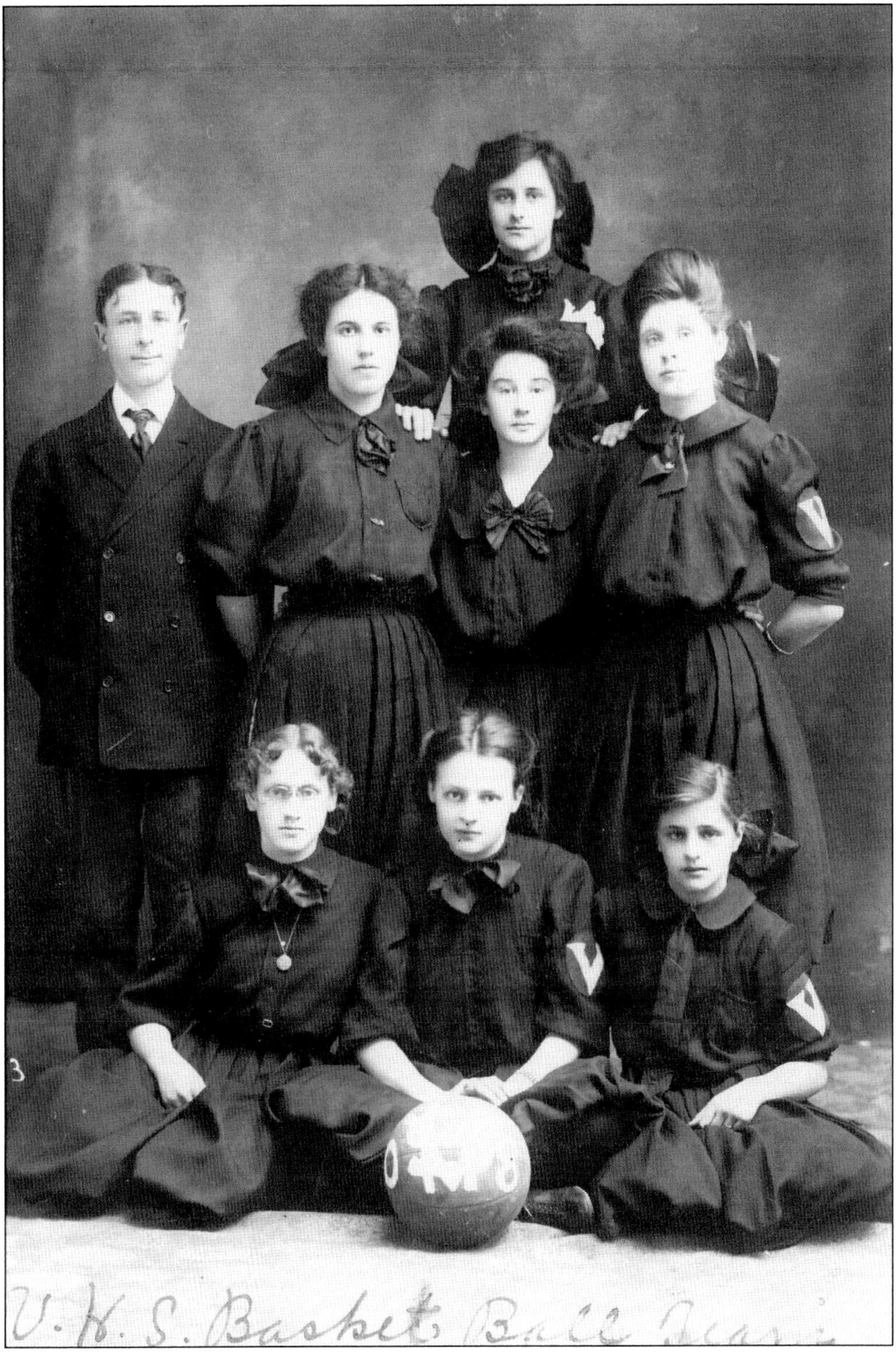

Vermillion High School's sports offerings included this early basketball team. One wonders how well the hair bows stood up to the rigors of the game.

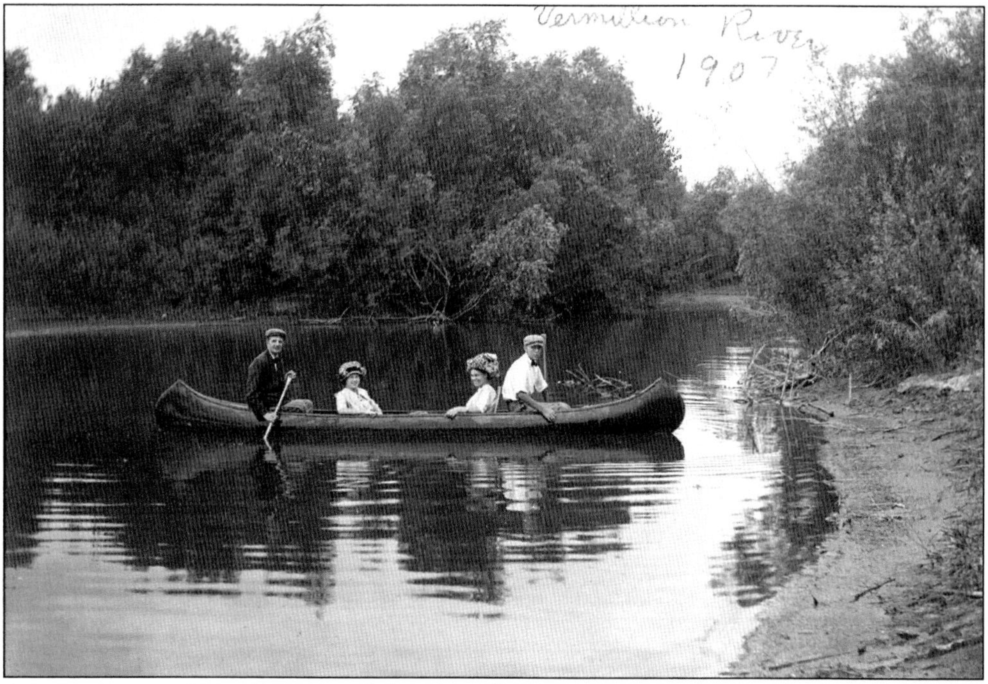

A canoe party takes advantage of the Vermillion River's quiet beauty. (Courtesy of W.H. Over Museum.)

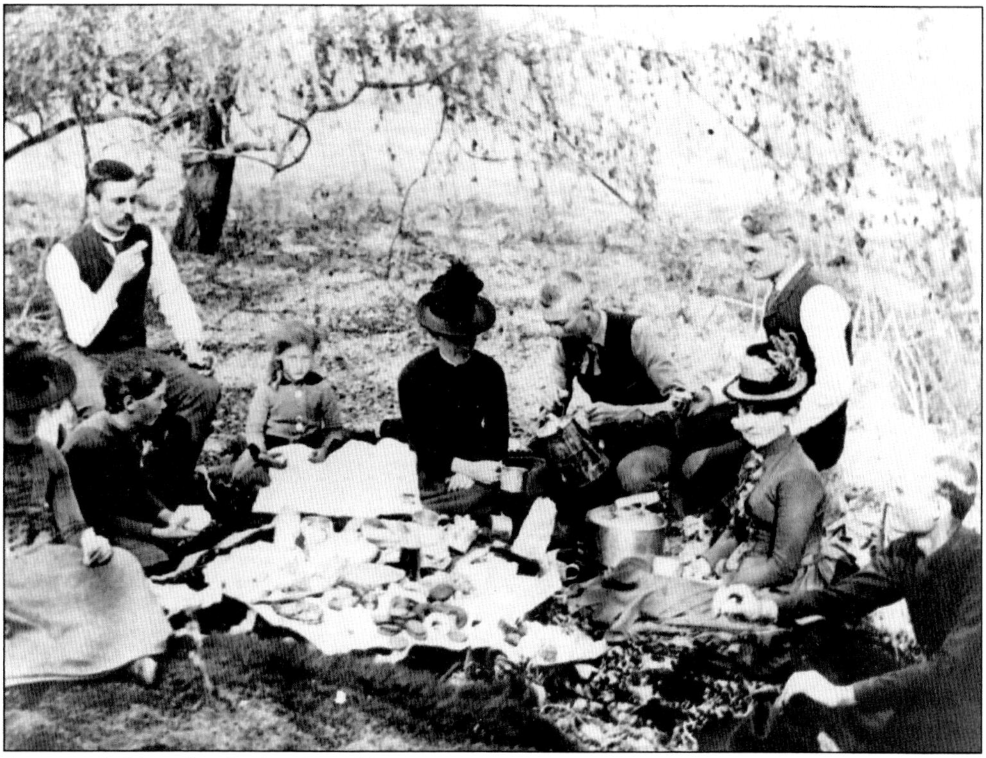
A picnic held in the shade of an old tree is pictured here. (Courtesy of USD Archive.)

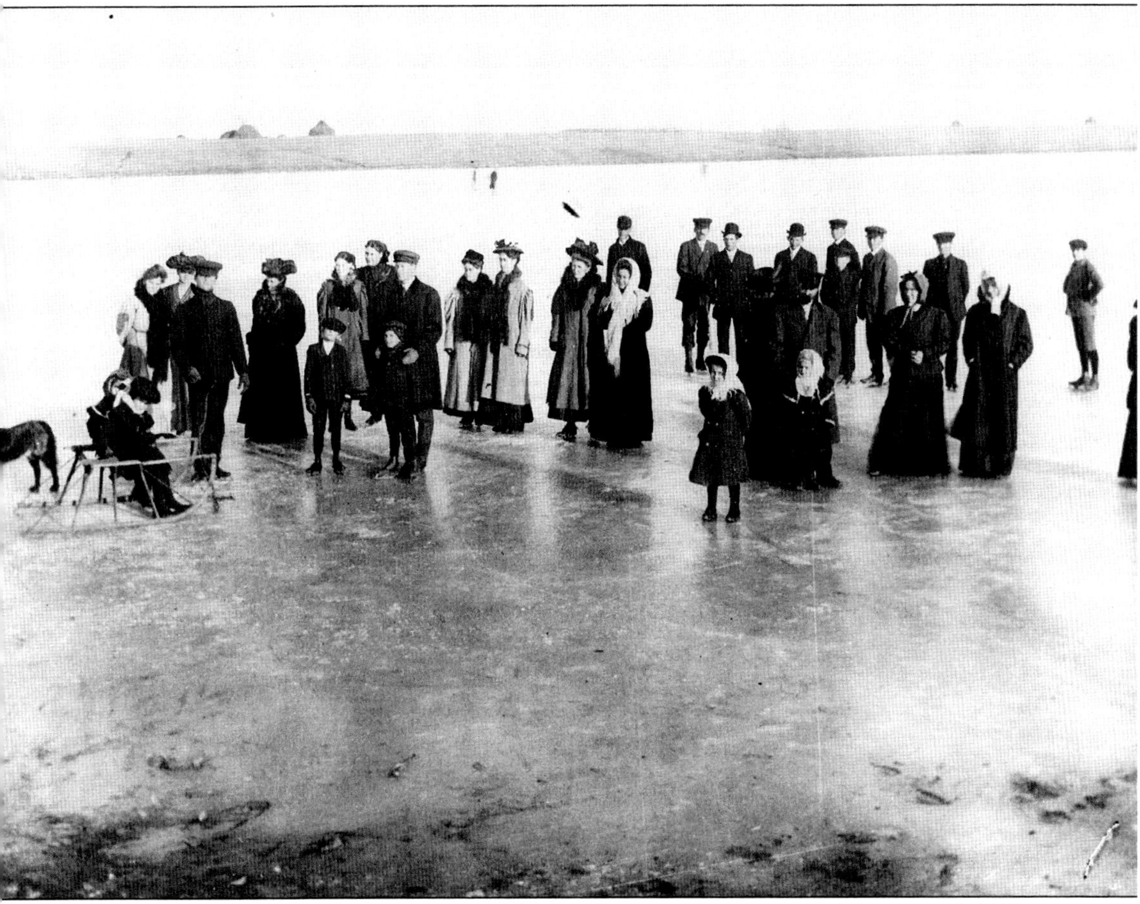

This photograph shows a skating party on Lake Emilene in Clay County. (Courtesy of W.H. Over Museum.)

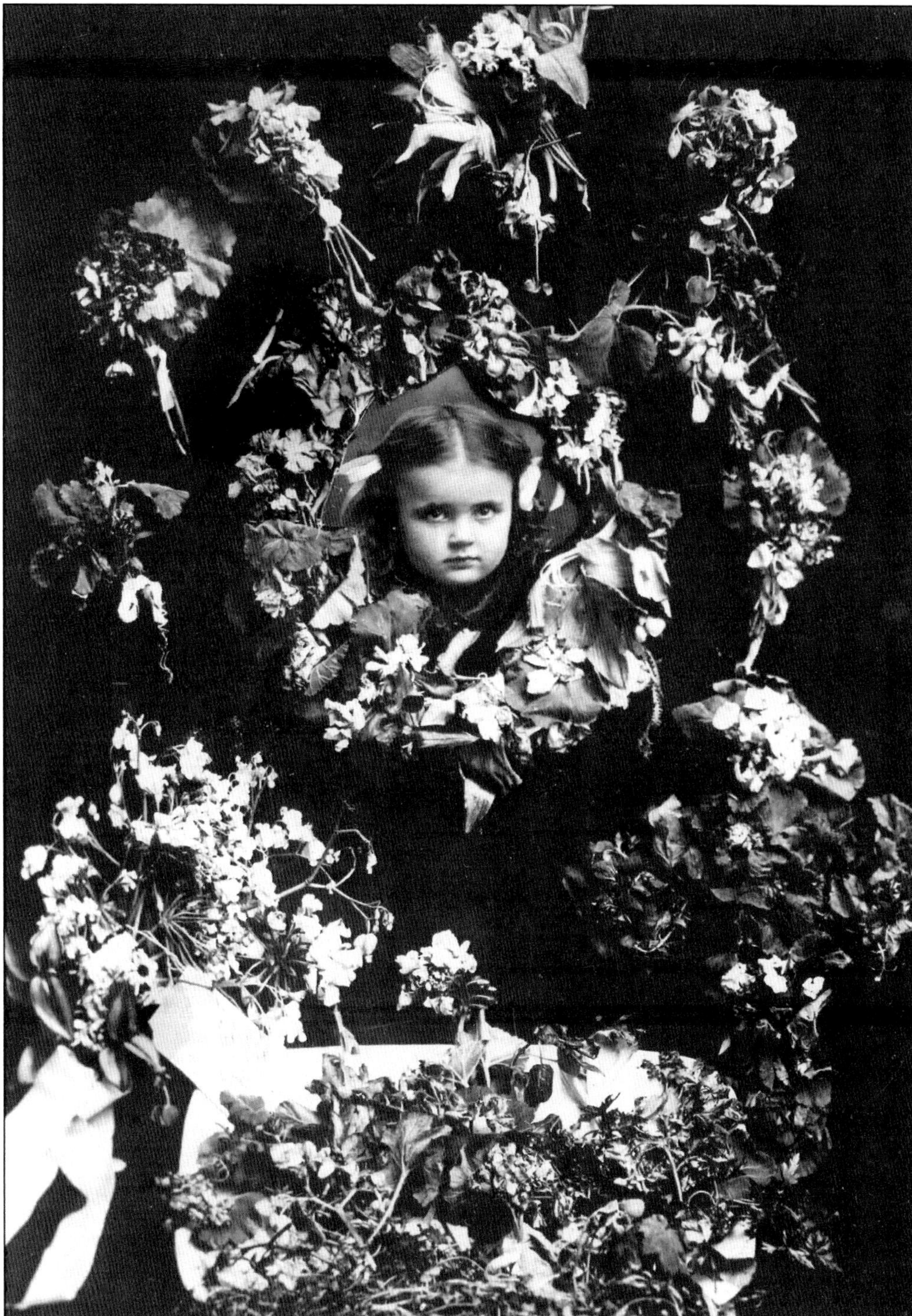

Funerals were a part of everyday life in Dakota Territory and funeral portraits were a way to commemorate the life of a beloved relation. This funeral portrait of a young girl is particularly touching. (Courtesy of the W.H. Over Museum.)

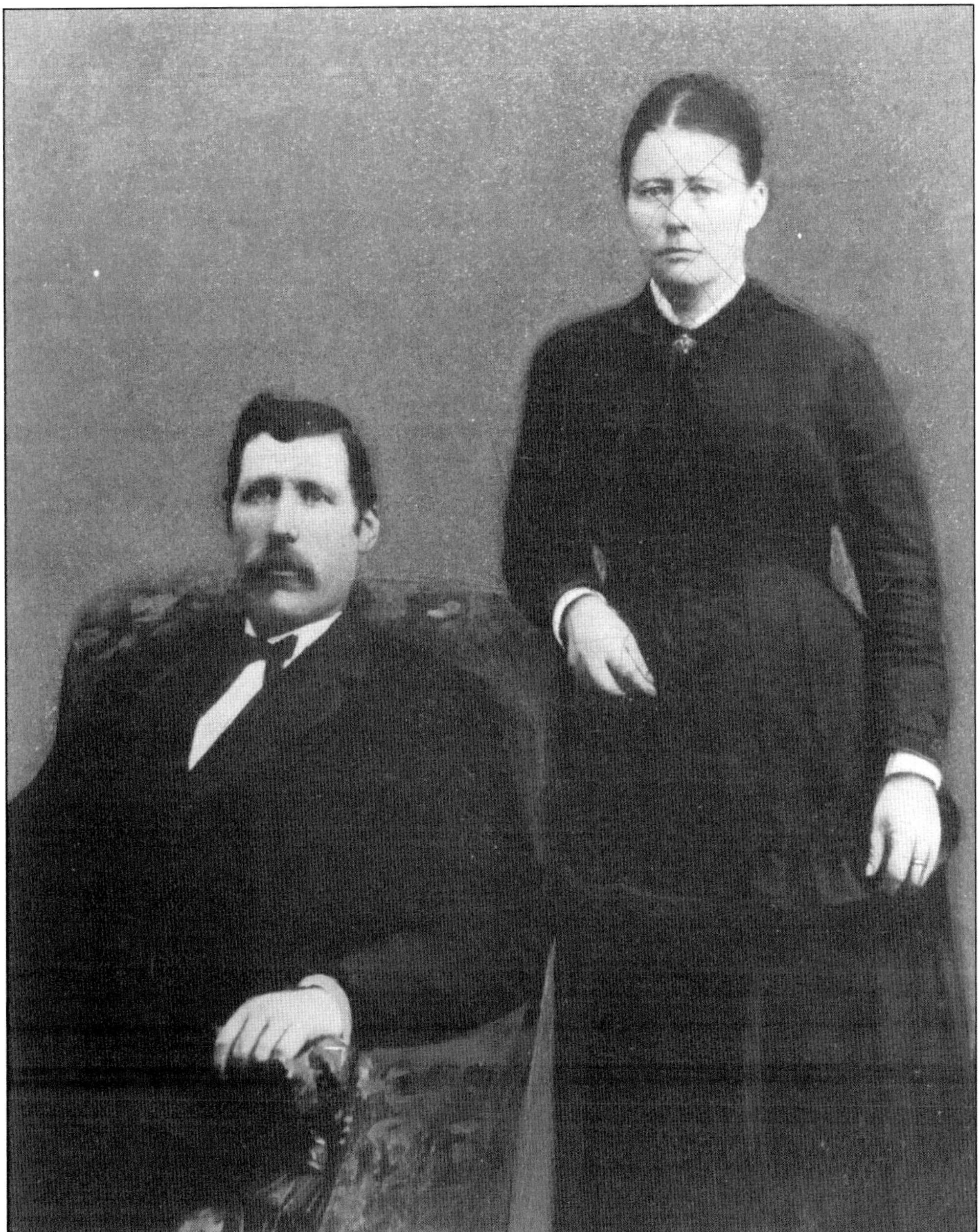

This couple received the first marriage license in Clay County and memorialized the occasion in this charming photograph. (Courtesy of the W.H. Over Museum.)

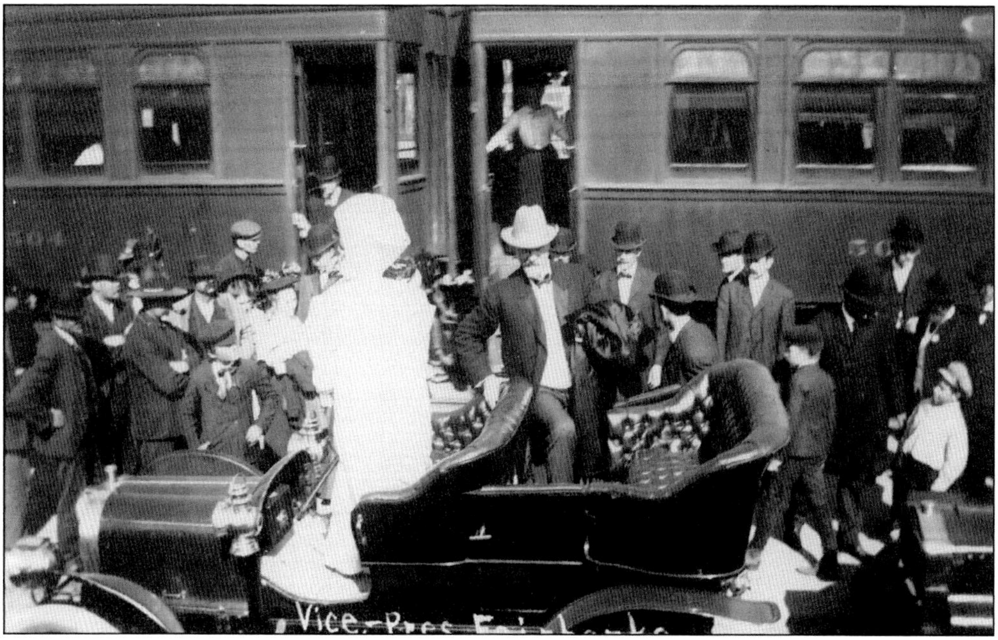

U.S. Vice President Charles Warren Fairbanks arrived in Vermillion on October 19, 1907 for a brief visit, and was met at the train station by local residents, including Mrs. Elley (in the front seat dressed in white), who had one of the first motorcars in town. (Courtesy of the W.H. Over Museum.)

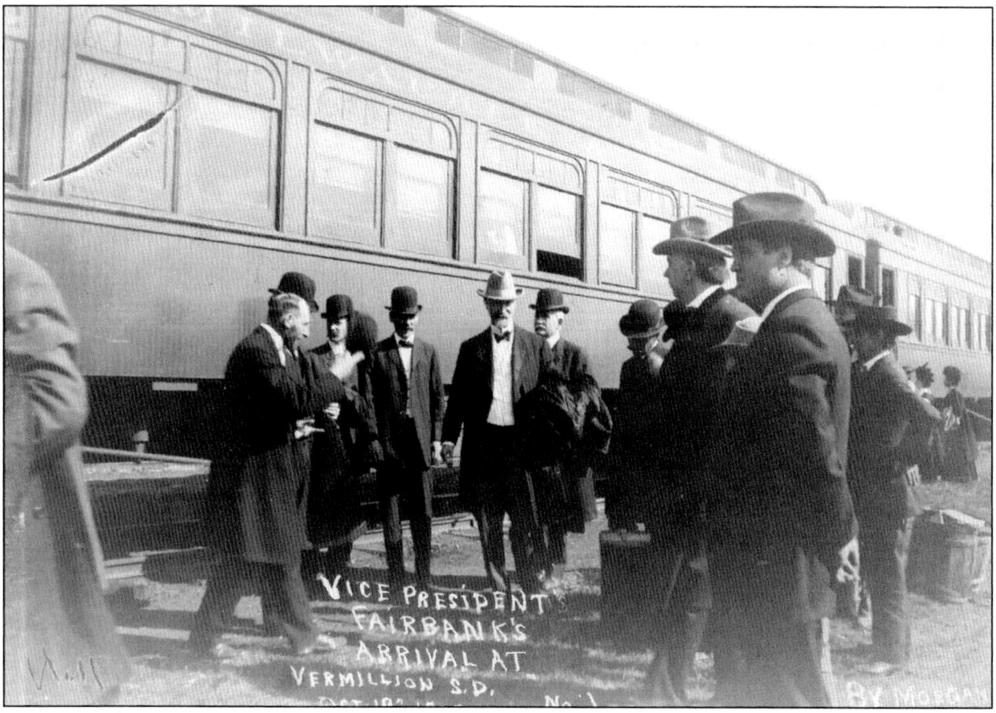

Vice President Fairbanks is welcomed to Vermillion by the town fathers. (Courtesy of W.H. Over Museum.)

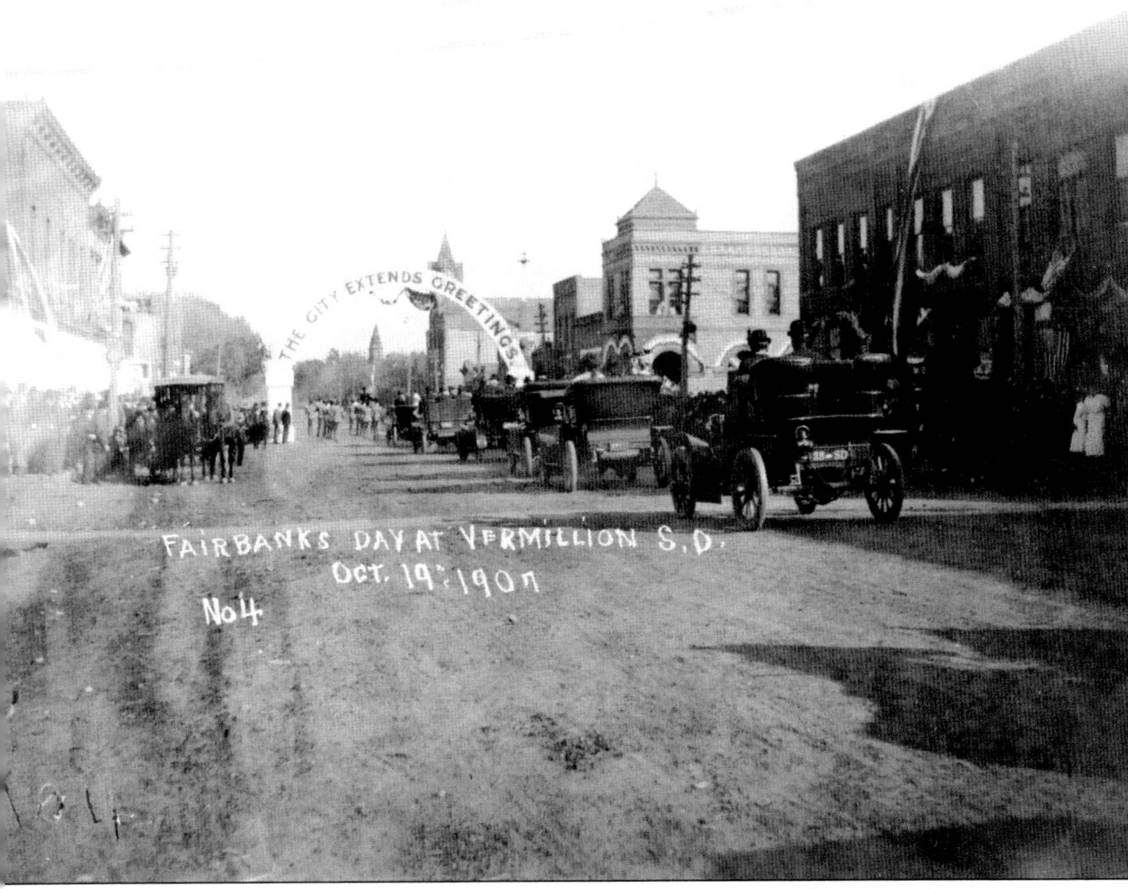

Local officials rolled out the welcome mat for Vice President Fairbanks. An archway was erected over Main Street, banners were hung, and Mr. Fairbanks was the honored guest in a parade of motorcars through the center of downtown Vermillion. (Courtesy of the W.H. Over Museum.)

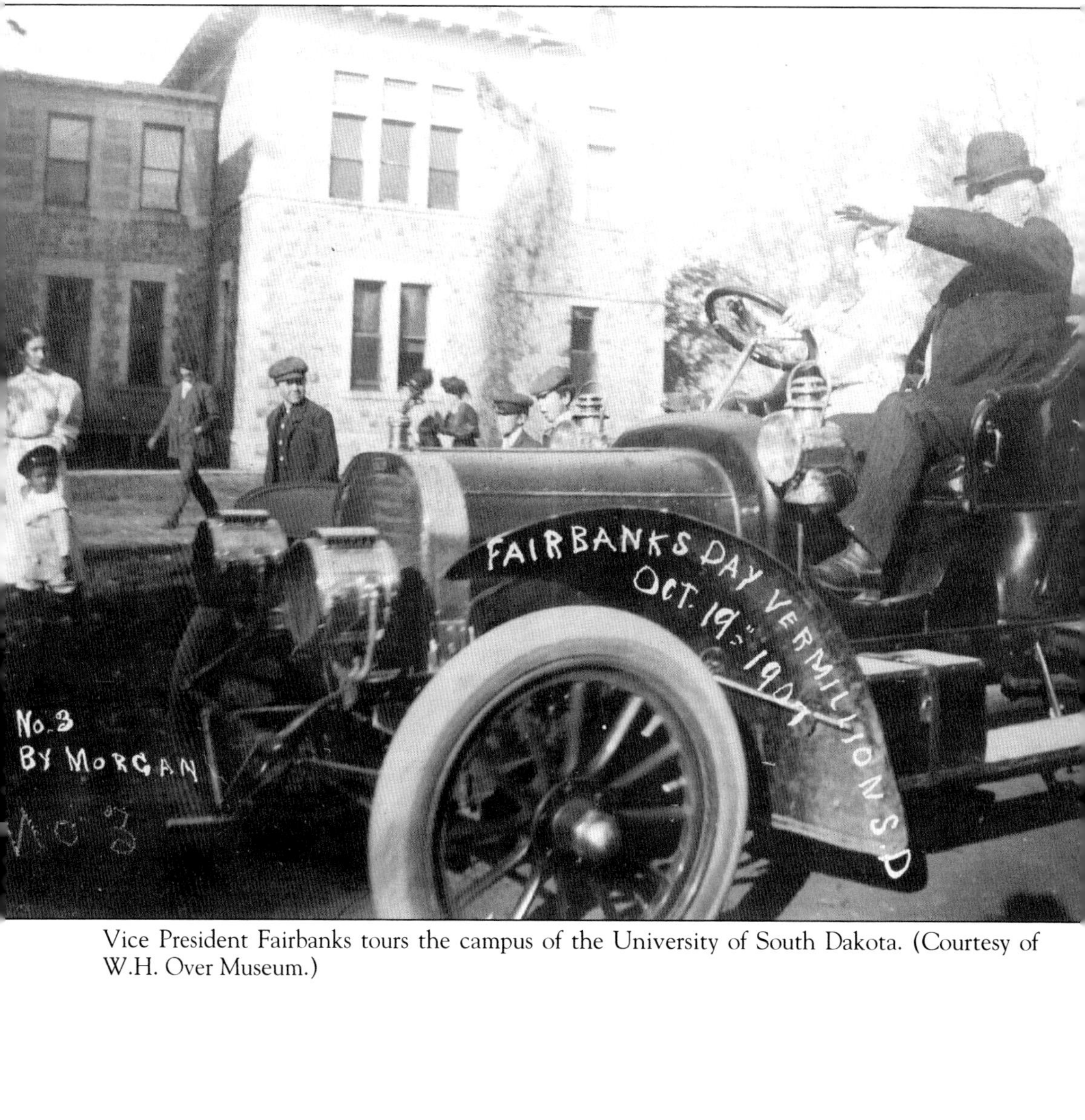

Vice President Fairbanks tours the campus of the University of South Dakota. (Courtesy of W.H. Over Museum.)

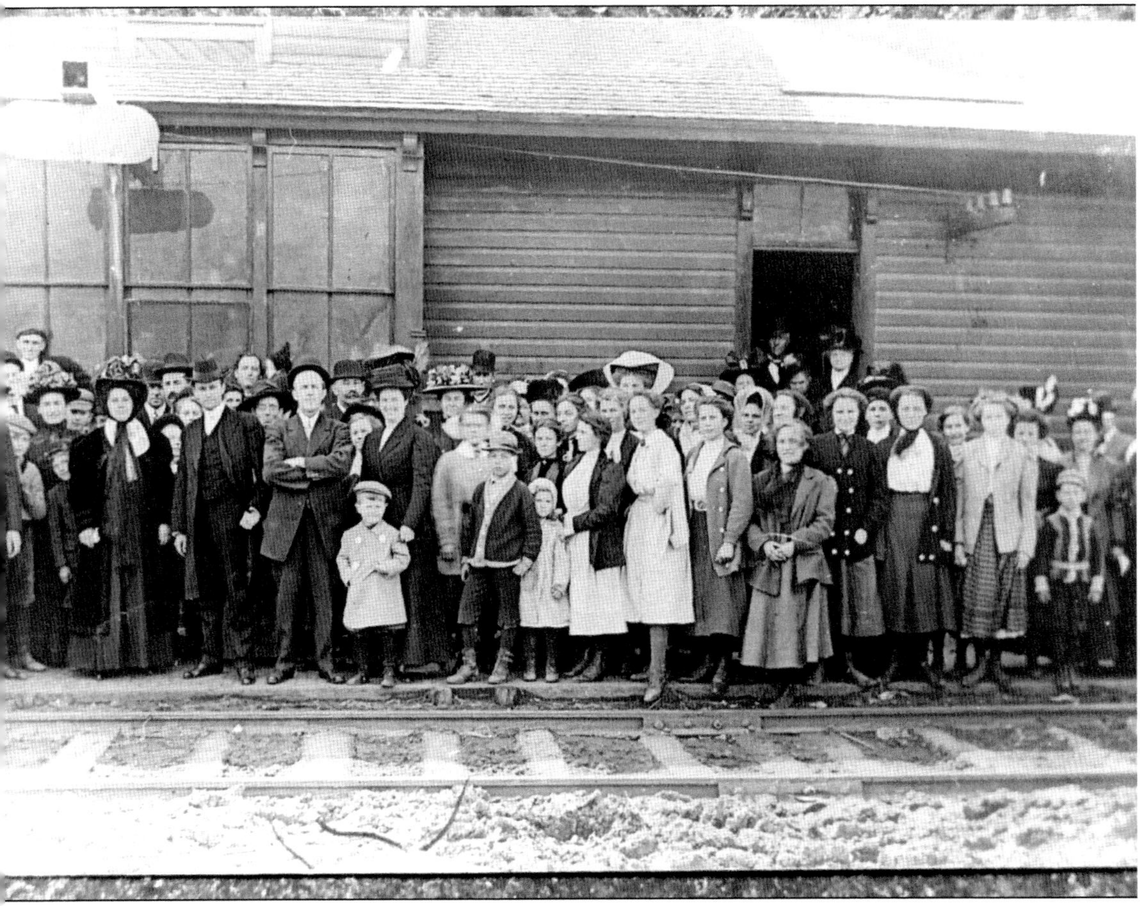

When Carrie Nation, the famous suffragist and organizer of the Women's Christian Temperance Union, came to town in March of 1910, the community offered her a warm welcome. She spoke at the Union Gospel Meeting and was later accompanied to the train station by the crowd pictured above. Carrie Nation is wearing a long cloak and standing in the front row, the third adult from the left.

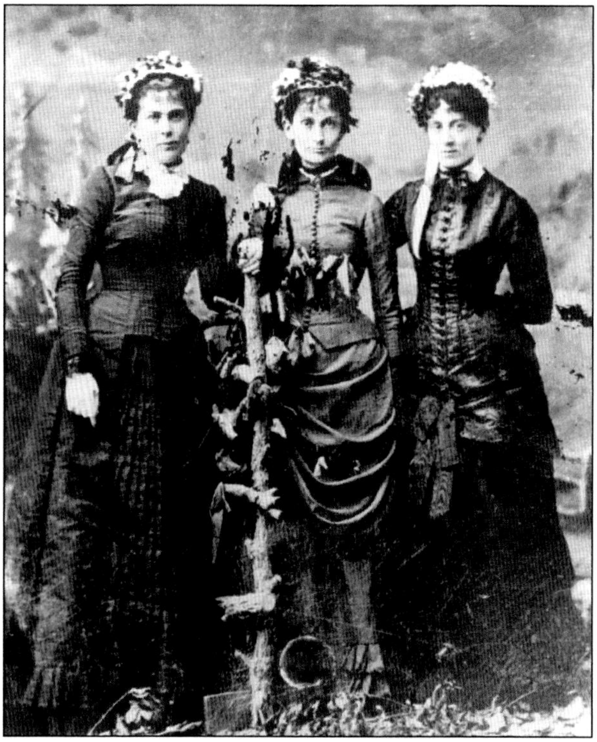

The Lewis Sisters married into three of Vermillion's elite families. From left to right the sisters are Anna Lewis Thompson, Adele Lewis Inman, and Lillie Lewis Morgan. (Courtesy of the Martin Weeks Collection at the W.H. Over Museum.)

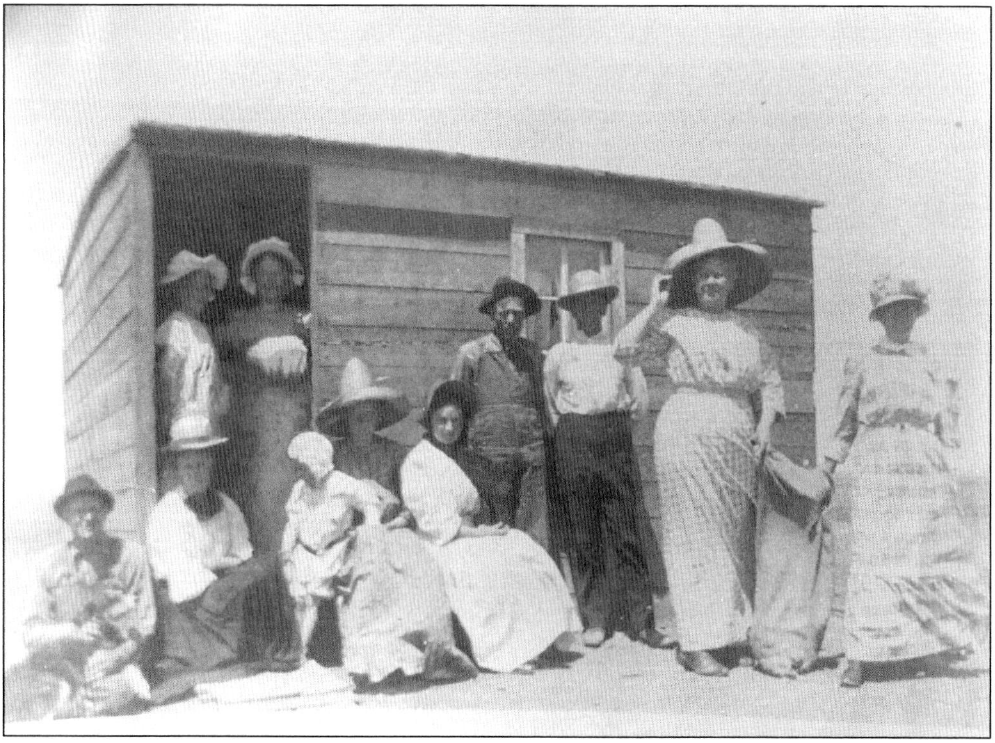

Members of the Anker Family from Clay County pose in front of a claim shanty in Meade County, South Dakota where they homesteaded. (Courtesy of W.H. Over Museum.)

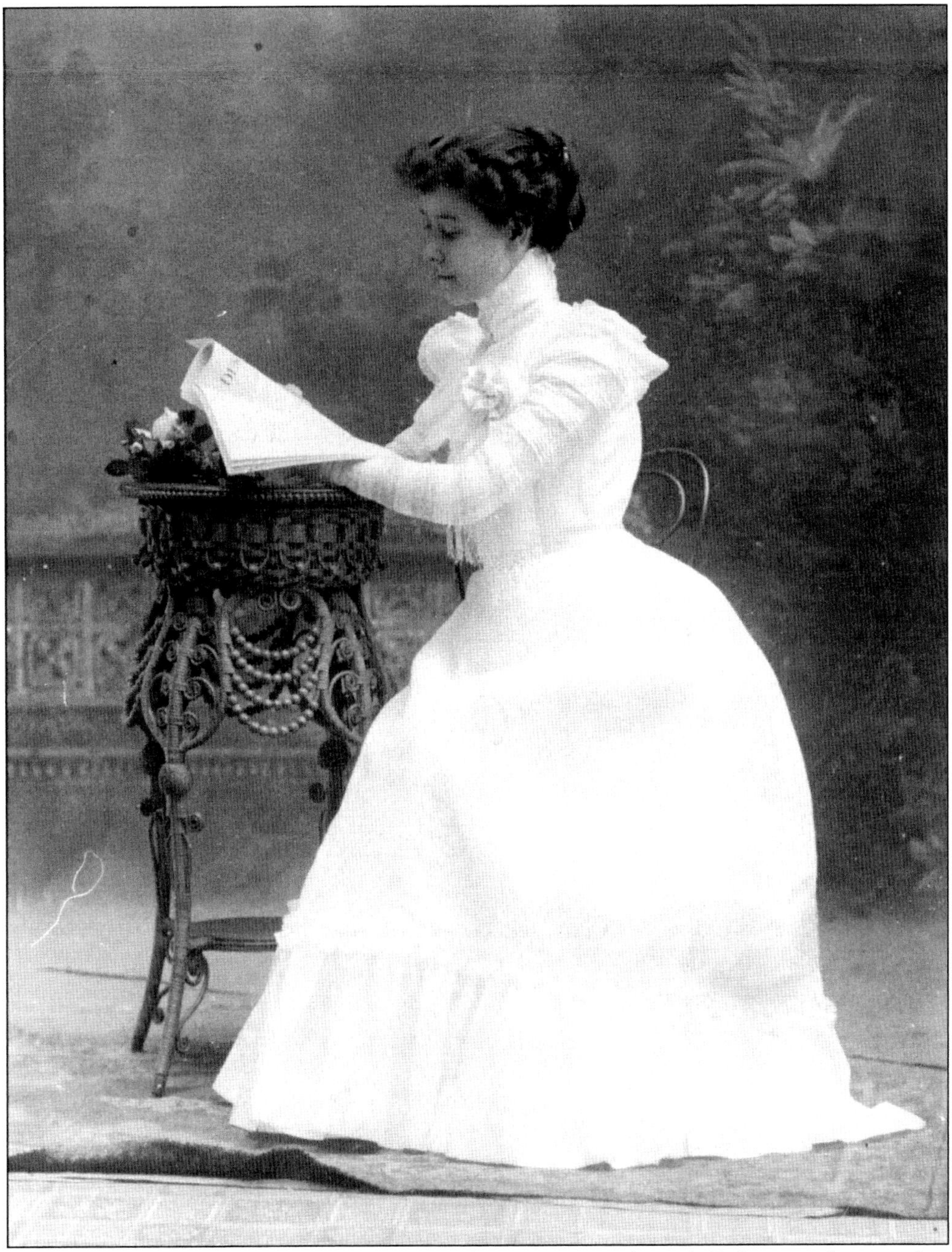

Mamie Weeks Gunderson was a member of the University of South Dakota graduating class of 1900. This is her graduation photograph. (From the Martin Weeks Collection at the W.H. Over Museum.)

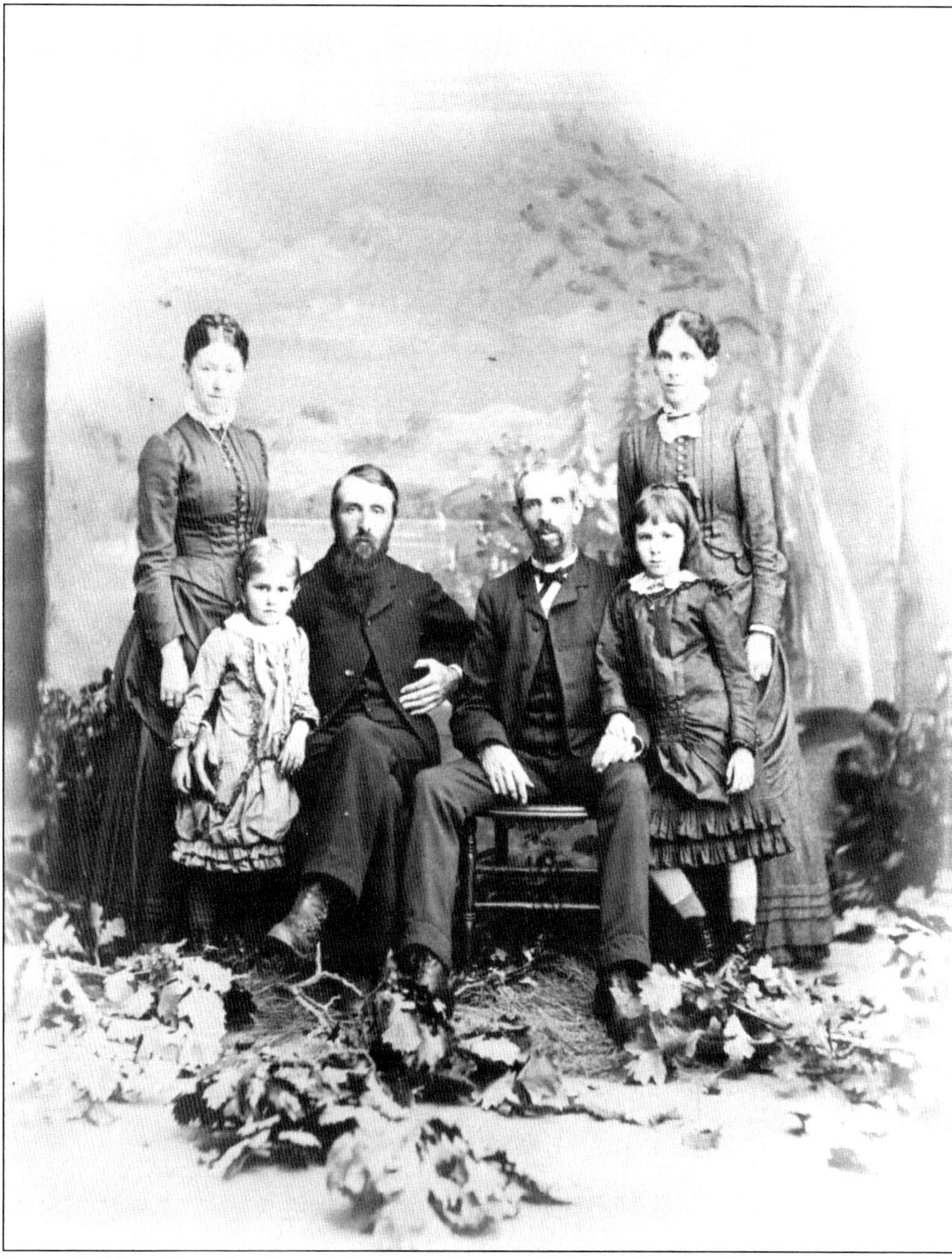

An early Vermillion family posed at the photographer's studio for this staged photograph. (Courtesy of the W.H. Over Museum.)

Seven

COMMUNITY LIFE

Vermillion was first incorporated on August 12, 1873 under a Board of Trustee form of government. The following month, the community came together to pass a series of ordinances relating to peace and order, licensing and regulation of intoxicating liquor, disorderly houses, the prevention of roaming cattle, hogs, and horses, and the taxation of dogs. In 1877, Vermillion elected its first mayor, Colonel John L. Jolley, a stalwart of the early community. Born in Canada, he fought in the Civil War and came to Vermillion in 1866. His many occupations included land official, lawyer, and teacher in the log schoolhouse. Vermillion's annual budget of $855.81 was largely funded by saloon licenses, which brought in $550 that year. Spending for sidewalks and roads topped the list of outlays each year.

Fire was a constant danger in the community and a city water system was the only defense. In 1891, a year after one of Vermillion's worst fires destroyed two blocks on Main Street, the Michigan Pipe Company proposed to build a city water system at a cost of $26,000. A company was formed of local citizens and the pipe company. Wooden pipes were laid and a pump house built below Market Street. Finally a wooden tank was built on top of the bluff. By early 1892, Vermillion had a reliable water supply.

Electricity came to Vermillion in 1895 when the town fathers granted a 20-year franchise to E.D. Brookman of the Vermillion Milling Company. The company's flour and gristmill, located on Center Street where City Hall now stands, purchased equipment that permitted power generation for the community as well. Residents and businesses found electricity to be unreliable in the early years. Finally, in 1898 Vermillion's first telephone exchange was installed for an initial 60 subscribers.

Residential neighborhoods were fairly utilitarian until the turn of the century. Those moving up from below the bluff were satisfied with meeting basic needs. A visitor in 1894 reported few nice residences and fewer nice yards. Houses had barns and outdoor toilets. The decade between 1900 and 1910 saw a building boom, and the city spread to cover most of the territory it would inhabit in 1950. The Civic Federation, and later the Civic Improvement League, worked to improve both the physical appearance and the spiritual character of the community by supporting park and street improvements while blocking the issuance of new saloon licenses. "Dandelion Day" was an annual attempt to engage all citizens in the task of "the destruction of the offensive plant that was marring the beauty of lawns and parkings." Arbor Day was observed annually. Prizes were awarded to the best gardens and the cleanest blocks.

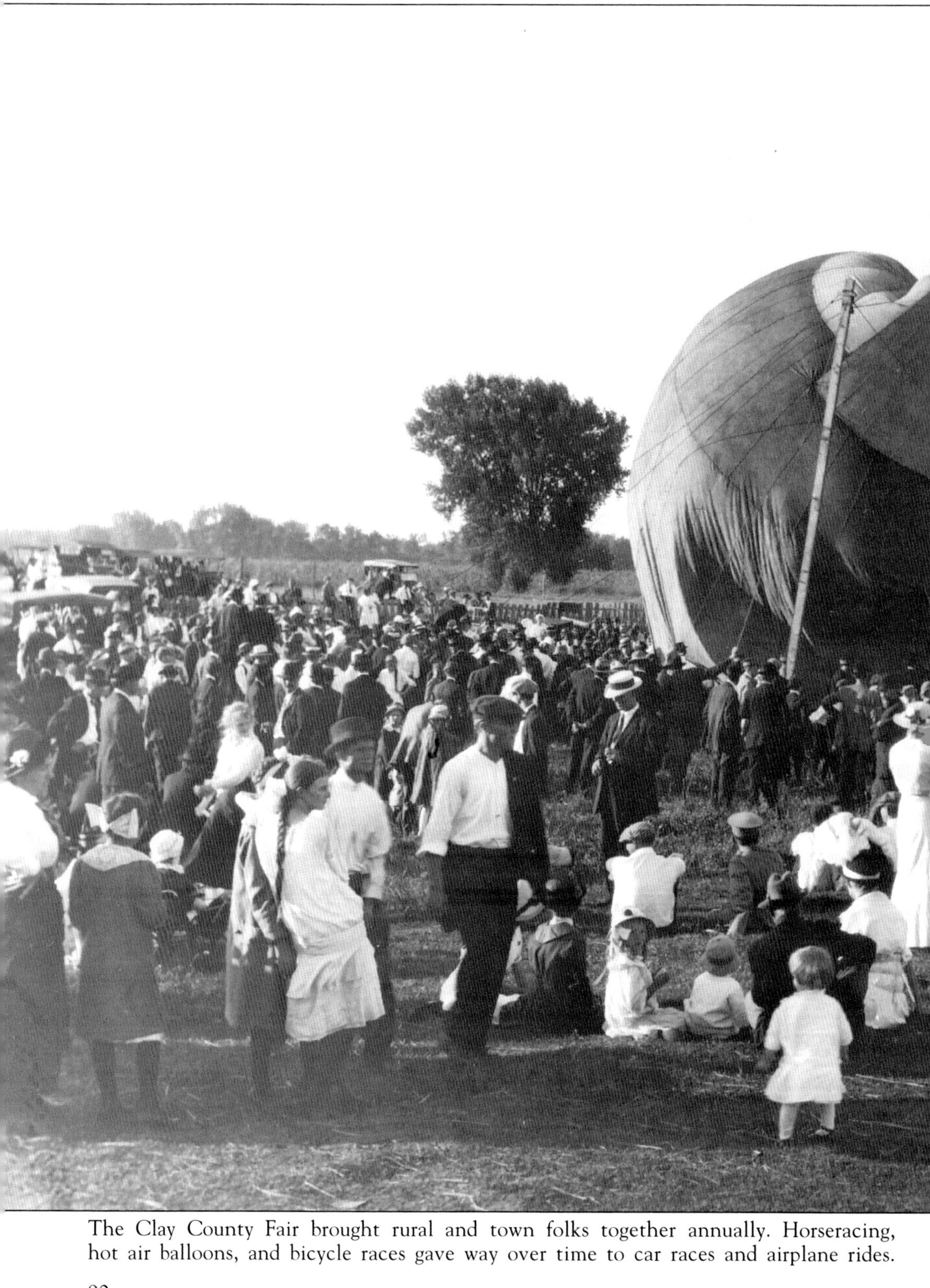

The Clay County Fair brought rural and town folks together annually. Horseracing, hot air balloons, and bicycle races gave way over time to car races and airplane rides.

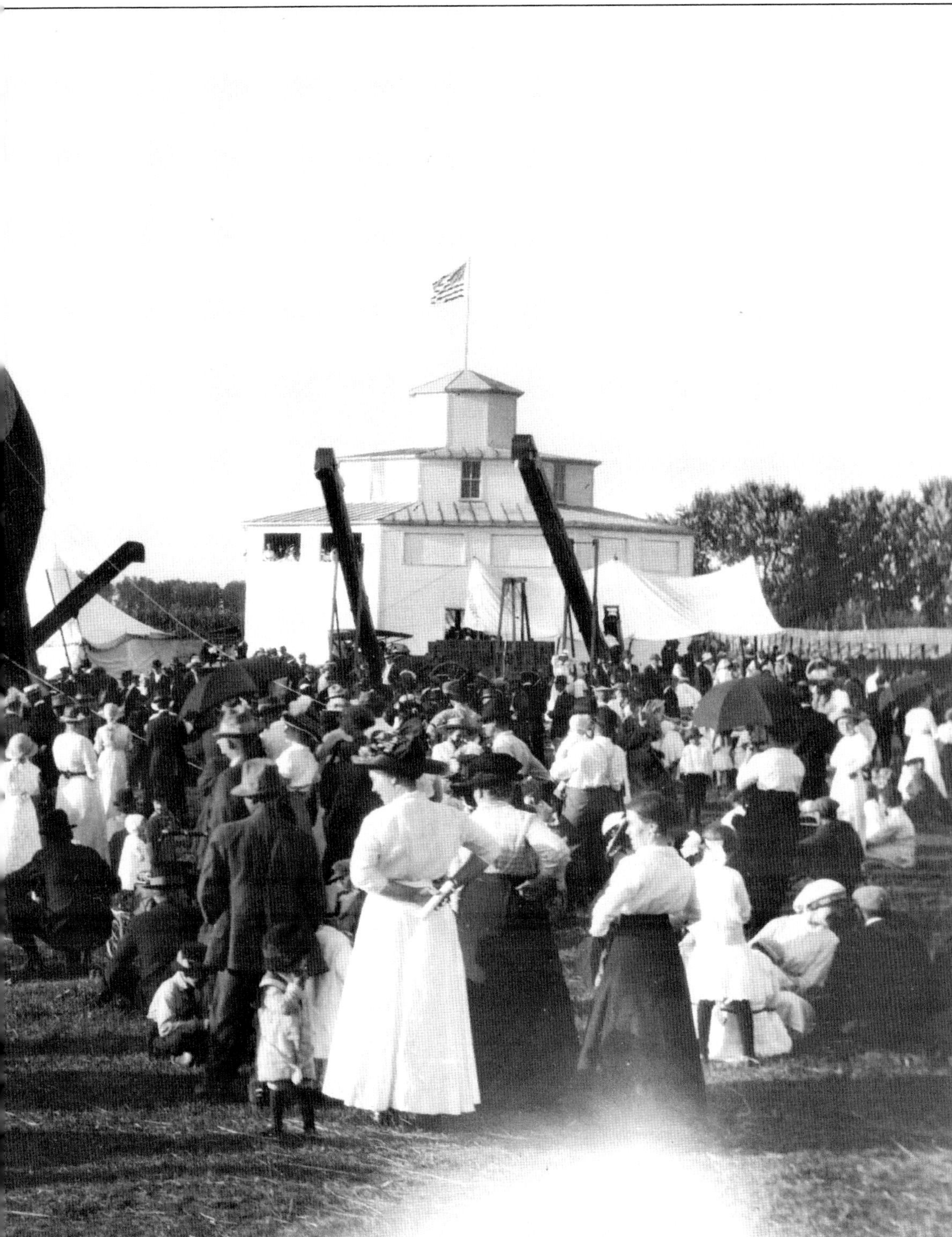

Here a hot air balloon is inflated on the Clay County Fairgrounds. (Courtesy of W.H. Over Museum.)

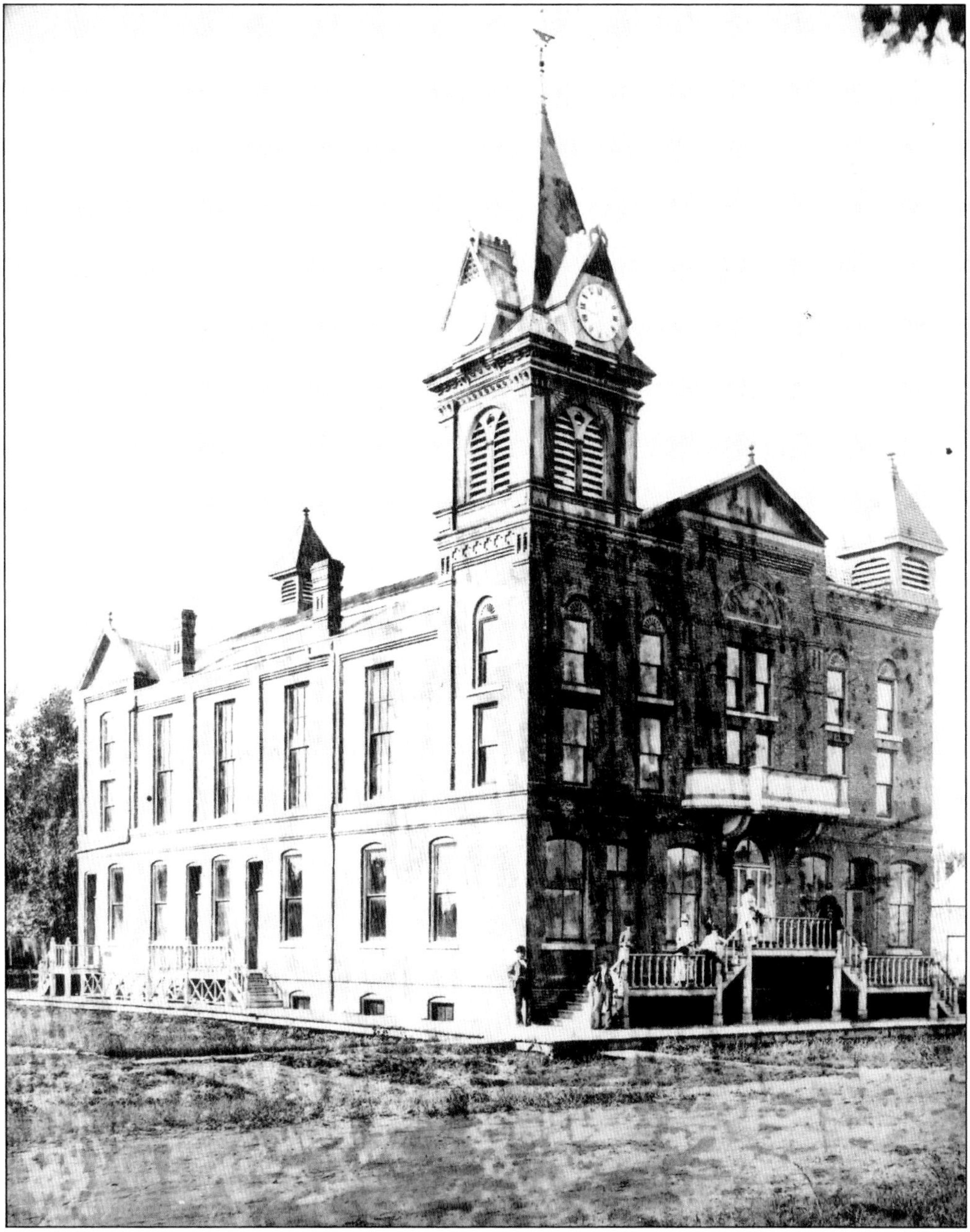

During the Great Dakota Boom, from the late 1870s to the early 1880s, optimism was high and civic improvements blossomed. A city hall was built in 1885 on the southwest corner of Church and Main Streets. (Courtesy of W. H. Over Museum.)

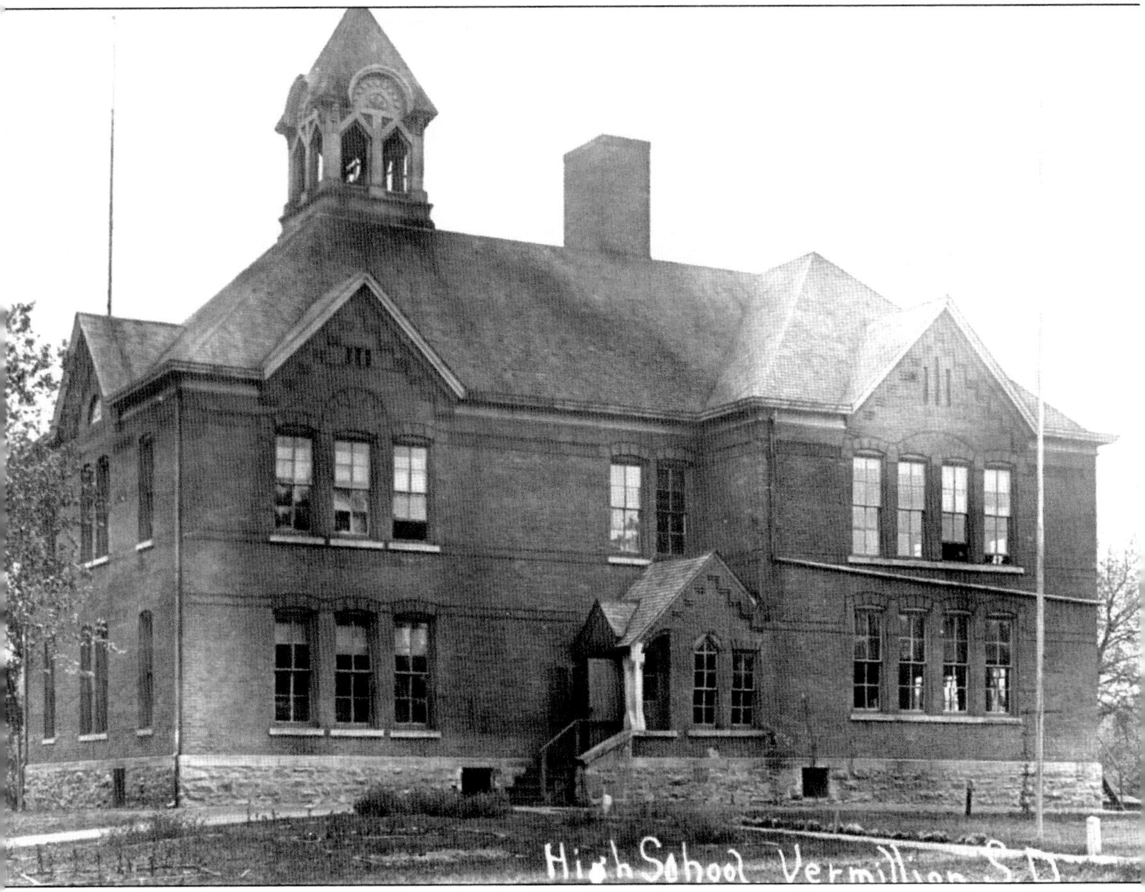

The old Vermillion High School was built of brick in classic turn-of-the-century style and featured a bell tower.

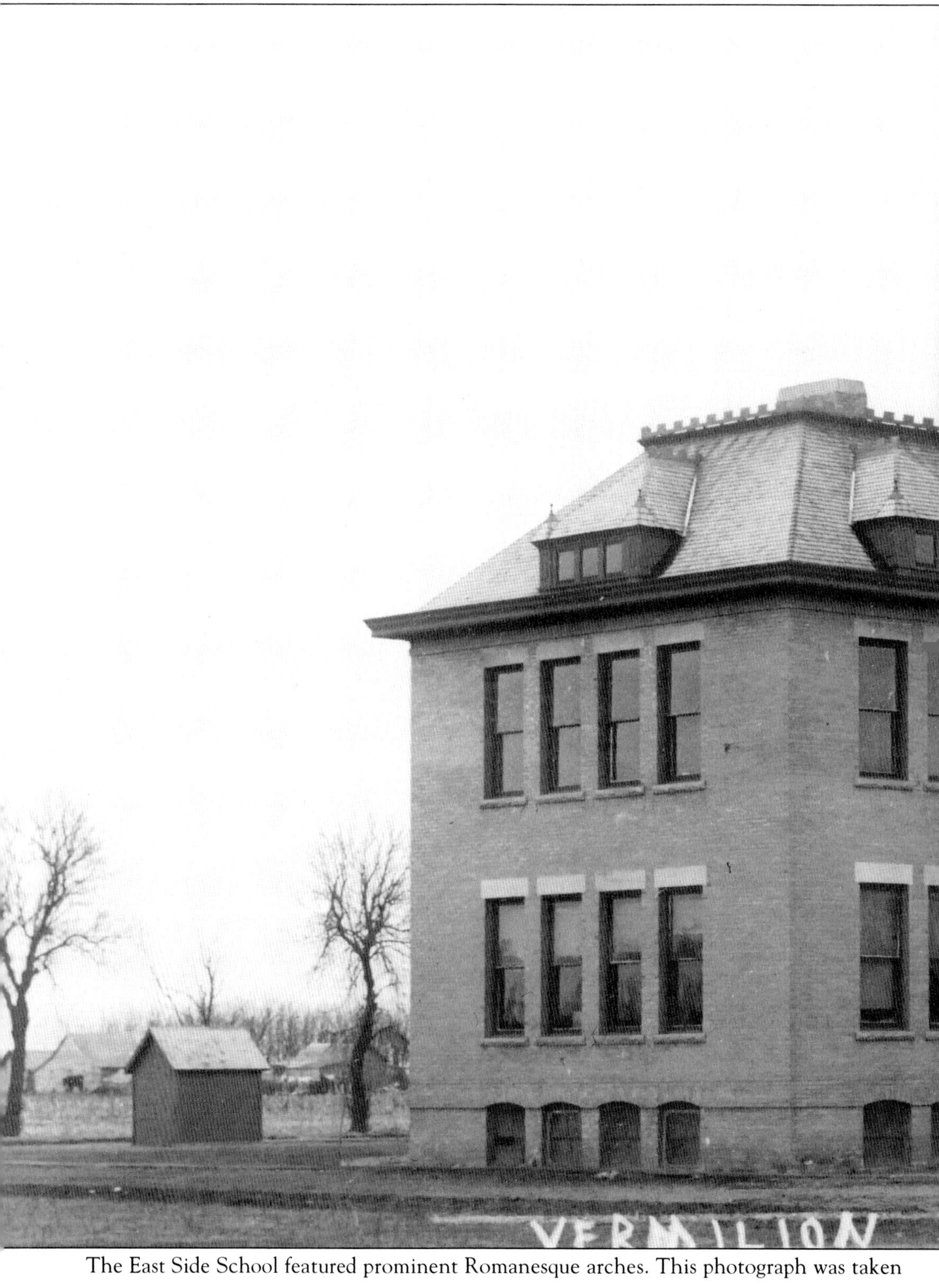

The East Side School featured prominent Romanesque arches. This photograph was taken

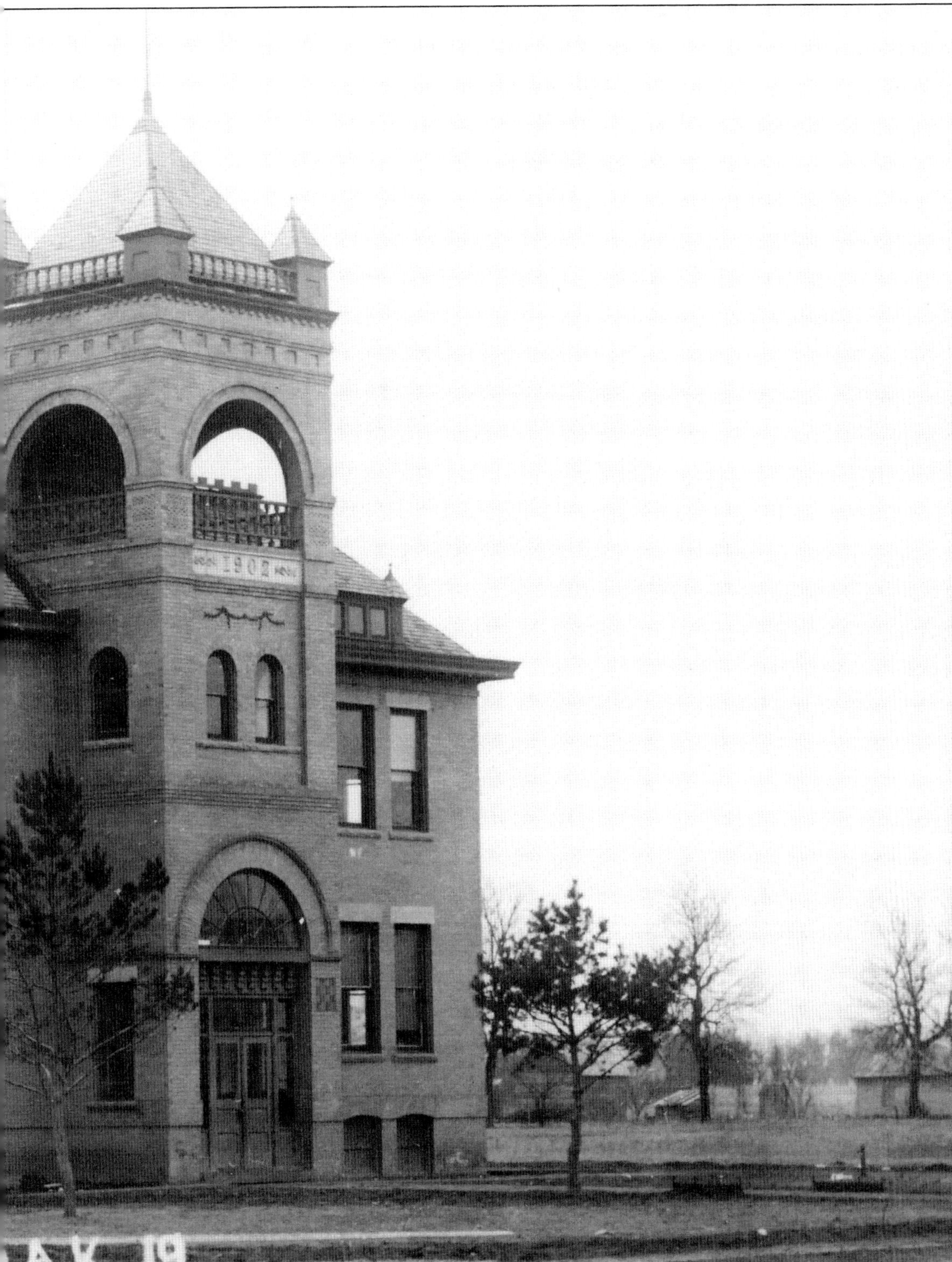

in 1919. (Courtesy of W.H. Over Museum.)

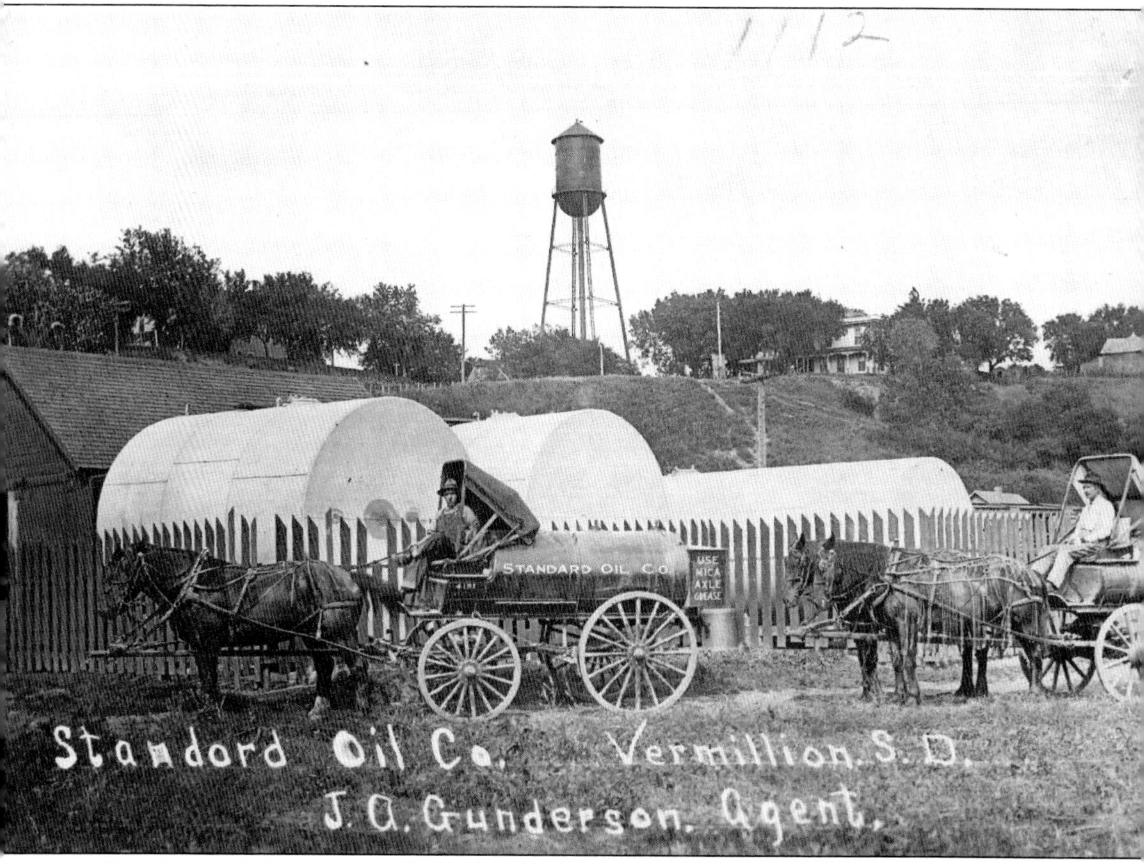

The Standard Oil Company had oil tanks below the bluff in Vermillion early in the century. Oil was delivered by horse and wagon, as shown here. J.A. Gunderson served as the local agent. (Courtesy of W.H. Over Museum.)

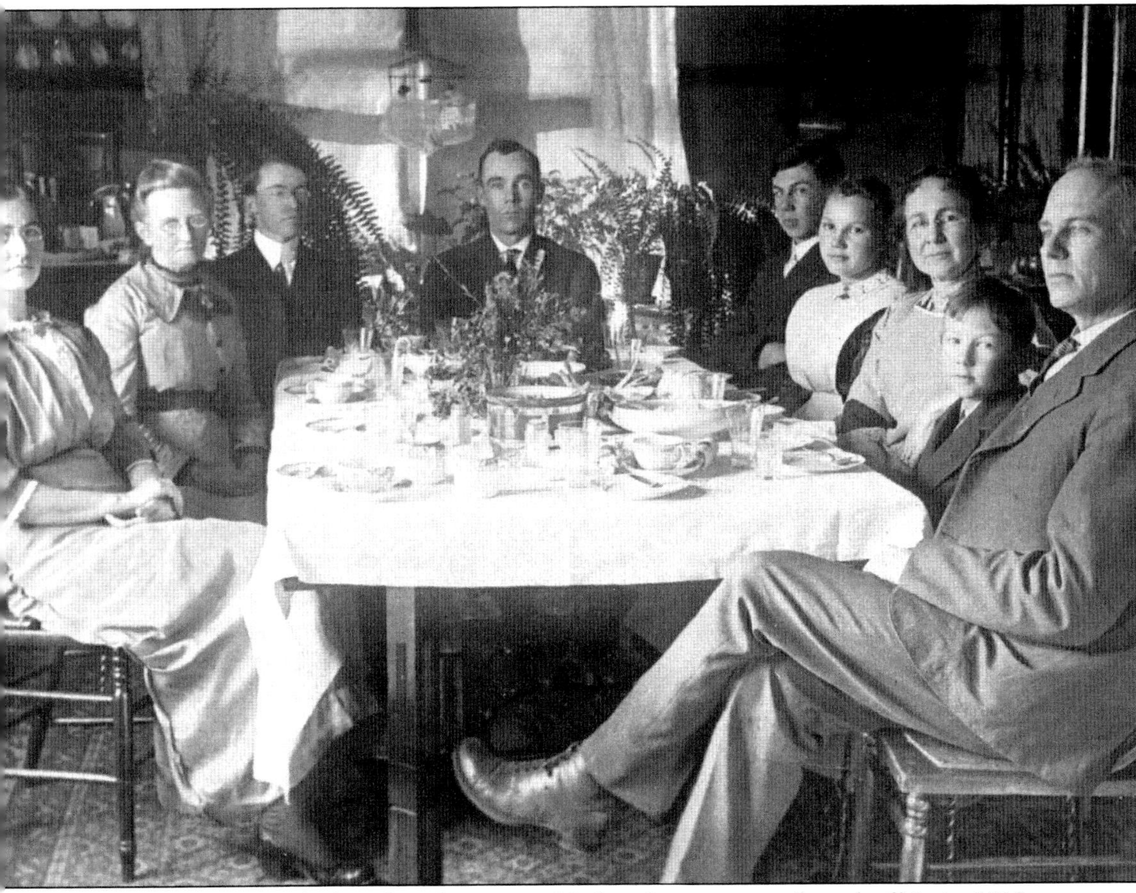

Dinner at Bertha Nagel's boarding house on Market Street was a formal affair in 1913. Pictured, from left to right, are Bertha Nagel, Mrs. Nagel, Lee Stevenson, Guy Morrison, Ralph Lawton, Edith Morrison, Mrs. Lawton, Sidney Lawton, and Will Lawton. (Courtesy of W.H. Over Museum.)

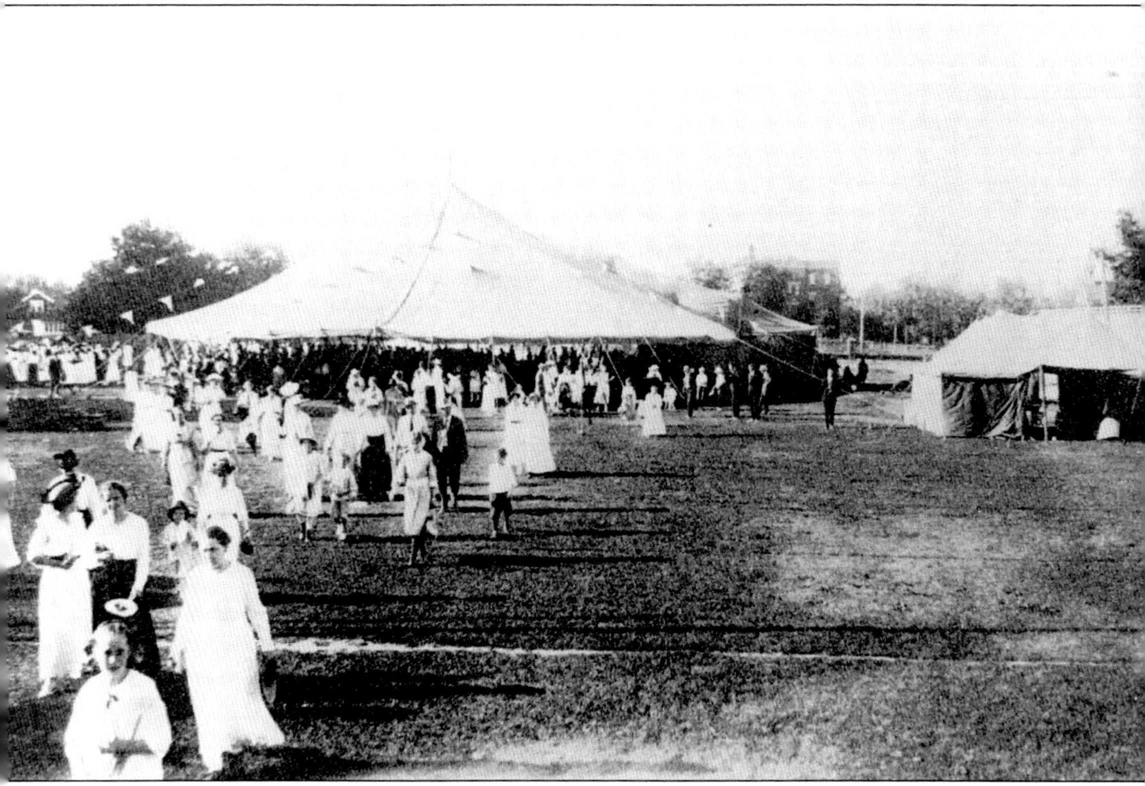

Chautauquas, such as the one pictured here, were important events in the life of Vermillion residents.

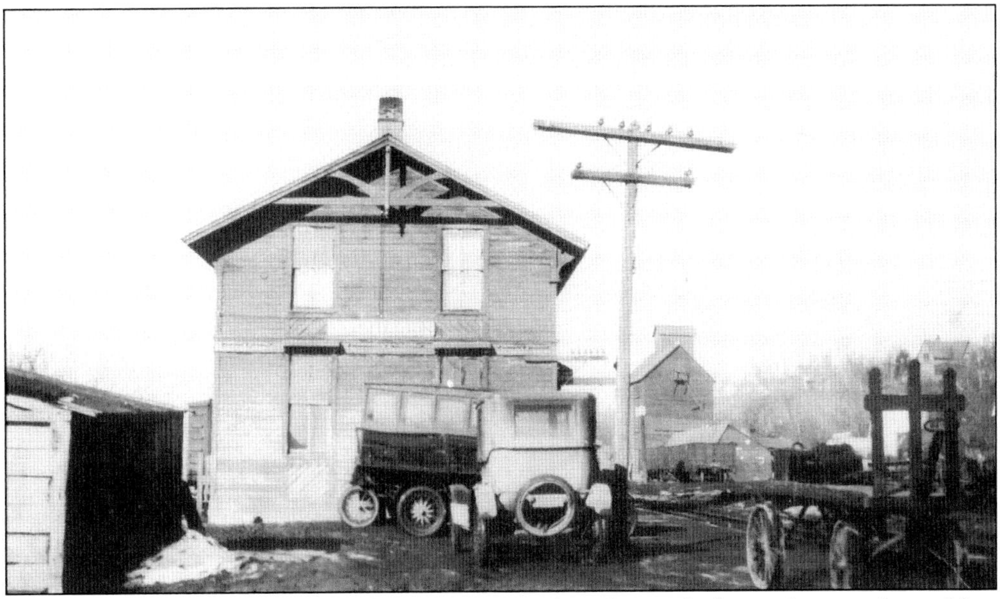

The coming of the railroad helped create new markets for goods, bring the outside world to Clay County, and connect residents to the outside world. The old Vermillion train depot was constructed below the bluff. (Courtesy of W.H. Over Museum.)

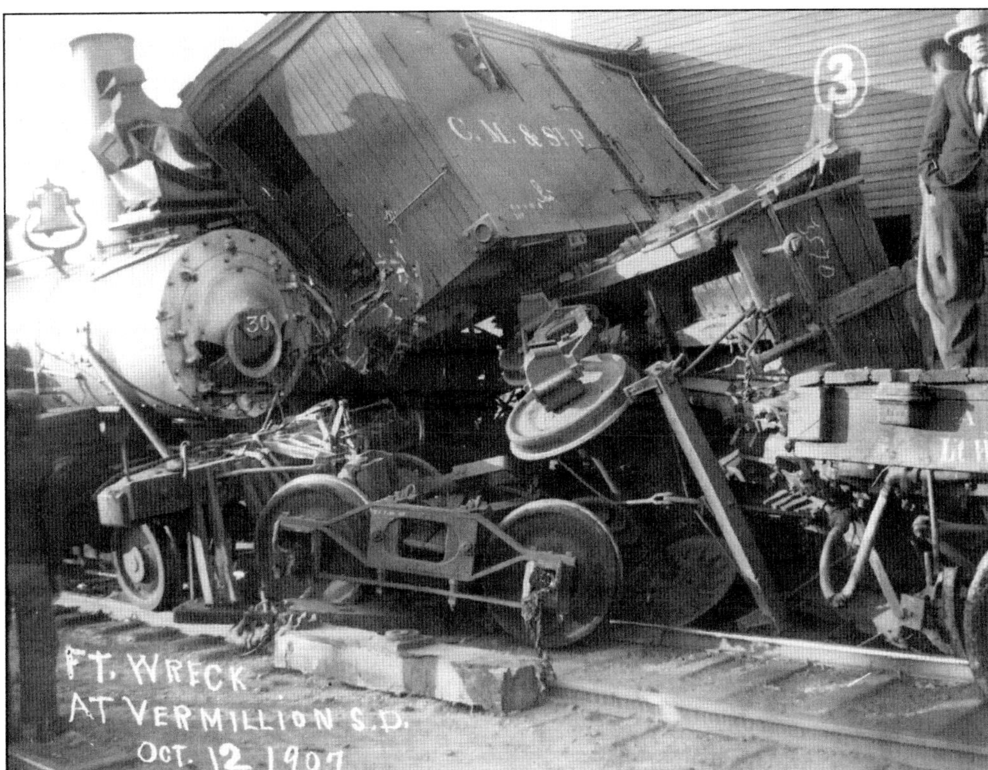

A train wreck in Vermillion in October of 1907 produced this mangled pile-up of cars. (Courtesy of W.H. Over Museum.)

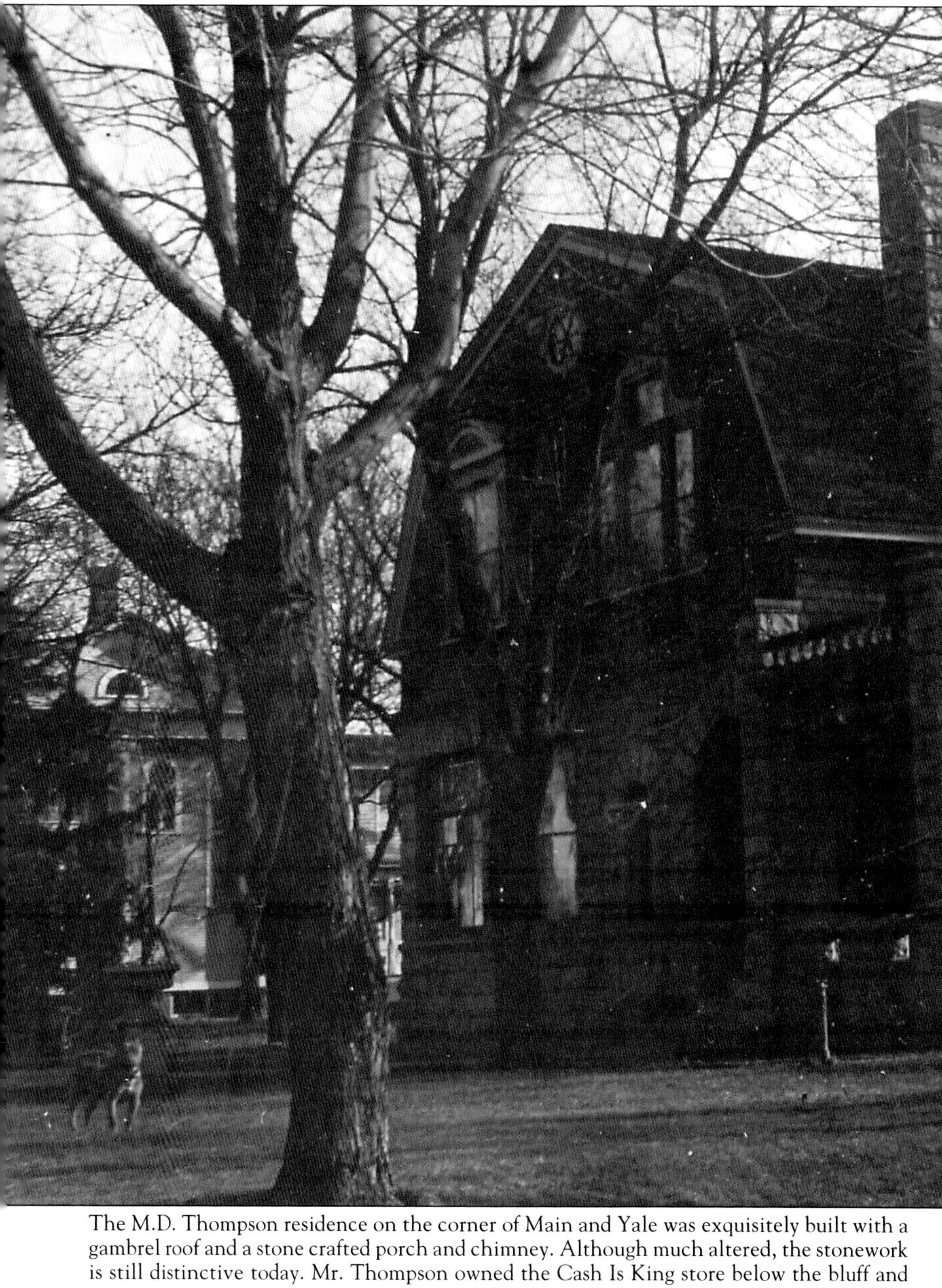

The M.D. Thompson residence on the corner of Main and Yale was exquisitely built with a gambrel roof and a stone crafted porch and chimney. Although much altered, the stonework is still distinctive today. Mr. Thompson owned the Cash Is King store below the bluff and

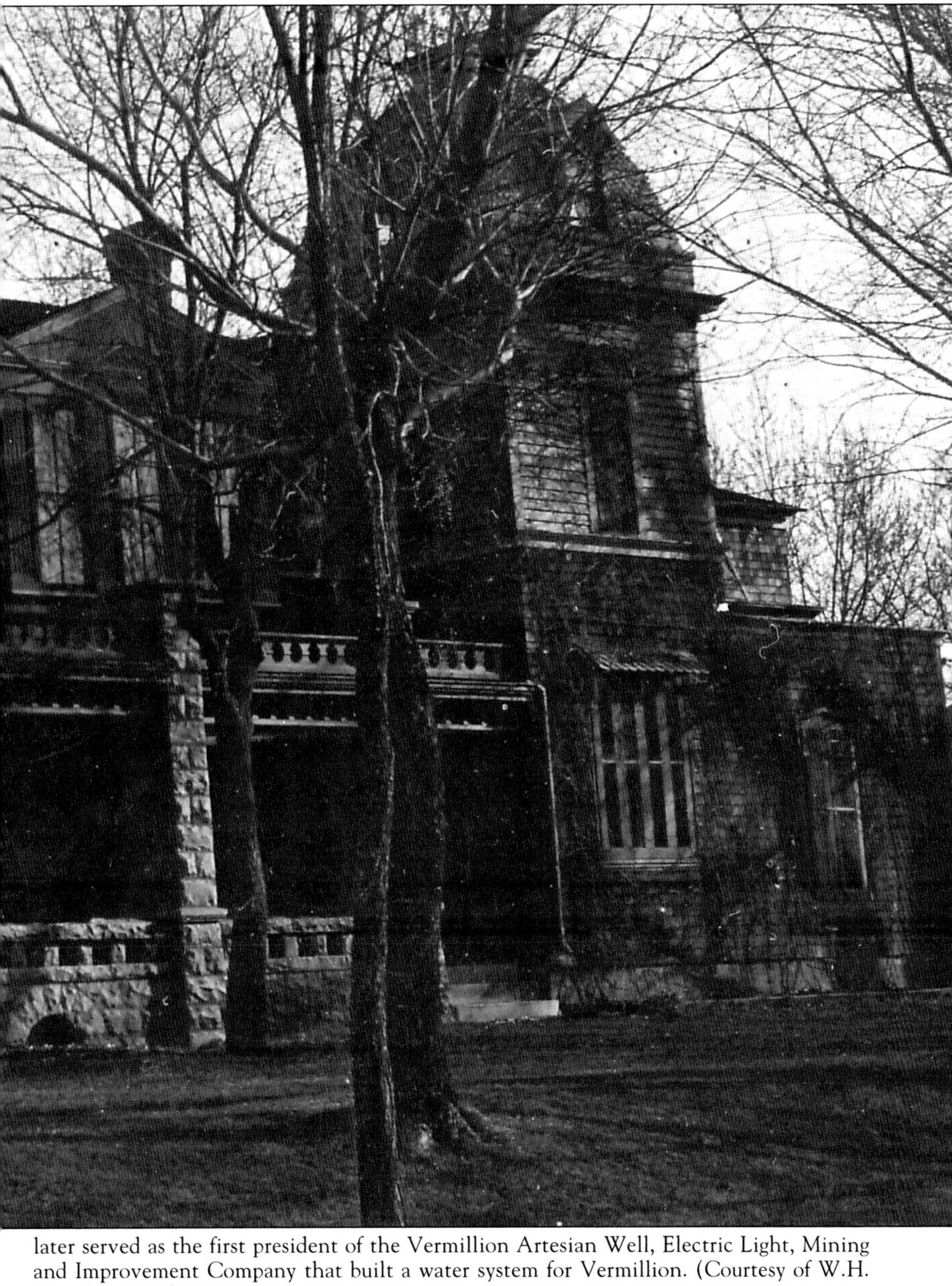

later served as the first president of the Vermillion Artesian Well, Electric Light, Mining and Improvement Company that built a water system for Vermillion. (Courtesy of W.H. Over Museum.)

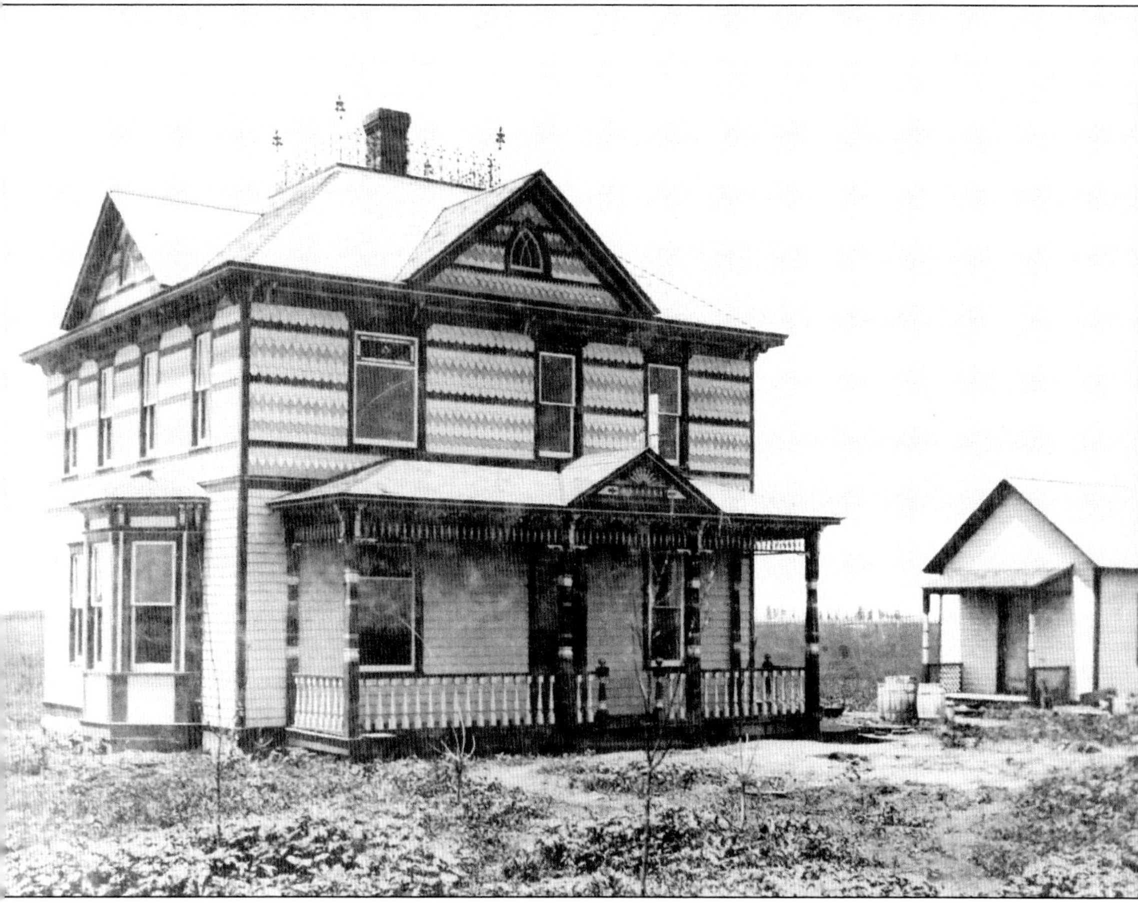

Mr. Charles Erickson built this house on the corner of his property and bought a piano for the parlor in hopes of finding a wife. However, he continued to live in the shack behind the main house as no wife materialized. (Courtesy of the W.H. Over Museum.)

Eight

The Farming Heritage of Clay County

Farming tall-grass prairie presented unique challenges to newcomers in Clay County. The customary 25 inches of annual rainfall required the adaptation of farming methods from more humid regions in order to survive. Grasshopper infestations devastated crops from time to time. Wind and weather could be severe, even alarming. Neighbors were spread thinly and loneliness was endemic to farm life.

Nonetheless, early settlers learned quickly that good soil preparation and diversification improved the odds of survival. Cows produced dairy products and creameries boomed. Oxen powered equipment and corn became an important crop. Hay production—especially in the Meckling and Gayville areas—fed an emerging cattle industry. In 1890, locals called this area the "hay capital of the United States." Orchards produced apples and plums, especially the indigenous wild plum, as early as 1868. Wakonda, Burbank, and Vermillion shipped fruit by railway, mostly to northern and western South Dakota. By 1900, Clay County was leading South Dakota in the production of these fruits. During the 1870s, the gold rush in the Black Hills created a new market for corn, oats, flour, cattle, hogs, poultry, eggs, and dairy products. When the price of wheat fell in the early 1890s many Clay County farmers began growing flax, which often commanded a better price. Tow mills that clean flax fibers sprang up in the area and locals produced linseed oil.

Scandinavians were prominent early immigrants. Over 200 Swedish families settled in the area east of the Vermillion River between 1868 and 1873. In 1880, Norwegians already made up about 22 percent of the population, concentrated in Norway Township to the west of Vermillion. Danish residents were spread in small groups over a number of communities. Lutheran churches sprang up throughout the county and used the homeland's language in church services and records. Traditional customs and interior church decoration reminded parishioners of home and their cultural identity.

The Clay County Agricultural Society formed and sponsored the first county fair in Dakota Territory in September of 1870. The fair was held near Nelson Miner's home with a dance at the Lee and Prentis Hall nearby. In subsequent years, horse racing, livestock exhibits, and theater all played a prominent role in this annual event.

Farmers' clubs provided a chance for farmers and their families to compare notes and to socialize. Meetings offered lectures, debates, and other opportunities to discuss the issues and problems of the day. Other events included oyster suppers, harvest festivals, and Fourth of July celebrations. At one time Clay County boasted six Grange lodges.

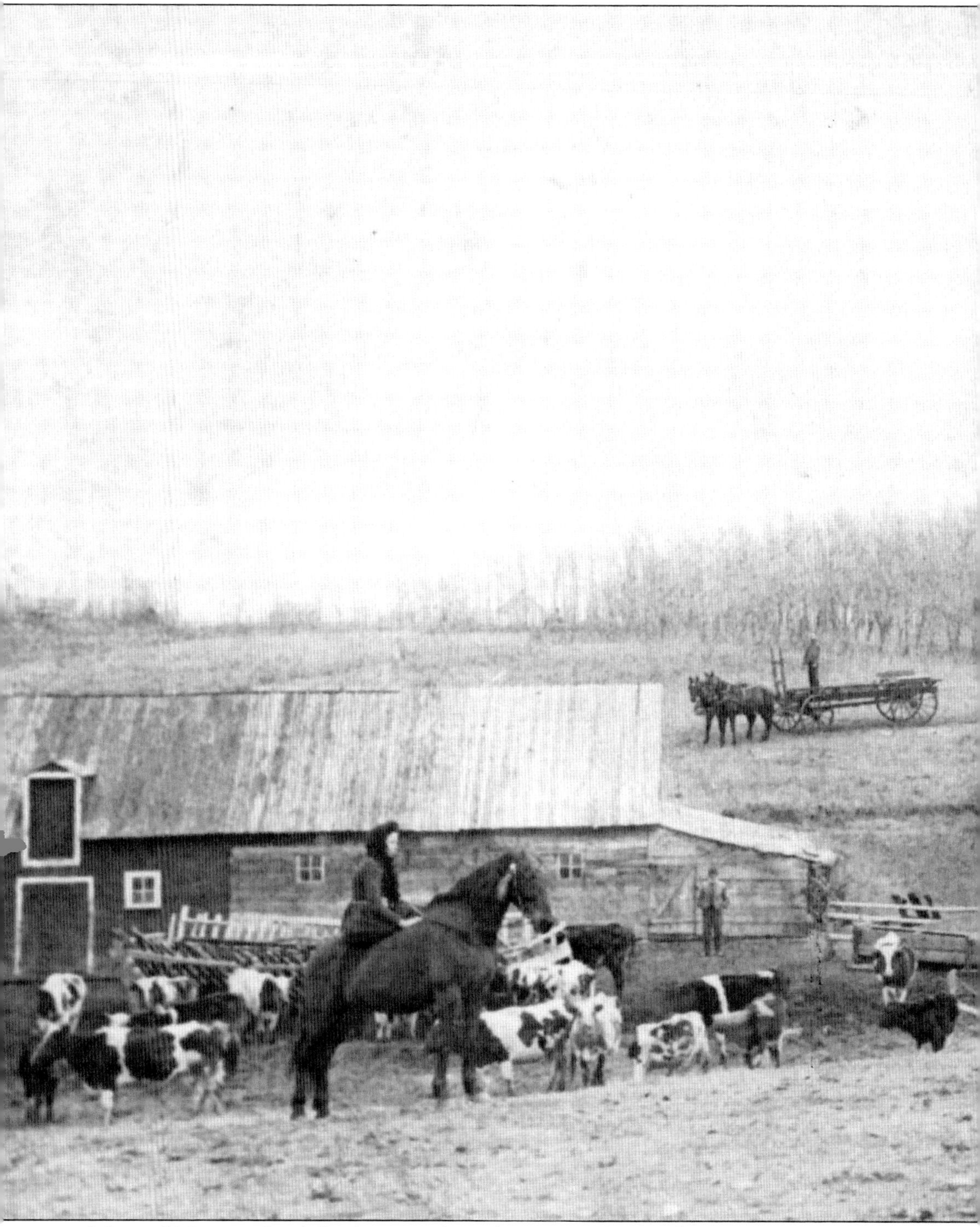

John and Margaret Sundell, who arrived in Clay County from Valbo Parish in Norway in 1870 with their two children, homesteaded the Sundell Larson Farm, which was located in section 1 of Pleasant Valley Township. A traveling photographer took this photograph of Margaret Sundell

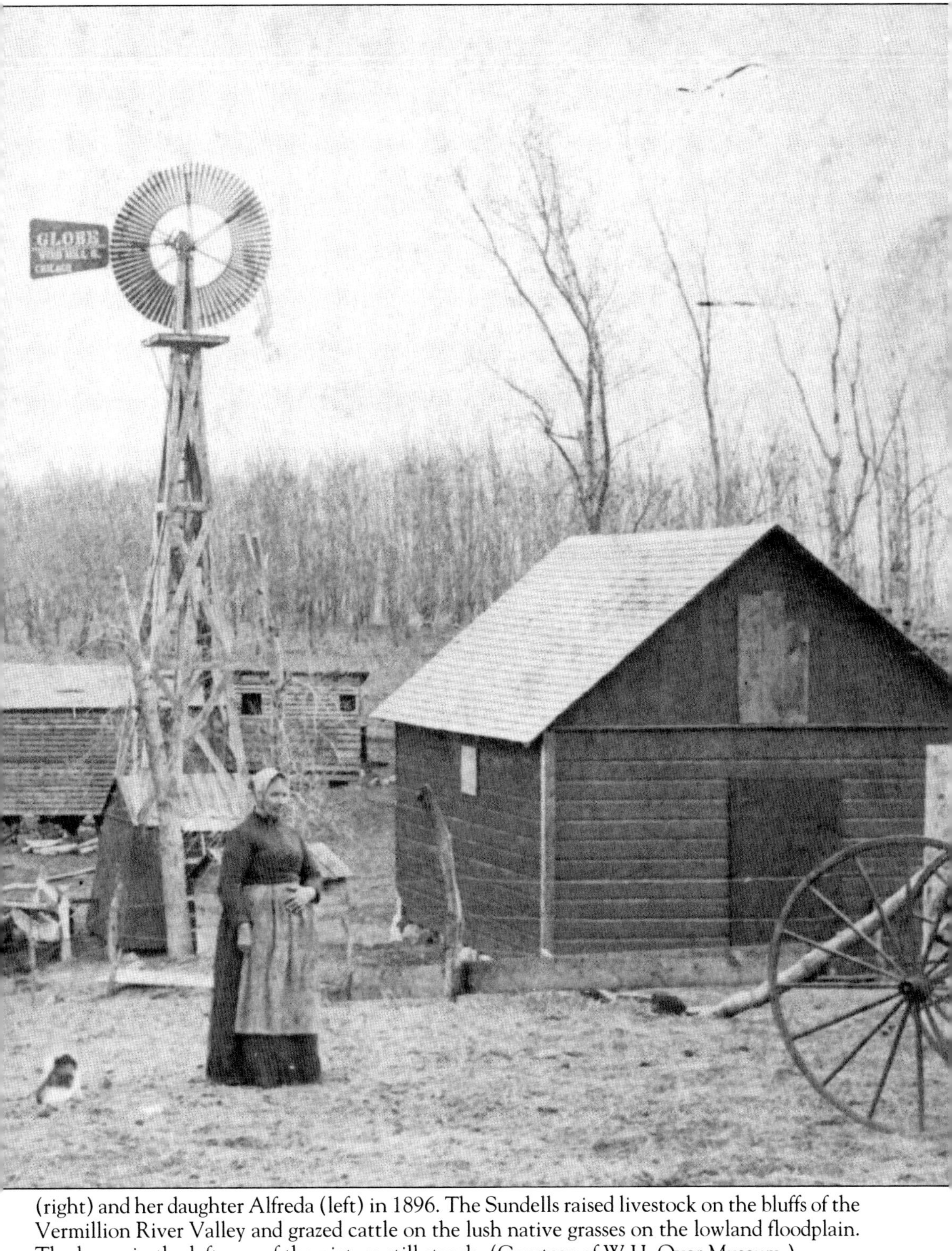

(right) and her daughter Alfreda (left) in 1896. The Sundells raised livestock on the bluffs of the Vermillion River Valley and grazed cattle on the lush native grasses on the lowland floodplain. The house in the left rear of the picture still stands. (Courtesy of W.H. Over Museum.)

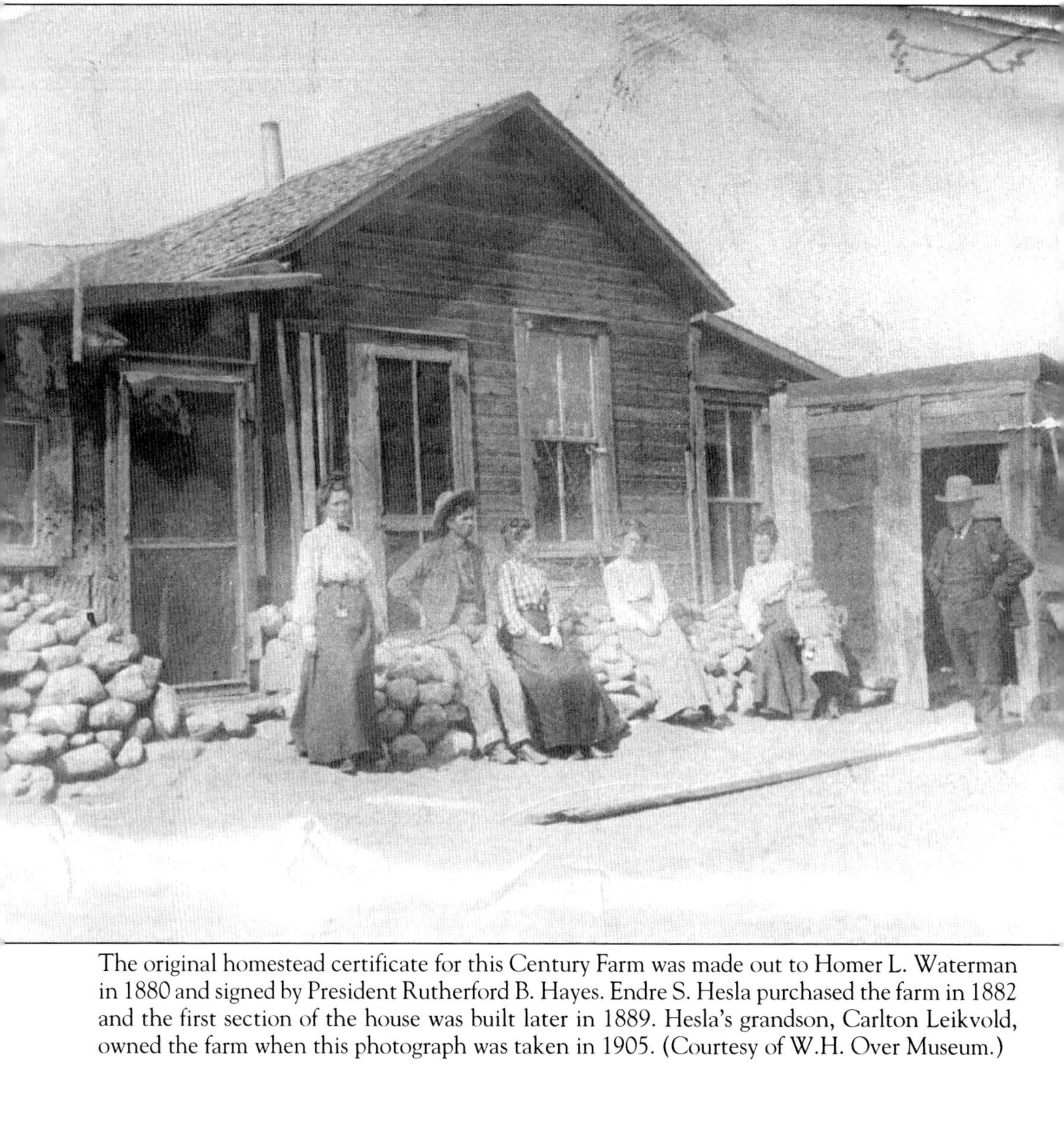

The original homestead certificate for this Century Farm was made out to Homer L. Waterman in 1880 and signed by President Rutherford B. Hayes. Endre S. Hesla purchased the farm in 1882 and the first section of the house was built later in 1889. Hesla's grandson, Carlton Leikvold, owned the farm when this photograph was taken in 1905. (Courtesy of W.H. Over Museum.)

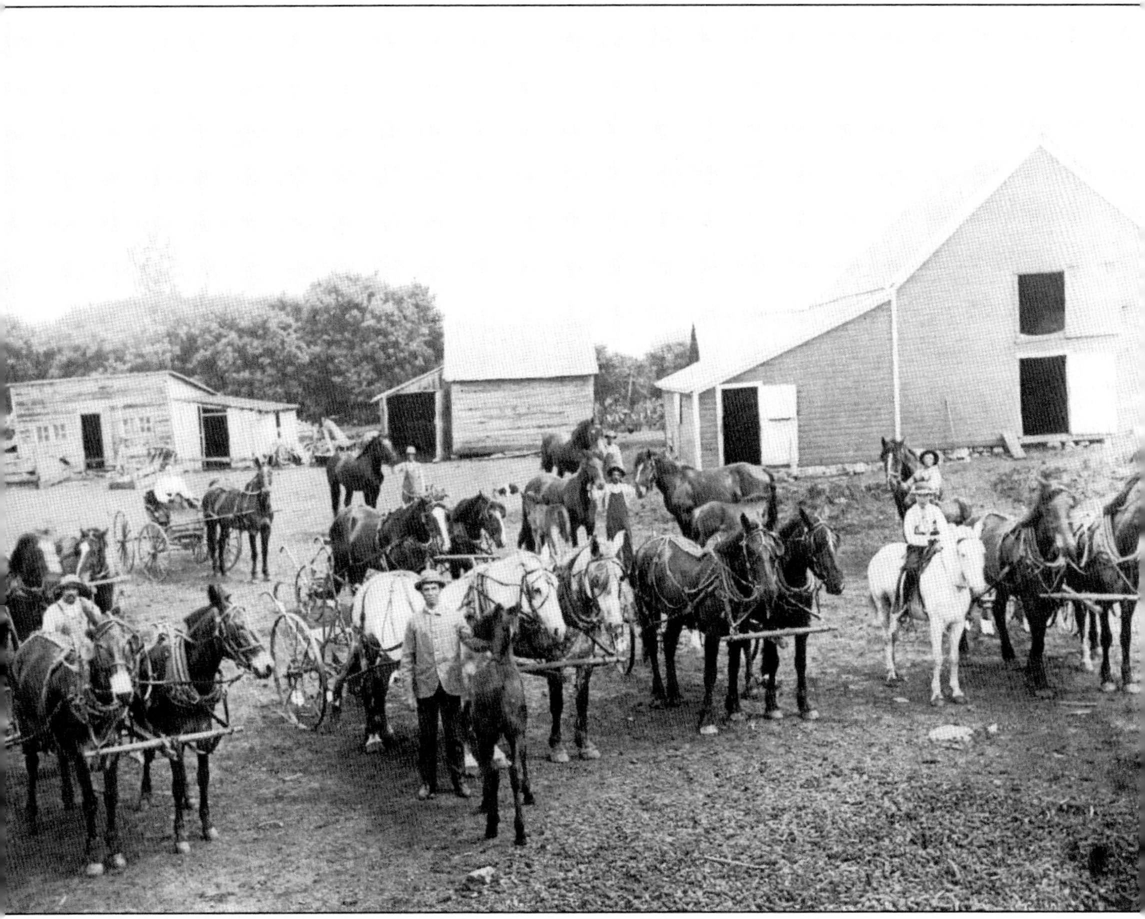

The Babb Farmstead is pictured above. (Courtesy of W.H. Over Museum.)

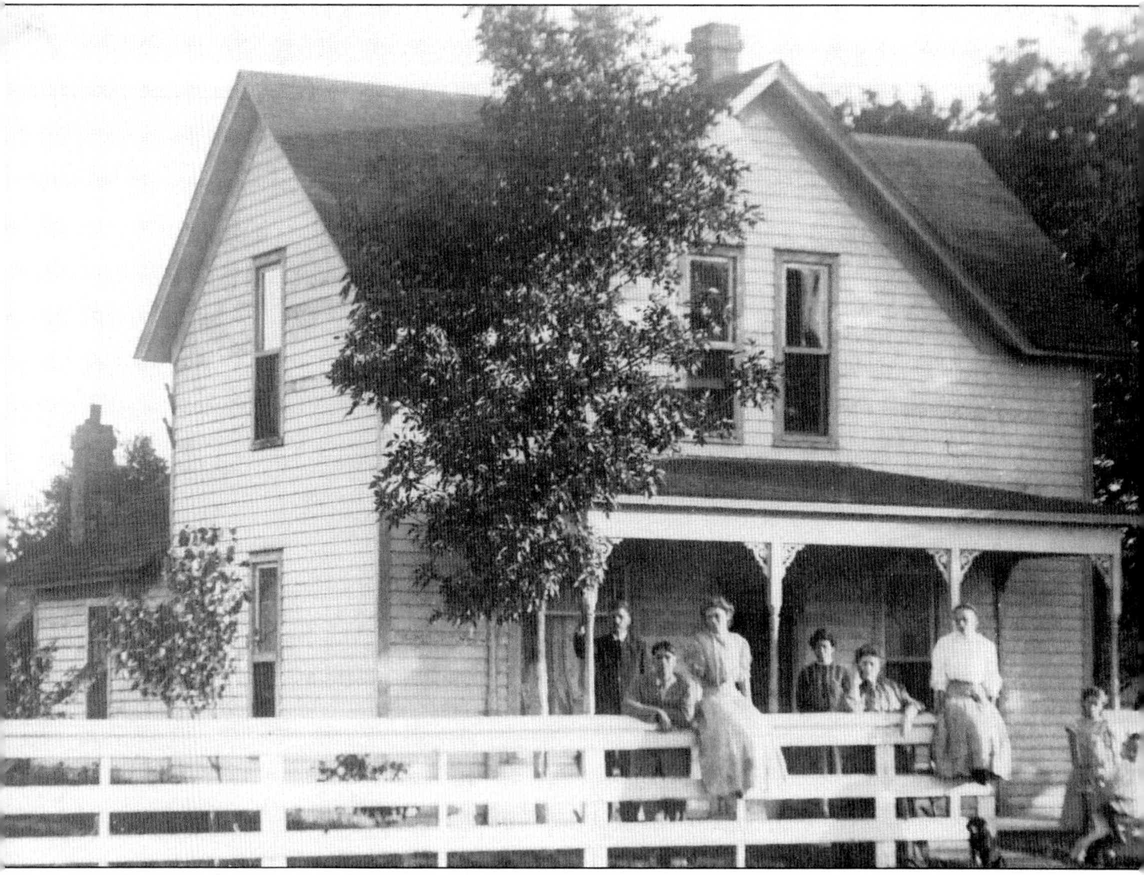

The Spensley Farmstead is pictured above. (Courtesy of W.H. Over Museum.)

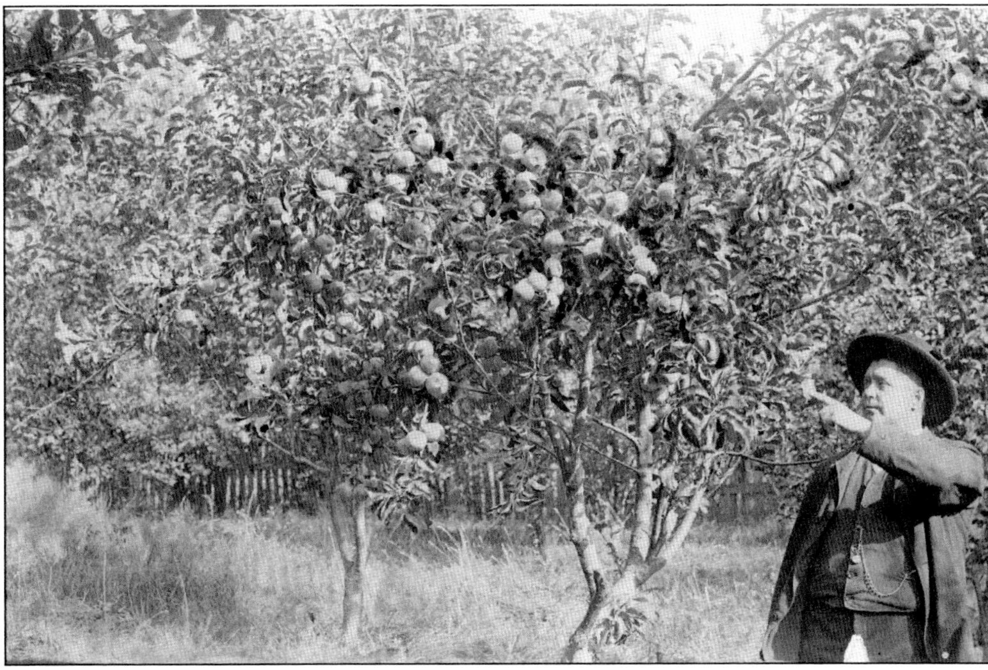

S.M. Kidder's orchard was located north of Vermillion on the Walter Harrington Farm. (Courtesy of W.H. Over Museum.)

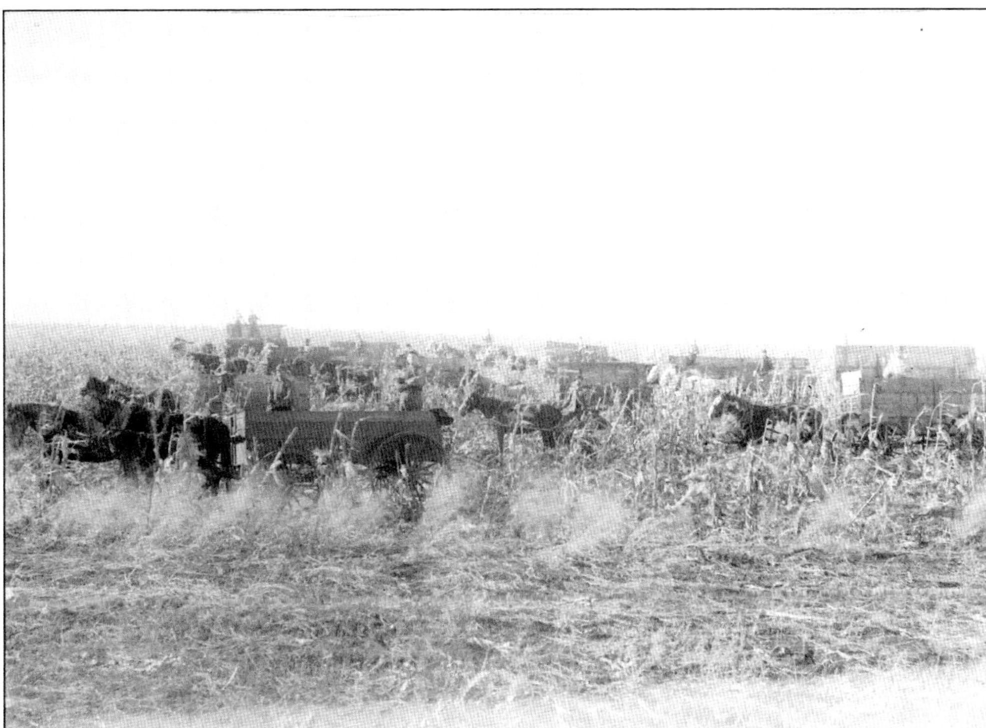

Corn husking was part of farm life on S.M. Kidder's farm near Vermillion. (Courtesy of W.H. Over Museum.)

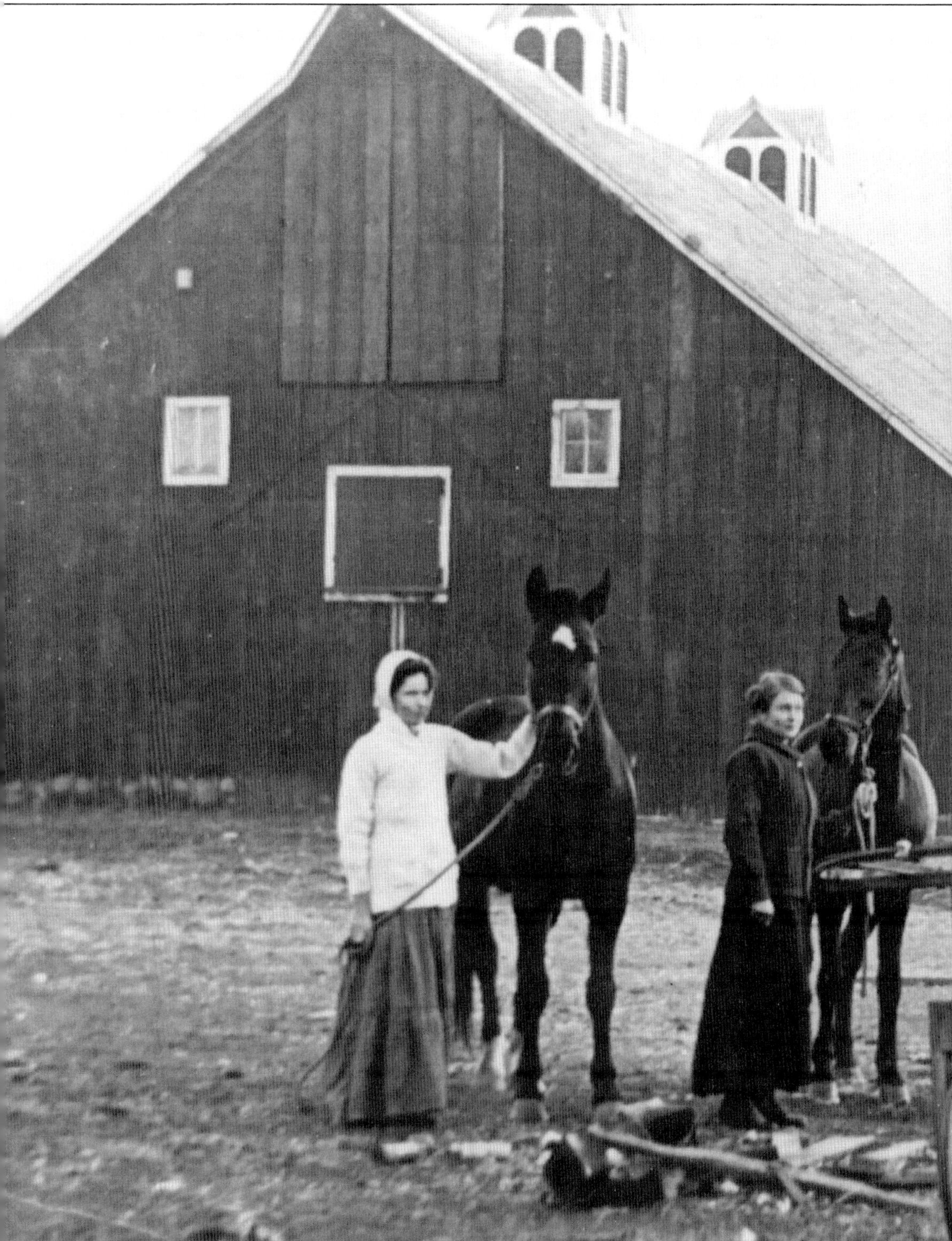

The Gunderson family posed with their tractor and horses in front of Gunderson Farm's barn,

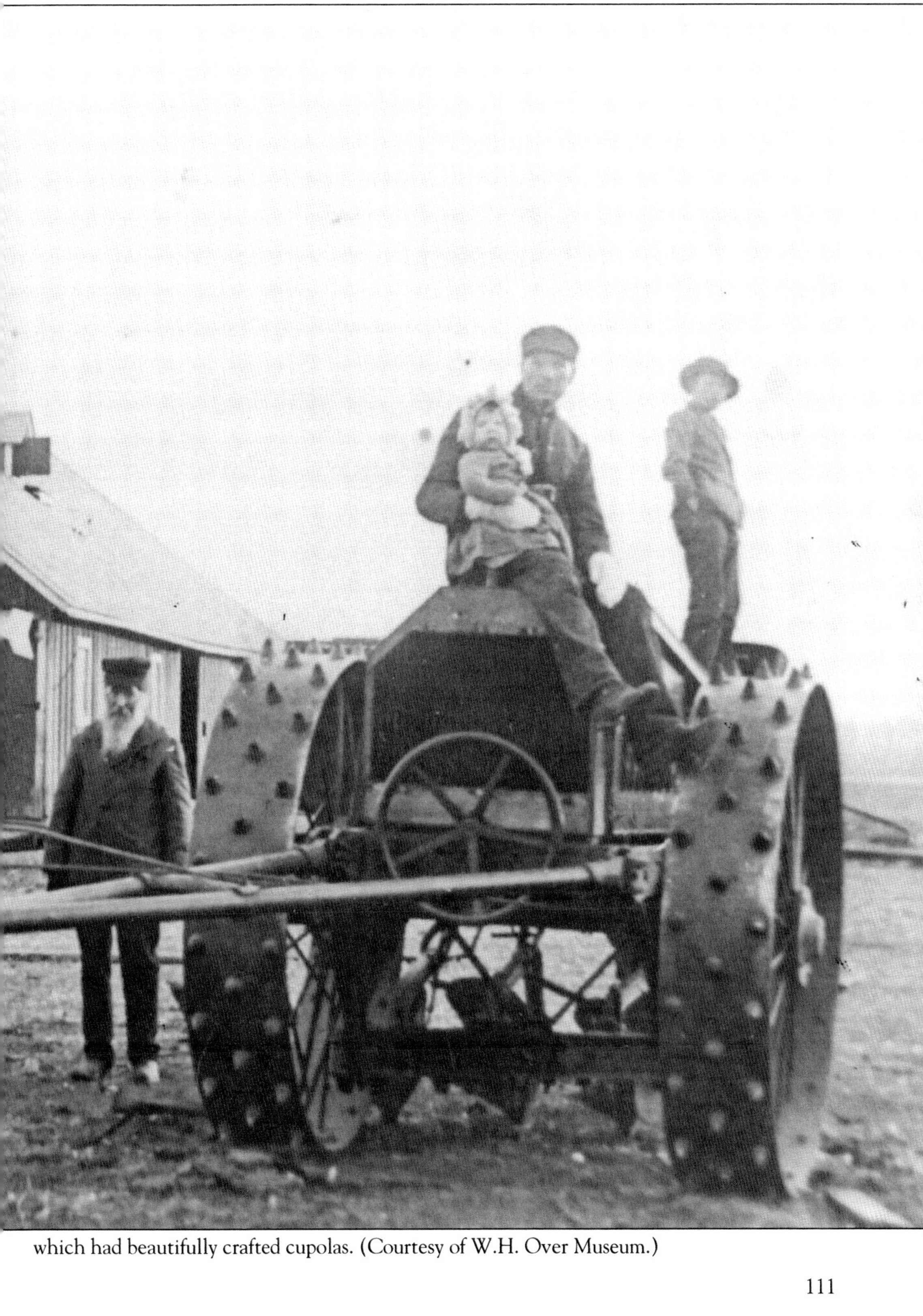

which had beautifully crafted cupolas. (Courtesy of W.H. Over Museum.)

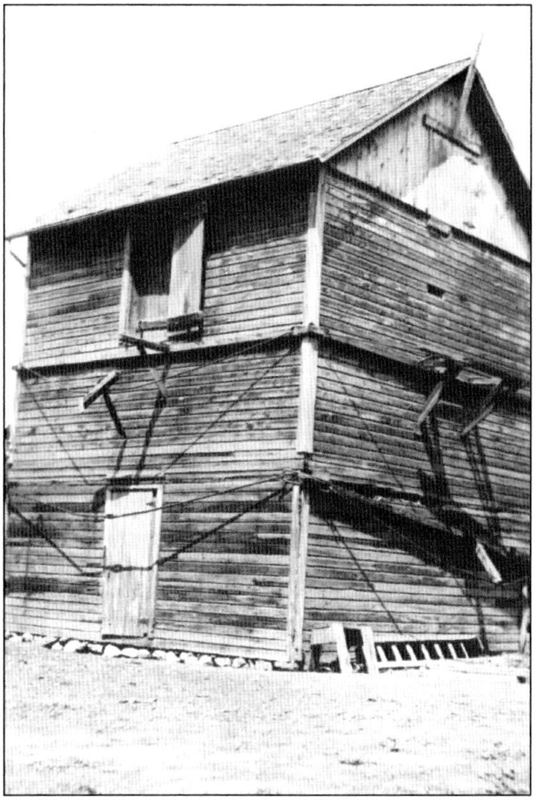

This is reputedly the first silo built in Dakota Territory. (Courtesy of W.H. Over Museum.)

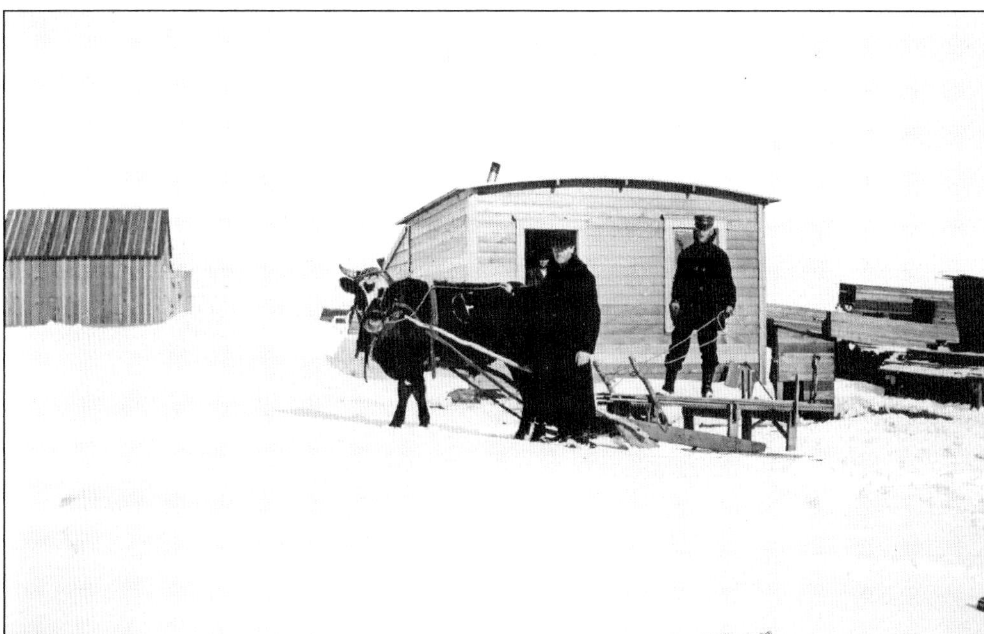

This picture shows an ox-drawn sled in snow in front of a small claim shack. (Courtesy of W.H. Over Museum.)

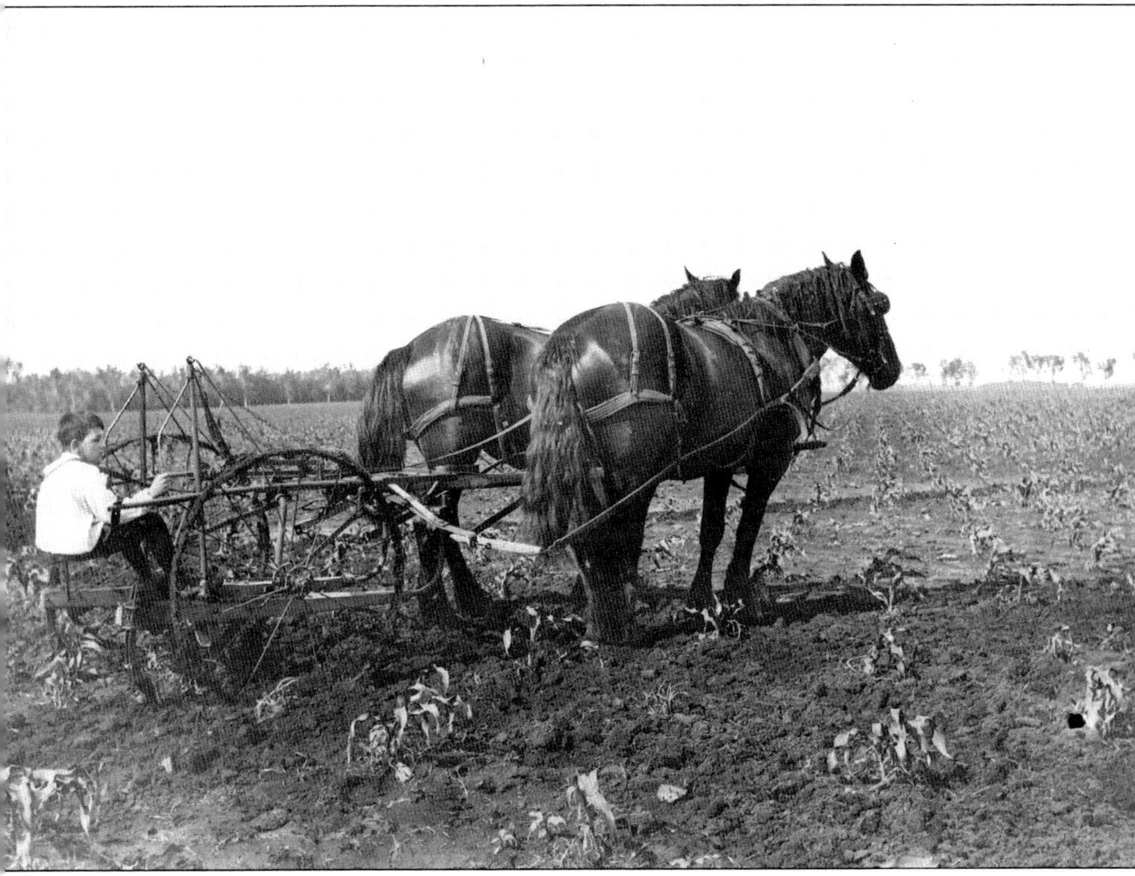

Young Swartzman guided a horse-drawn cultivator on the Norin Farm in Glenwood Township. His father was a traveling optometrist who left his son in the care of the Norin family. The Norin Timber Claim is in the background. (Courtesy of W.H. Over Museum.)

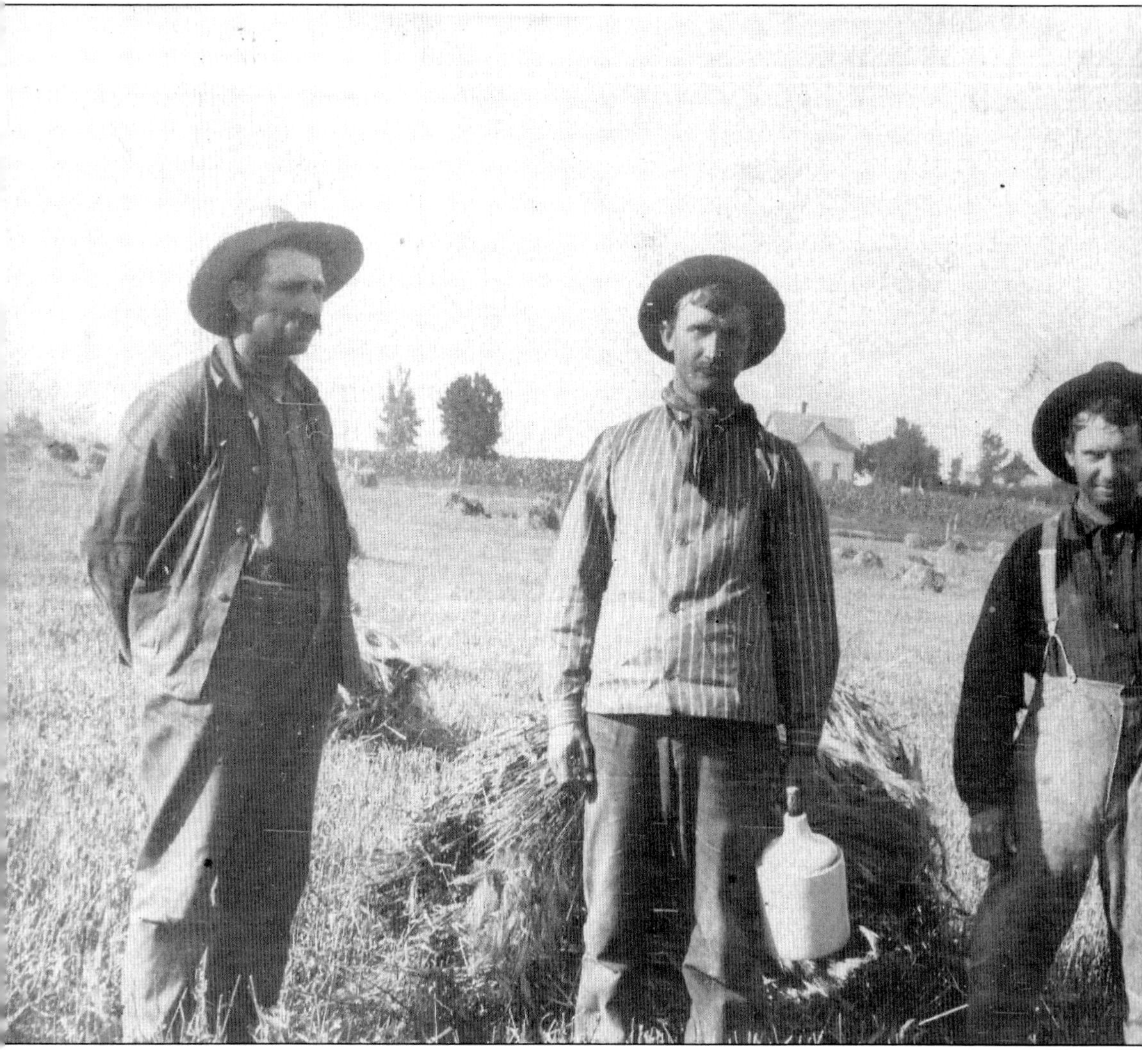

Grain shockers take a break and share the water jug. (Courtesy of W.H. Over Museum.)

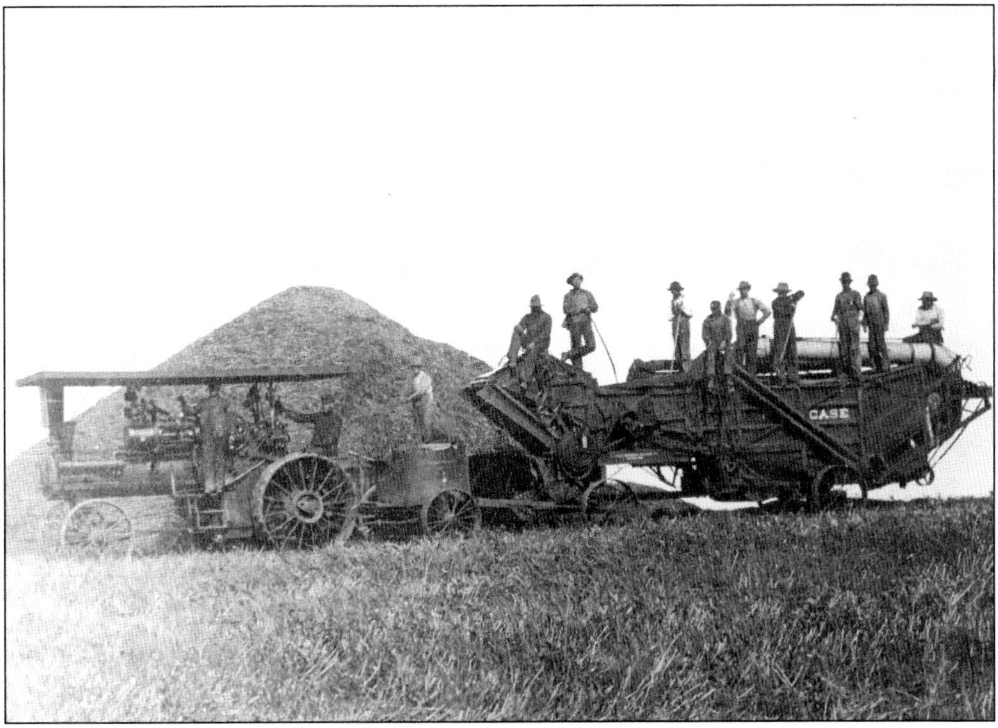

A threshing crew operates a large mechanized thresher. (Courtesy of W.H. Over Museum.)

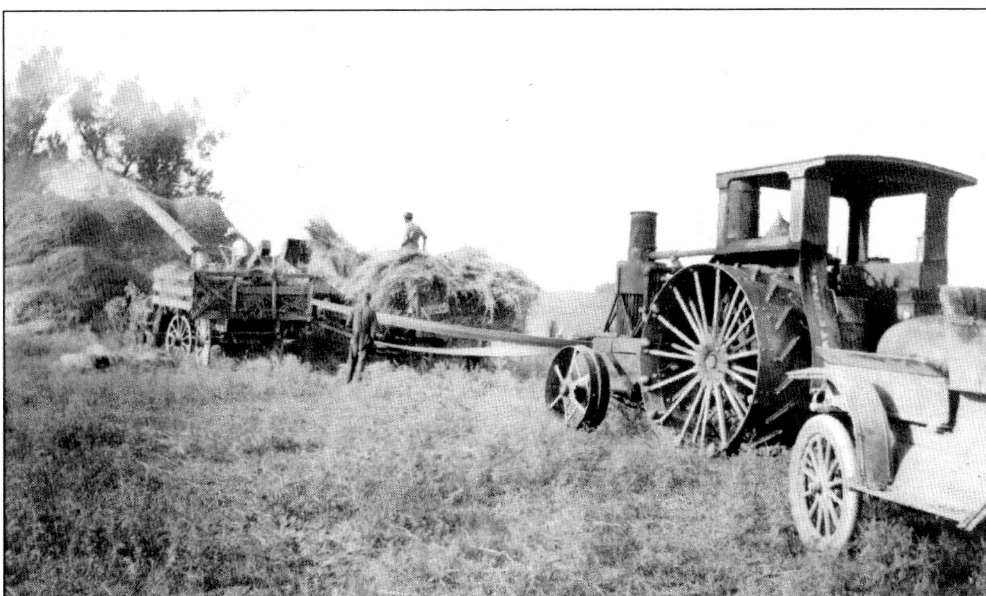

Mechanization made the farmer's life much easier. The above rig was used in Clay County in the 1910s. (Courtesy of W.H. Over Museum.)

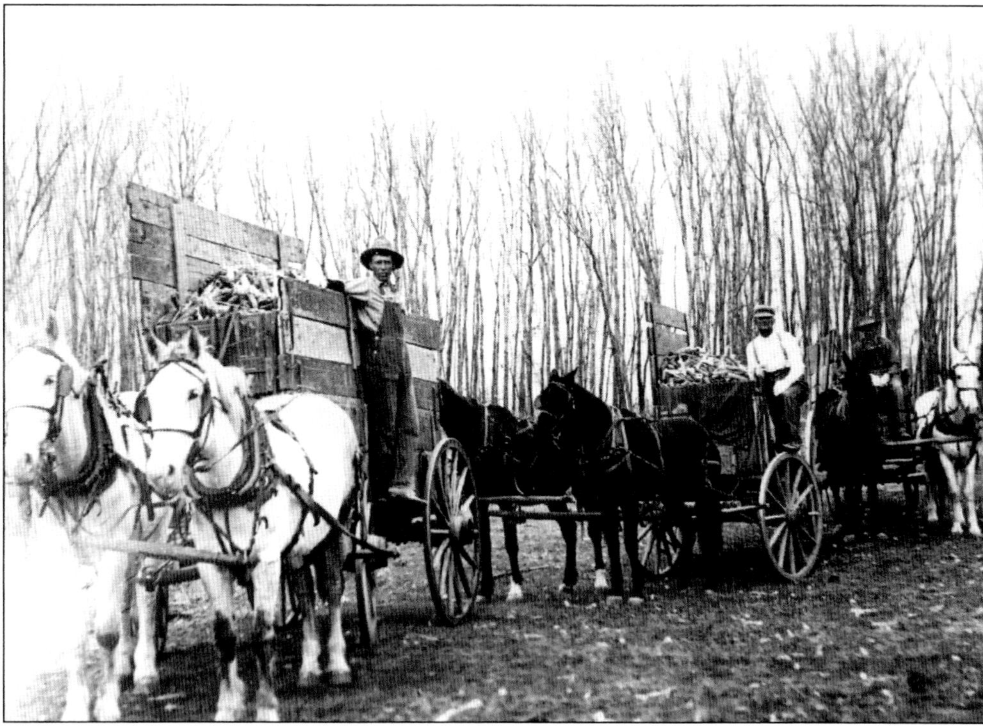

Three wagons with horse teams bring in the harvest. (Courtesy of W.H. Over Museum.)

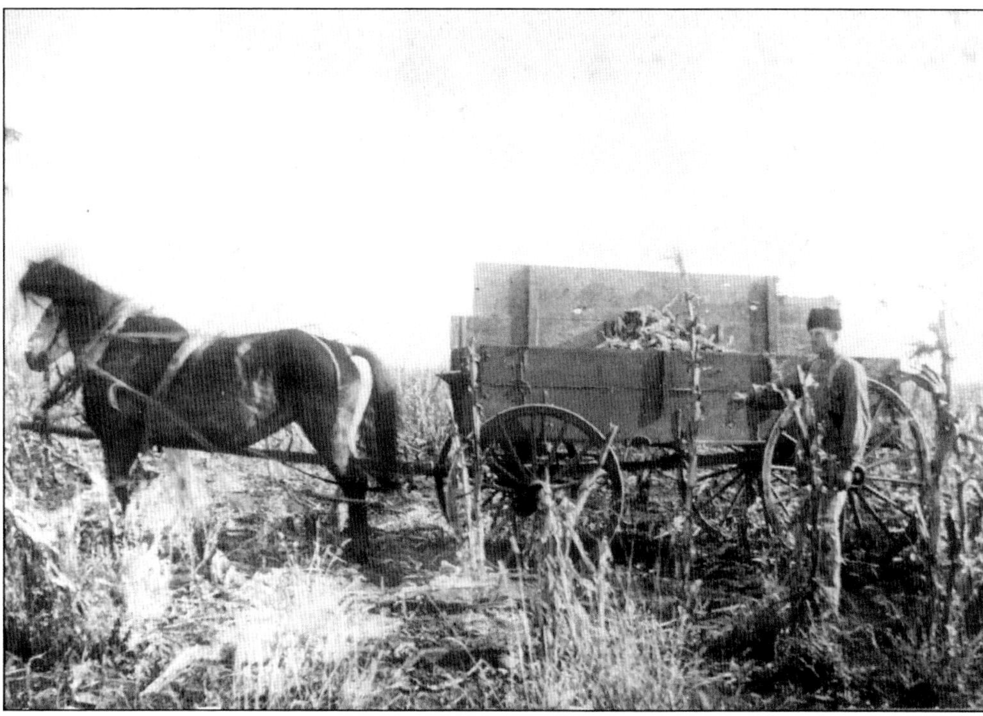

Husking corn had to be done by hand. (Courtesy of W.H. Over Museum.)

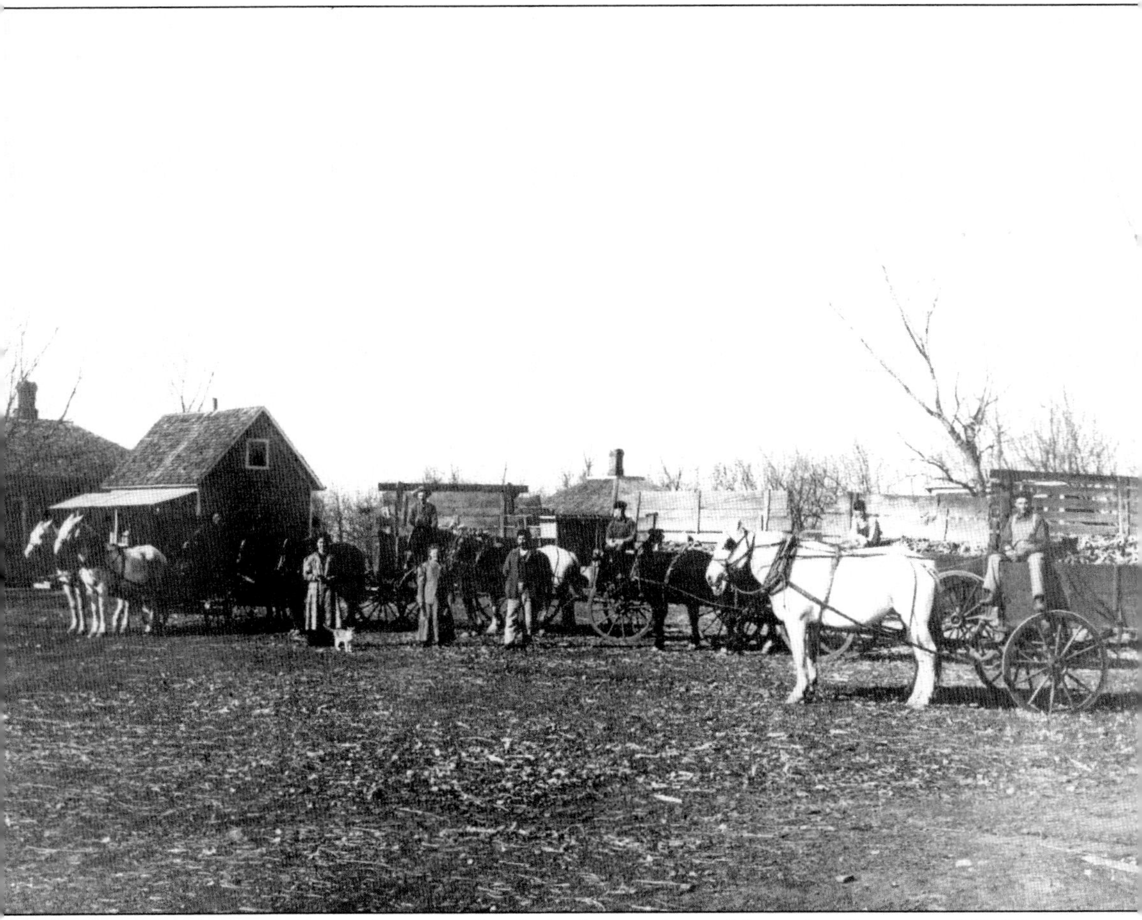

Farmers loaded carts with produce, much of which was shipped by rail. (Courtesy of W.H. Over Museum.)

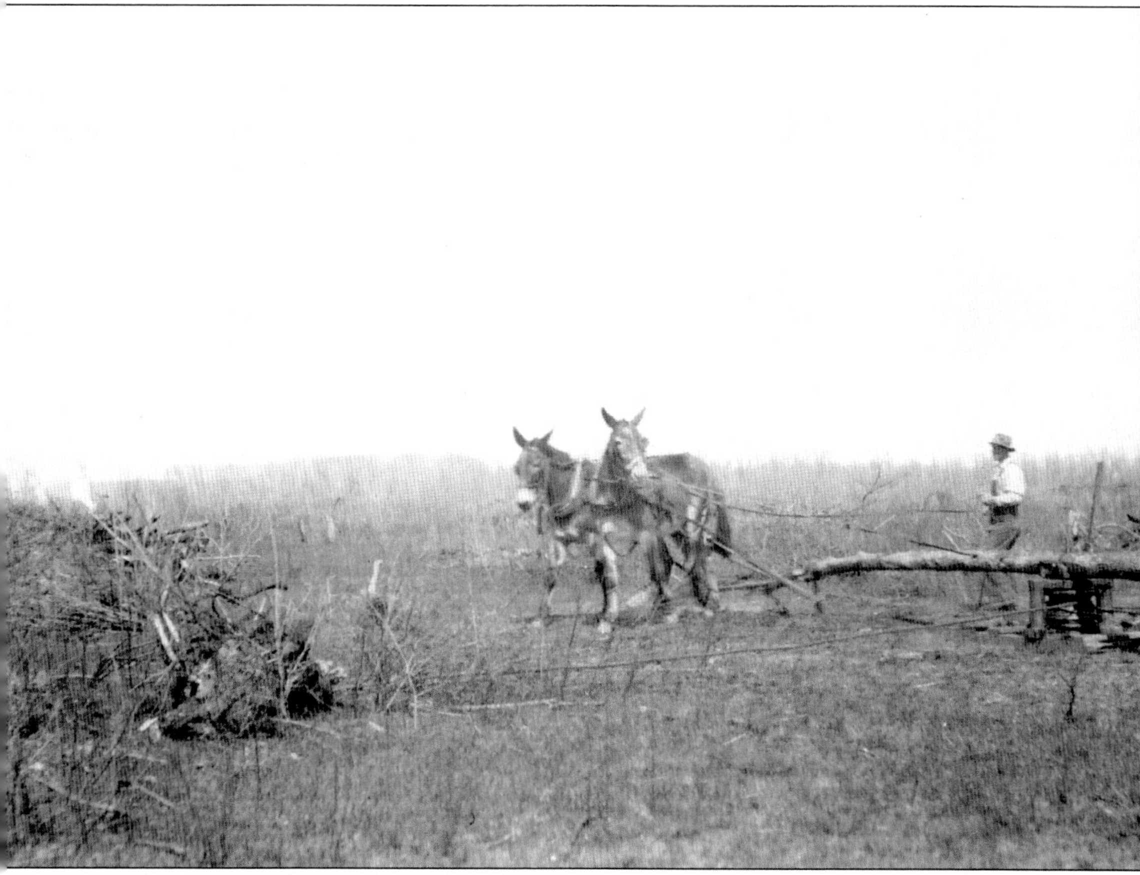

Early farmers had to be clever about building labor-saving devices, as life on a farm could be hard. A homemade capstan powered by a team of horses made this farmer's life a bit easier. (Courtesy of W.H. Over Museum.)

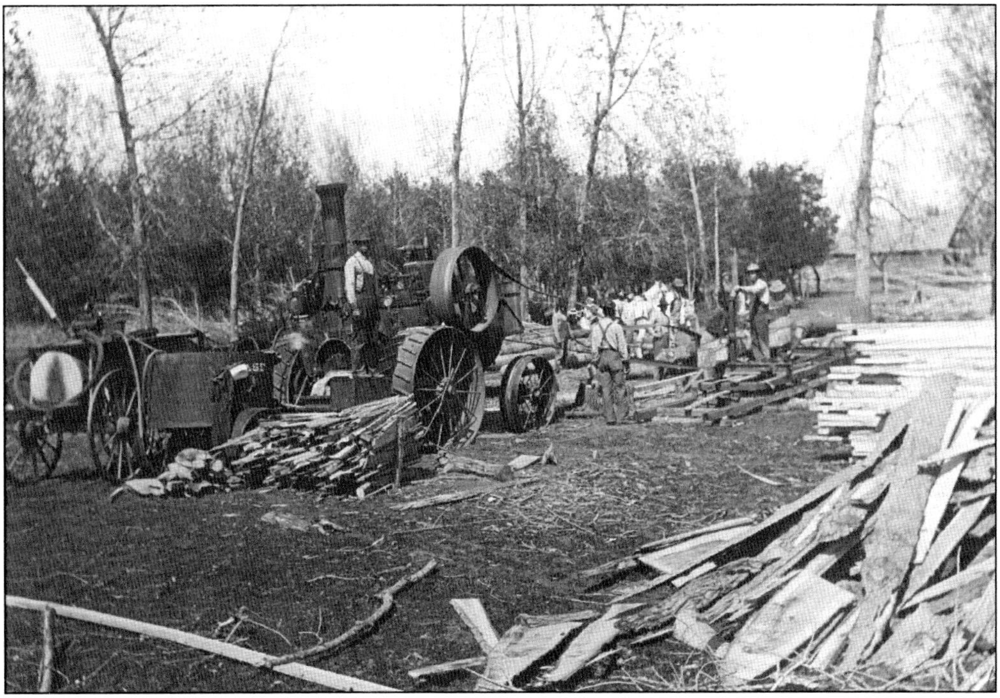

Cornelius Andrews operated a sawmill using steam-powered machinery on Four Knolls Farm. (Courtesy of W.H. Over Museum.)

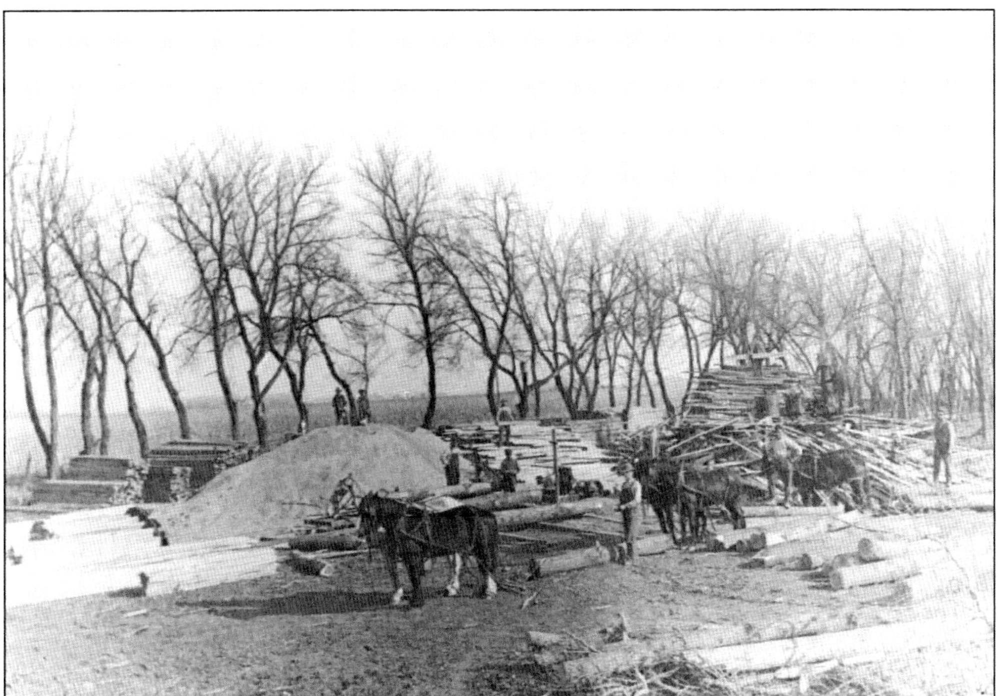

Teams of horses did the majority of the heavy lifting at Cornelius Andrews' sawmill. (Courtesy of W.H. Over Museum.)

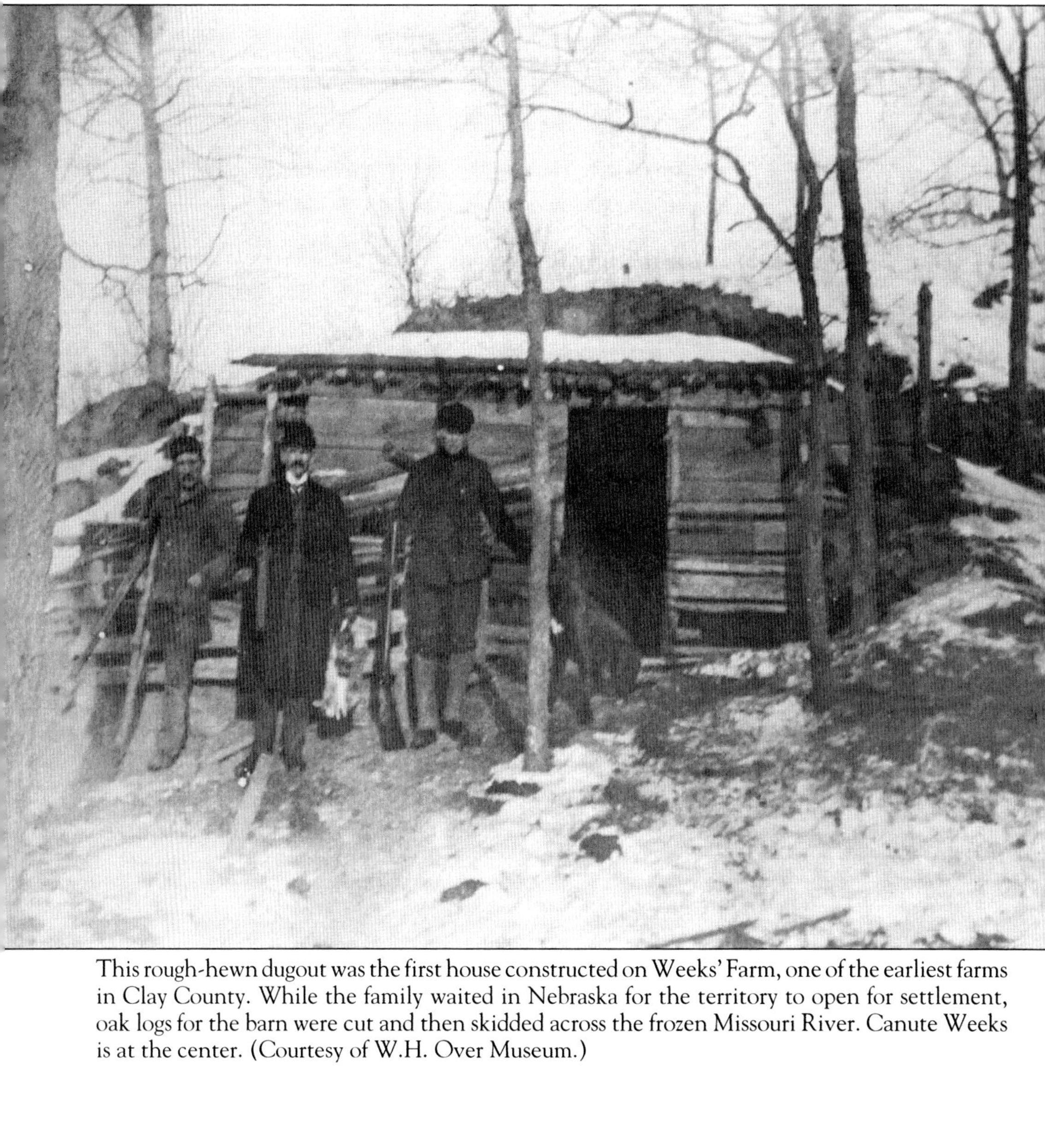

This rough-hewn dugout was the first house constructed on Weeks' Farm, one of the earliest farms in Clay County. While the family waited in Nebraska for the territory to open for settlement, oak logs for the barn were cut and then skidded across the frozen Missouri River. Canute Weeks is at the center. (Courtesy of W.H. Over Museum.)

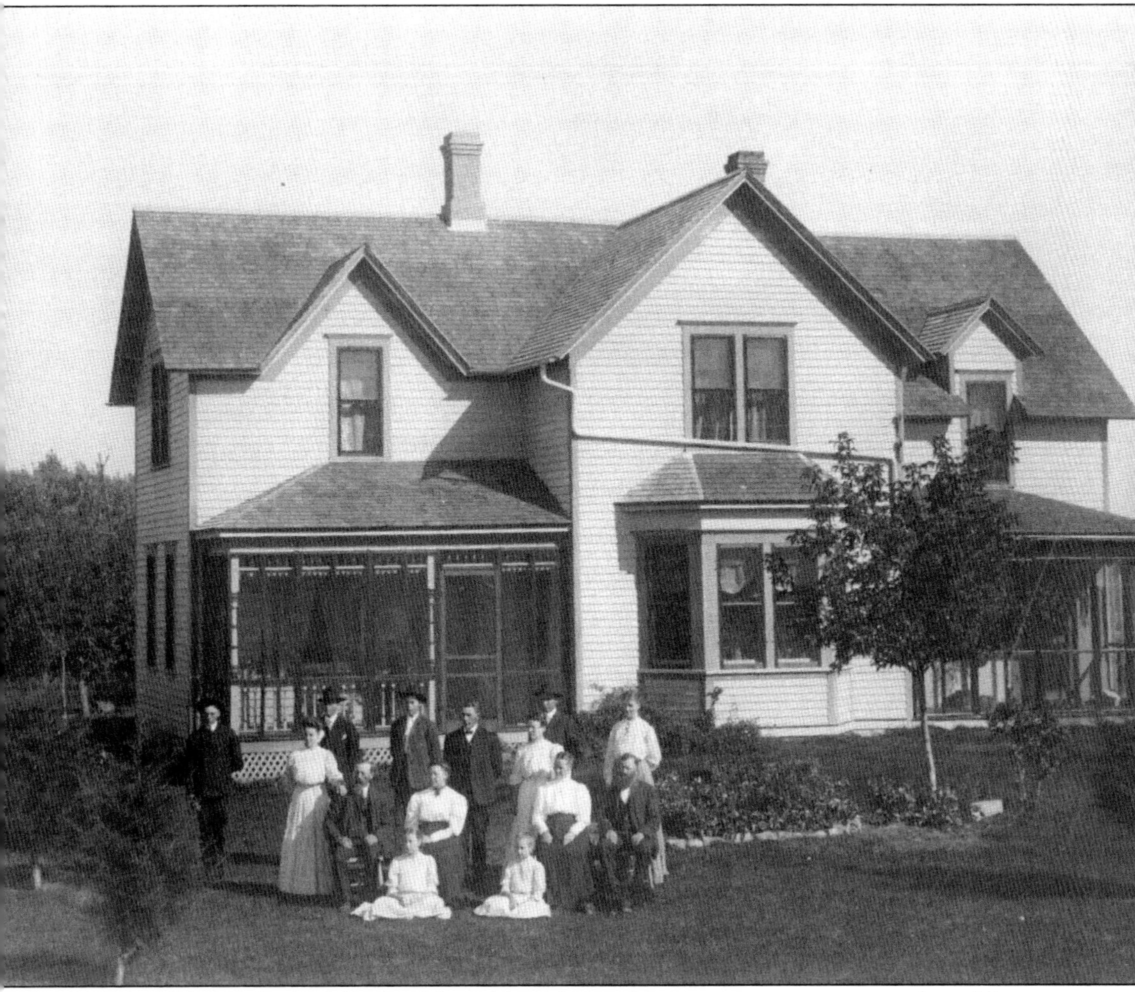

Life on early farms required hard work and long hours. Leisure time was scarce and neighbors were important resources. The Weeks Family visited a neighbor on Bluff Road near the Weeks Farm. (Courtesy of Martin Weeks Collection, W.H. Over Museum.)

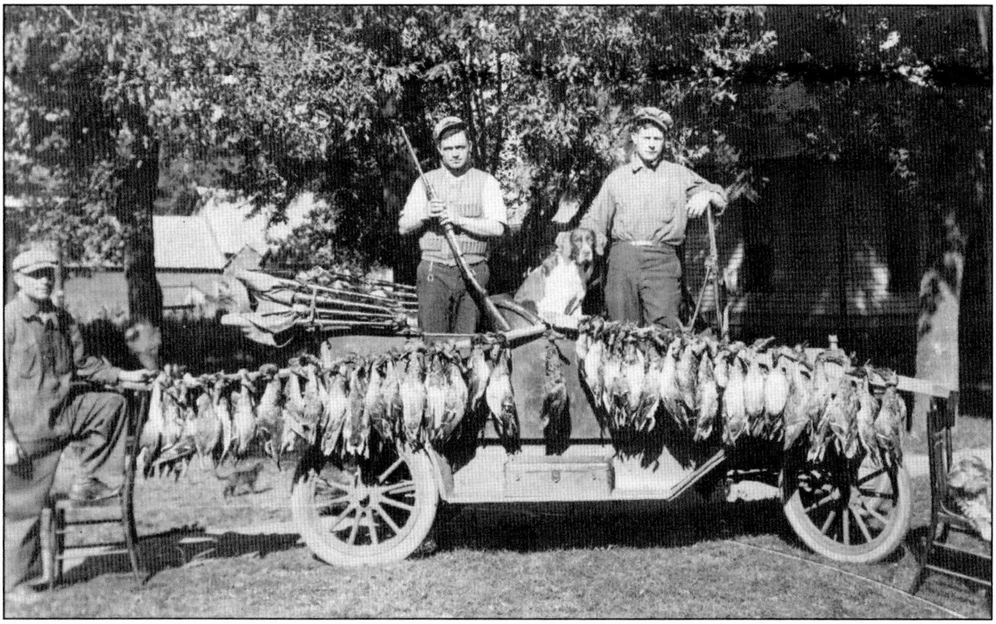

Hunting was an important source of food for early residents and has become an important tradition for many Clay County families. (Courtesy of W.H. Over Museum.)

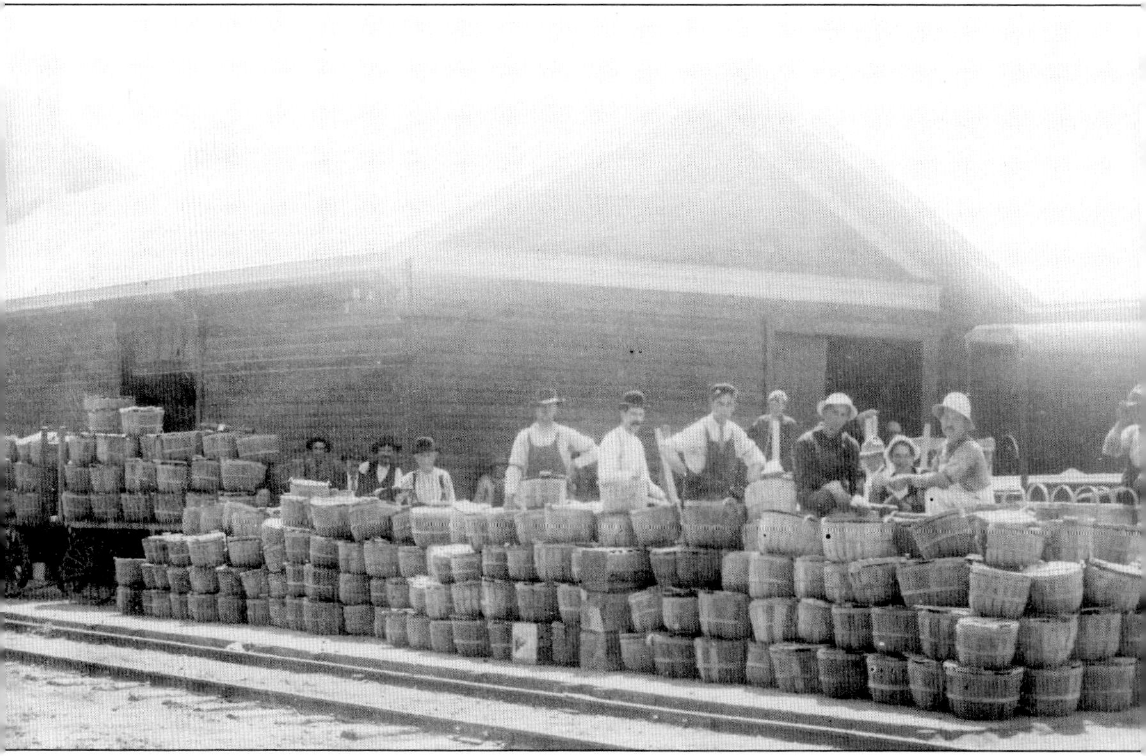

These locally-grown plums were shipped by rail from Vermillion's depot to markets in northern and western South Dakota. Fruit shipments were also made from Burbank and Wakonda. (Courtesy of W.H. Over Museum.)

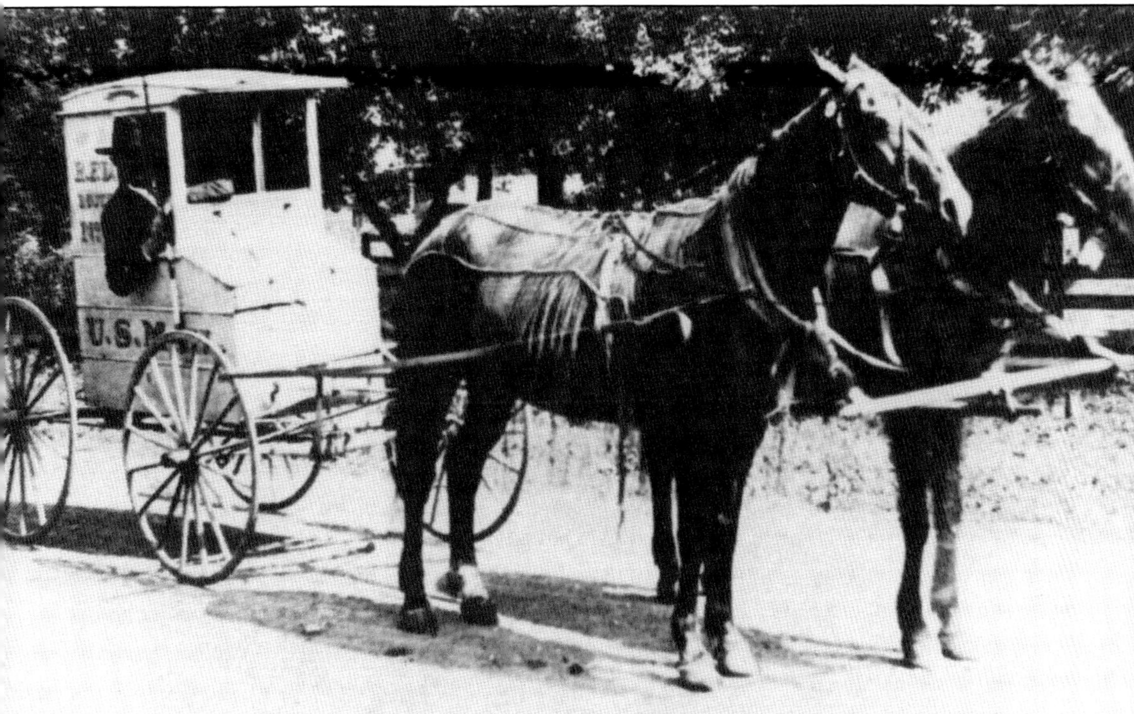

Rural mail delivery was accomplished by means of horse and buggy such as this one, which delivered mail in rural Clay County early in the century. (Courtesy of W.H. Over Museum.)

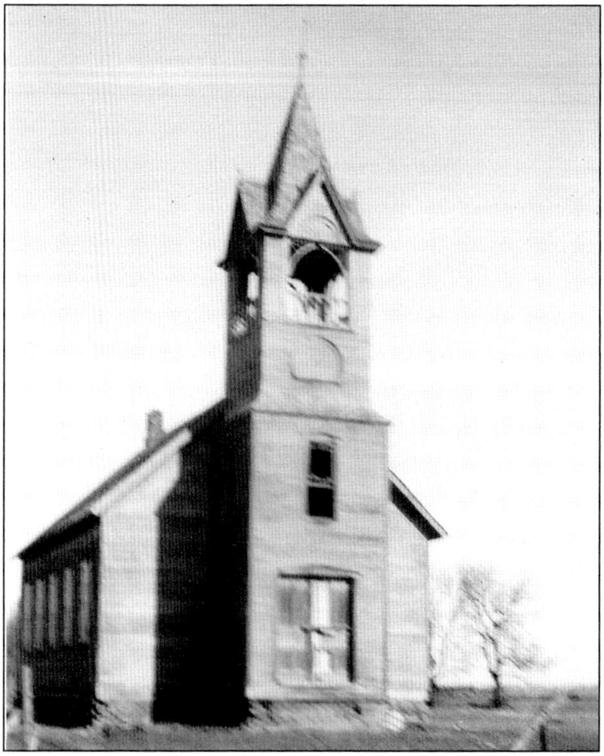

Small wooden churches like this one dotted the rural prairie and were central to the social as well as the religious life of Clay County's farm communities. Cleland Church was situated about seven miles north of Vermillion and is built in the classic prairie style. (Courtesy of W.H. Over Museum.)

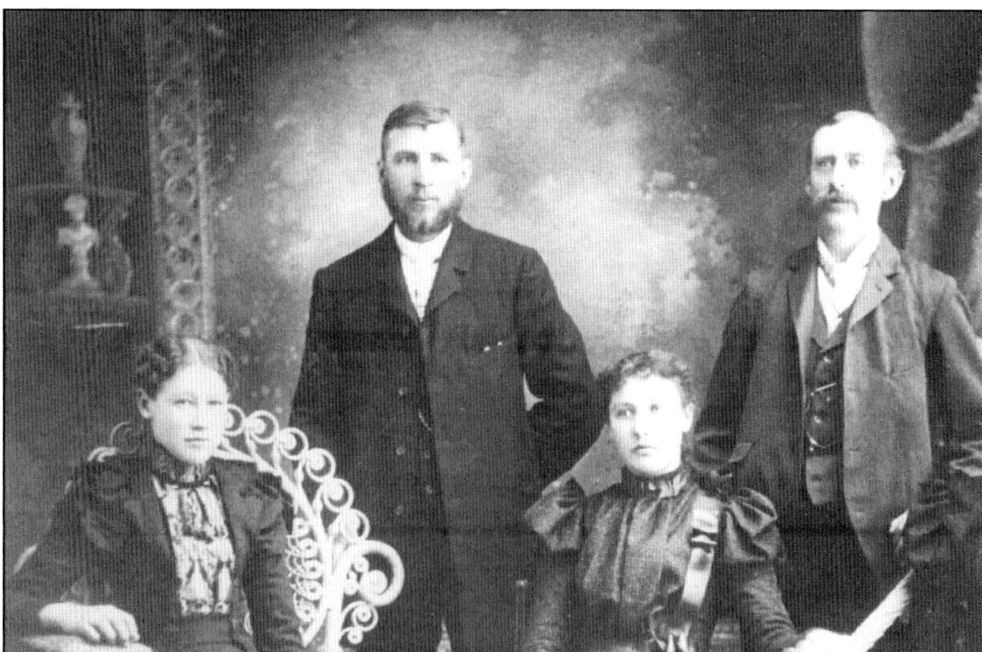

The First Rockfield Church Choir posed for a formal portrait in the 1890s. Rockfield is north of Greenfield in Clay County. From the front left, choir members are Sister Anna Hansen, soprano; Paulina Jacobsen Christiansen, alto; Sister Clara Hansen, organist. In the back row are Hans Christensen, bass; and Christ Christensen, tenor.

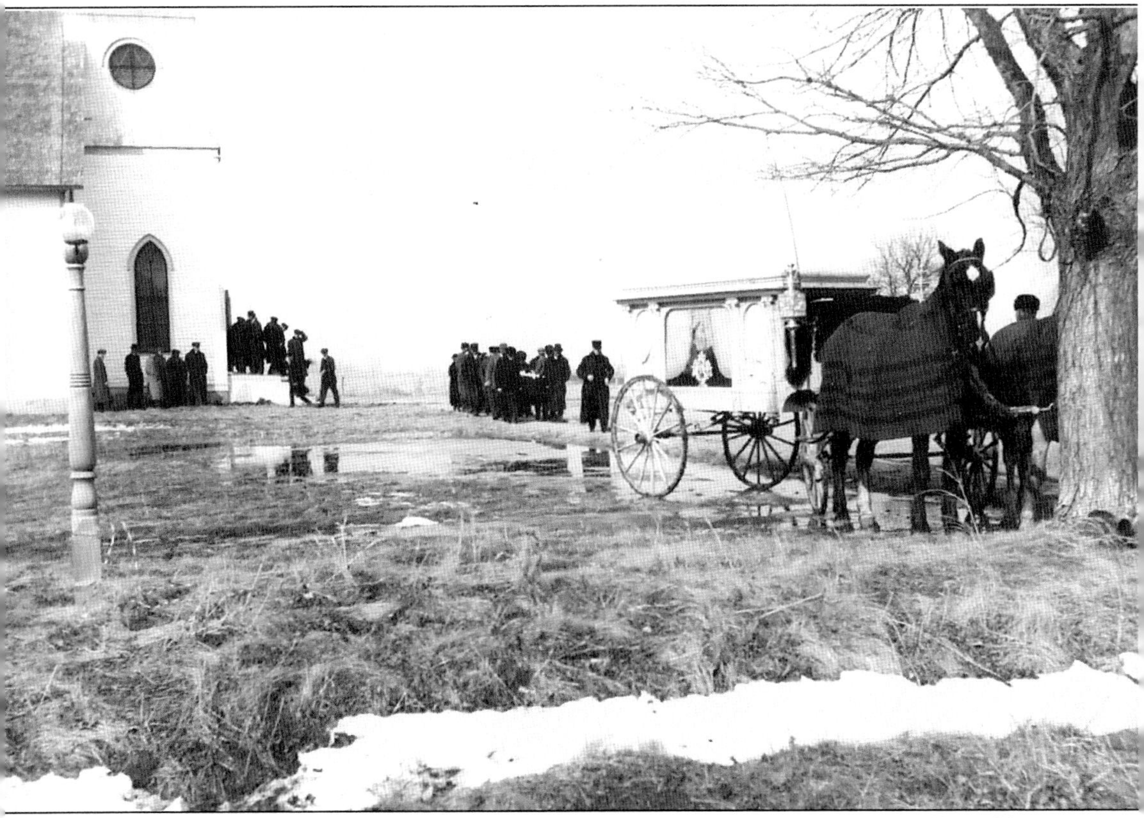

A funeral in 1920 at the Dalesburg Lutheran Church featured a horse-drawn hearse followed by mourners. The predominantly Swedish church was organized in 1871 and its first services were held in a dugout. (Courtesy of W.H. Over Museum.)

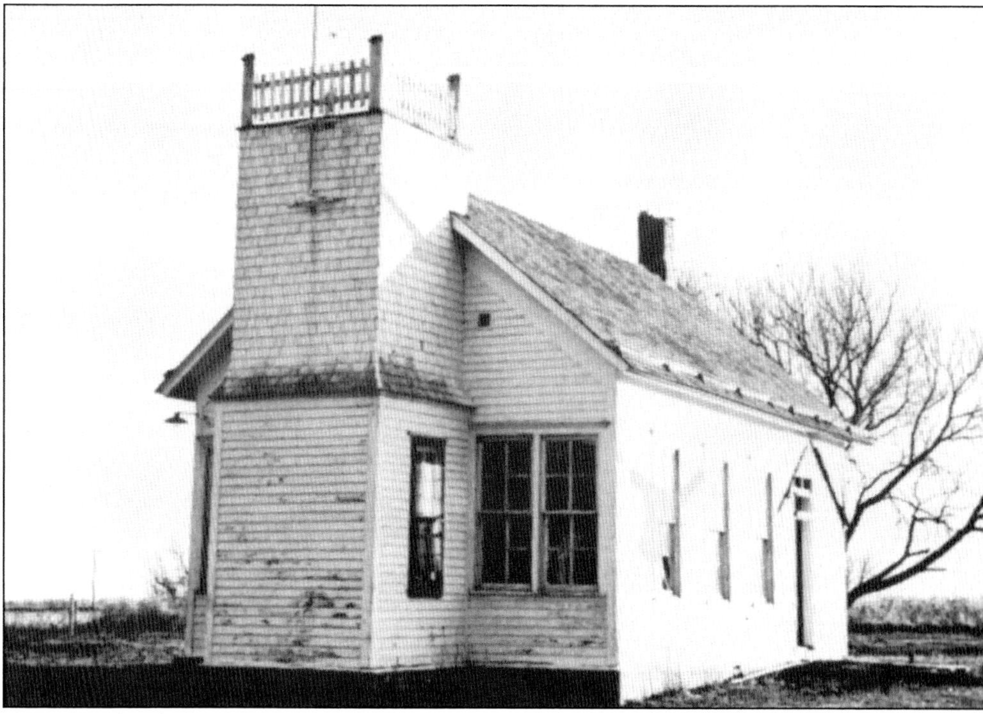

Country schools are an important part of South Dakota's rural heritage. Independent School #1, built in 1867, was the first rural school in Clay County. It was situated about a mile north of Vermillion until it closed in 1969. It has been moved about 1.5 miles north of its original site. (Courtesy of W.H.Over Museum.)

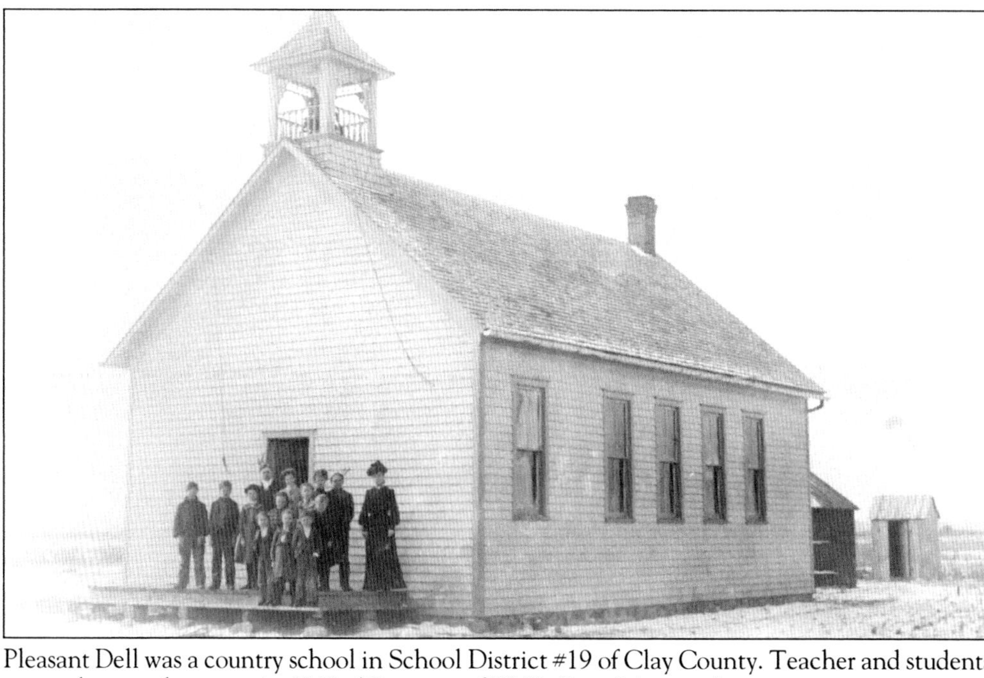

Pleasant Dell was a country school in School District #19 of Clay County. Teacher and students appear here as they were in 1903. (Courtesy of W.H. Over Museum.)

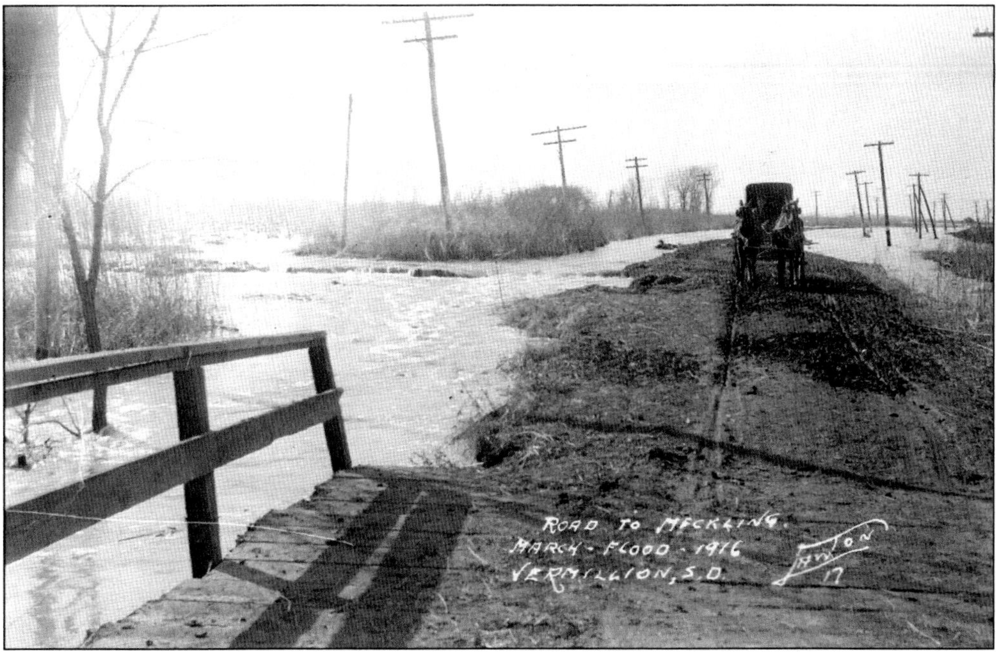

This is the road to Meckling during March of 1916 when floods again inundated Clay County. (Courtesy of W.H. Over Museum.)

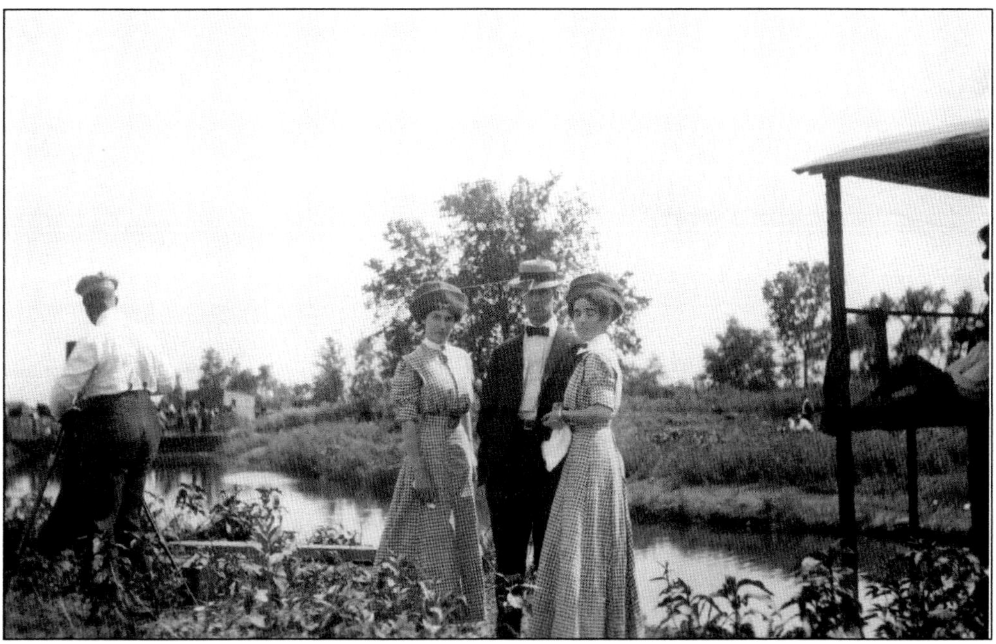

The city undertook the dredging of the Vermillion River. (Courtesy of USD Archive.)

Historical Resources

W.H. Over Museum

The museum has an excellent exhibit on Lewis and Clark's journey as well as an interesting gift shop with books and crafts oriented to the region. In addition, the museum sponsors a walk that retraces the Corps of Discovery's trek from the Vermillion River to Spirit Mound each year on the anniversary of the event. Short talks on the geology, history, flora, and fauna of the area are provided.

The Austin-Whittemore House

The Clay County Historical Society provides tours of this elegant 19th century home. The Austin-Whittemore House also is a repository for local genealogical information and many artifacts of life in early Vermillion.

Publications

Beierle, BA and Rheba Massey. *Clay County Historic Preservation Plan*. Vermillion, South Dakota: Clay County Historic Preservation Commission, 2002.

Clay County Historic Preservation Commission. *Guide to Historic Sites in Clay County, South Dakota*. Clay County Historic Preservation Commission, 1994.

Cummins, Cedric. *The University of South Dakota, 1862-1966*. Vermillion, South Dakota: University of South Dakota, 1975.

A.H. Lathrop. *Life in Vermillion Before the 1881 Flood and Shortly After*. Vermillion, South Dakota: Clay County Historical Society, 1970.

————. *Vermillion Reminiscences, Notes on the Early Days of Vermillion, South Dakota; Its People and Institutions*. Reprint of a series of articles written by A.H. Lathrop for publication in the *Vermillion Plain Talk*. Undated.

Schell, Herbert. *Clay County: Chapters Out of the Past*. Vermillion South Dakota: Vermillion Chamber of Commerce, 1985.

Sterling, Everett W. *Vermillion Story*. Vermillion, South Dakota: State University of South Dakota, 1959.

W.H. Over Museum. *Exploring Spirit Mound*. Vermillion, South Dakota: W.H. Over Museum, August 26, 2000.